Fortress Europe

ALSO BY MATTHEW CARR

Blood and Faith: The Purging of Muslim Spain
The Infernal Machine: A History of Terrorism

Fortress Europe

Dispatches from a Gated Continent

Matthew Carr

Requests for permission to reproduce selections from this book should be mailed to:
Permissions Department, The New Press, 38 Greene Street, New York, NY 10013.

Published in the United States by The New Press, New York, 2012
Distributed by Perseus Distribution

LIBRARY OF CONGRESS CATALOGING-IN-PUBLICATION DATA

Carr, Matthew, 1955–
    Fortress Europe : dispatches from a gated continent / Matthew Carr.
      p. cm.
    Includes bibliographical references and index.
    ISBN 978-1-59558-685-8 (hc. : alk. paper)
    1. Borderlands—Europe.   2. Border crossing—Europe.   3. Illegal aliens—
Europe—Social conditions.   4. Illegal aliens—Government policy—Europe.
5. Border security—Government policy—Europe.   6. Europe—Emigration and
immigration—Government policy.   I. Title.
    JV7590.C39 2012
    363.28'5094—dc23
                                                                                                2012012225

Now in its twentieth year, The New Press publishes books that promote and enrich public
discussion and understanding of the issues vital to our democracy and to a more equitable
world. These books are made possible by the enthusiasm of our readers; the support of a
committed group of donors, large and small; the collaboration of our many partners in the
independent media and the not-for-profit sector; booksellers, who often hand-sell
New Press books; librarians; and above all by our authors.

www.thenewpress.com

Composition by Westchester Book Composition
This book was set in Adobe Caslon

Printed in the United States of America

2   4   6   8   10   9   7   5   3   1

In this world, shipmates, sin that pays its way can travel freely, and without passport, whereas Virtue, if a pauper, is stopped at all frontiers.

—HERMAN MELVILLE, *Moby-Dick* (1851)

Contents

Acknowledgments   xi

INTRODUCTION: Incidents on the Border   1

PART ONE: Hard Borders

  1. A Gated Continent   11

  2. Postcards from Schengenland   25

  3. Policing the Spanish Frontier   45

  4. Mare Schengen   64

  5. The Greek Labyrinth   84

  6. Small Island: British Borders   107

  7. The Internal Border   124

PART TWO: Border Crossings

  8. Difficult Journeys   147

  9. Traffic   164

 10. Hands Across the Border   185

 11. Blurred Edges: Europe's Borderlands   207

12. The Western Borders   230

EPILOGUE: Beyond the Border   245

Notes   255

Index   267

Acknowledgments

This book has taken almost two and half years of my life to write and research, and it could not have been written without cooperation and assistance from many different people in various countries. There are too many of them to list here, but I would like to thank some of the individuals and organizations who were especially helpful to me in my journeys to Europe's borders.

Liz Fekete from the Institute of Race Relations encouraged and supported this project from the outset and helped my research in a number of ways. Eva Ottavy from Migreurop provided a constant list of contacts. Thanks are also due to Johaina Taleb, to Christine Majid from PAFRAS in Leeds, to Vebi Kosumi from the Dover Detainees Visitors Group, and to Tony Fuller, director of the Kent Refugee Action Network. Rakiba Khatun provided invaluable feedback and commentary on the section on destitute asylum seekers. During my visit to Dover, Detective Inspector Charlie Stokes from the Frontier Crime Unit and the officers from the Joint Intelligence Unit in Folkestone generously gave me an invaluable firsthand police perspective on the U.K. border.

In Calais I want to thank Dominic Fitch and Steven Greaves, whose powerful and moving photographs of migrants in the city led me to places that I might not otherwise have discovered. Steve was also a great companion during my first trip to Greece—our bizarre escapades in Evros prefecture will always be ingrained on my memory. William Spindler from UNHCR was generous with his time in Calais and also helped my research in other countries.

Victor Fiorini from the Dover Detainees Visitors Groups went out of his way to help me with information and contacts in his native Malta. In Malta I also wish to thank Matthew Vella, Maria Pisani, Joe Abela from the Maltese Peace Lab, and Roberta Buhagiar from the Jesuit Refugee Service.

Médecins Sans Frontières in London were helpful to me at various stages of my research, but I owe a special thanks to Jorge Martín and the MSF team in Morocco. Thanks also to Hicham, Mohammed, and Noureddine from the ABCDS in Oujda for their hospitality and assistance; Morocco's migrants could not find more dedicated advocates.

I also wish to thank the Civil Guard in Melilla and Ceuta for their cooperation and for their extensive tours of the frontier fences. José Palazón was an indispensable source of information on the migrants in his home city of Melilla, and also in Morocco and on the Spanish mainland. A special thank-you to José Nanclares Mendia in San Isidro, Almeria, for his generous hospitality and for guiding me through the hidden world of Almeria's migrant workers. Thanks also to Amine el-Khiari in Nador, Morocco, to Estefanía Acién at the University of Almeria, to Andrés de la Peña in Algeciras, and to Imma Gala and Helena Malena Garzón in Tangier.

In Greece I would not have got very far without crucial assistance from Salinia Stroux, an intrepid and tenacious campaigner for the rights of Europe's migrants, who opened pathways for me in various parts of the country. Thanks also to Haris and Sotiris from the Migrant Solidarity Group in Igoumenitsa for their hospitality and assistance, to Greg Kavarnos from the Villa Azadi in Lesvos, to Melina in Samos, to the Hellenic Coast Guard in Samos, and to Alex Anastasiou and Spyros Koulocheris from the Greek Refugee Council in Athens.

In Poland the Nadbuzanski branch of the Polish Border Guard provided me with more time and assistance than I had any right to ask for. I also wish to thank the Fundacja Pogranicze (Borderland Foundation) in Sejny for their invitation to the 2011 Milosz centennial and an unforgettable three days. A special thank-you to Ksenija Konopeck for patiently dealing with my complicated travel arrangements; also to Arnold Markovitz for his amusing and intelligent company and his moving insights into his father's past and the lost world of Jewish Sejny.

In Slovakia I wish to thank the Slovak Ministry of Interior and Colonel Jan Vinc and his colleagues from the Border Police Directorate in Sobrance. Thanks also to Vladimir Bilcik from the Slovak Foreign Policy Association in Bratislava for his detailed overview of the Slovakia-Ukraine border, and to Oksana from the Border Monitoring Project Ukraine in Uzhgorod.

During my two visits to Italy, Vittorio Longhi from *La Repubblica* provided me with crucial contacts in Lampedusa and in Brescia and gave me a place to stay in Rome. Thanks also to Ilaria Vecchi in Lampedusa, to Stefania Ragusa in Milan, and to Simona Giovanna Lavo and Louise Bolzoni in Brescia.

I am also indebted to the Lipman Miliband Trust and the Society of Authors, whose generous awards helped finance my research.

I also wish to extend a general thank-you to all the migrants and refugees who took time to share their stories and experiences with me, many of whom had more pressing priorities than talking to an English writer researching a book. All these individuals and organizations helped make this book possible. Responsibility for any errors or mistakes is of course mine alone.

As always, I owe a special debt of gratitude to Jane for her patient and uncomplaining support during my frequent absences abroad.

This book is dedicated to her.

Fortress Europe

Incidents on the Border

Until 2005 not many Europeans were aware that Europe begins in Africa. Lying 155 miles apart on the Moroccan coast, the two designated "autonomous cities" of Ceuta and Melilla are an incongruous legacy of Spanish colonialism that has never been recognized by Morocco. Both exclaves are entirely enclosed by massive two-tiered wire fences that mark the southern boundaries of the European Union.

In the summer of 2005, some three thousand sub-Saharan African *sin papeles* (irregular migrants) were camped in Moroccan territory outside the two exclaves, waiting for an opportunity to cross the hated *grillage* (wire fence). Most of them were young men, some of whom had been living in the rocky hills and forests for months, evading the Moroccan police patrols who periodically raided their camps and destroyed their plastic shelters and bivouacs. That year the raids intensified, as the Moroccan government came under increasing pressure from Spain and the European Union to clear the camps. In February more than six hundred Moroccan police and soldiers tore through the forests at Ben Younech near Ceuta, burning and looting the migrant camps and arresting their occupants. By the summer these raids had become so frequent that migrants of more than a dozen nationalities held a series of meetings in the forests, in which they resolved to "fight the *grillage*" en masse in the hope that at least some of them would get across the fence.

On June 23, two hundred people attempted to scale the fence at Melilla, using homemade ladders built from ropes and branches, only to be driven back by the Civil Guard and Spanish Foreign Legion. On August 29, three hundred migrants made another attempt on the Melilla fence with a hundred homemade ladders. This time 180 men managed to cross to the other side; most were immediately pushed back into Moroccan territory by the Spanish security forces.

At first these clashes received little attention in the European media. On the night of September 28, however, more than five hundred migrants scaled the fence at Ceuta. Some wore gloves and cardboard suits to avoid lacerating themselves on the rolls of razor wire that lined the top of the fence. Others used strips of carpet or attempted to scramble over with their bare hands. A closed-circuit camera image shows a group of African migrants in the space between the two fences, leaning their ladders against the inner barrier. The cameras did not show the brutal events that followed, as Civil Guard and Moroccan soldiers and police converged on the fences from both sides, attacking the border crossers with batons, rifle butts, tear gas, rubber bullets, and—at least on the Moroccan side—live ammunition. In the ensuing melee one man broke his neck falling from the fence, another slashed his throat on the razor wire and bled to death, and three others were shot dead.

By the morning most of the intruders had been driven back into Morocco, leaving strips of torn clothing on the fence and a detritus of shoes, gloves, baseball caps, piles of ladders, and patches of blood on the nearby ground. Shocked by what the Spanish media referred to as a "human avalanche," the Socialist government of José Luis Zapatero hurriedly deployed 480 soldiers to Ceuta, while 1,600 Moroccan police and security forces were brought in to reinforce the other side of the fence. On the night of October 6, however, hundreds of unarmed migrants attempted once again to storm the Melilla fence, where they were driven back by Spanish police and Civil Guard and Moroccan security forces bearing shotguns and fixed bayonets. This time six men died and dozens were injured while climbing over the fence or being beaten back with truncheons and rifle butts. Some managed to break through the security cordon and ran with bleeding hands and feet to the local police station, where they were legally entitled to apply for asylum, having entered EU territory, and sang and prayed to give thanks for their deliverance.

In the aftermath of this incursion, Moroccan soldiers and police began rounding up all migrants in the area and transporting them in trucks and buses to the border with Algeria near the city of Oujda and farther south at the edge of the Sahara, where they were shunted into the desert with little or no food or water and told to make their way back to their countries of origin. Over the next few days, nongovernmental organizations, reporters, and human rights activists began receiving desperate mobile phone calls from migrants appealing for help. On October 7, workers from Médecins Sans Frontières rescued five hundred African migrants stranded without food or water in the desert near El Aouina–Souatar in southern Morocco. Other groups were found wandering the desert by guerrillas from the Polisario Front, which is fighting for the independence of Western Sahara from Morocco. Faced with strong criticism from Amnesty International and other international NGOs—but not from Spain or the European Union—the Moroccan government began to mount its own rescue operations. Eventually some 3,500 migrants were deported by plane, by which time an unknown number had already died.

Border Wars

The "battles" at Ceuta and Melilla were the most dramatic expression of a nightmare that has haunted the European imagination ever since the end of the Cold War. From Ceuta and Melilla in the south to the 1,800-mile frontier that marks Europe's new eastern frontier with Belarus, Ukraine, and Moldova, from the Greece-Turkey border to the English Channel, from the Mediterranean to the Adriatic and the Aegean, European governments have reinforced their borders with police, soldiers, border guards, naval patrols, physical barriers, and detection technologies in the most sustained and extensive border enforcement program in history.

This massive deployment of technology and personnel is not a response to a military threat. Though terrorism, security, and crime are sometimes presented as justifications for these reinforced borders, their overriding objective is the prevention of "illegal" immigration, primarily from the global South. The result is a tragic and often lethal confrontation between some of the richest countries on earth and a stateless population from some of the world's poorest, a conflict that has been unfolding for more than two decades at Europe's territorial borders and which also extends inside and beyond them. It is a struggle that is being waged on land and at sea, at remote Slovak border posts and on isolated Greek islands, in the ports and airports of major cities, in the Sahara Desert and the heart of Africa, in urban housing complexes and immigrant detention centers.

Statistics give an indication of the lethality of this confrontation. According to a 2006 study carried out by the Berlin Wall Association and the Centre for Contemporary Historical Research, 125 people were killed trying to cross the Berlin Wall throughout its entire history. Between 1988 and April 2011, 15,551 migrants died trying to cross Europe's borders, according to the antiracist organization United.[1] The majority of these deaths took place during the perilous journeys across Europe's southern sea borders, where thousands of men, women, and children have drowned in overcrowded and unseaworthy vessels.

At least two thousand people are estimated to have died in the Sahara Desert trying to reach Europe. Migrants have suffocated in truck containers, fallen from trains and buses, or frozen to death in the wheel carriages of passenger planes. In the winter of 2007 three Chechen girls, ages six, ten, and thirteen, froze to death trying to cross the Tatra Mountains between Ukraine and Poland with their mother, who survived with her two-year-old daughter. On September 27, 2008, five migrants were blown up when they strayed into a minefield on the Greece-Turkey border.

Such events have become so routine that they rarely attract more than cursory media attention, broken by occasional moments when the death toll rises to a new level of obscenity. One of those moments took place in December 2001, when thirteen mostly Kurdish migrants paid $4,000 to "people smugglers" to transport them to England, where they intended to seek asylum. On the last leg of their journey they were smuggled from Zeebrugge in a P&O freight container loaded with Italian office furniture and told that they would arrive in England two hours later. Instead their ship arrived in Ireland after a convoluted fifty-six-hour journey, where it remained for two more days in an enterprise park in Wexford. By the time the container was finally opened, eight passengers had died from suffocation and hyperthermia, including four children.

Migrants have also died inside the countries they wanted to reach. Between 1998 and 2008, 150 people killed themselves in Germany because they were due to be deported. On August 27, 2003, an Iranian asylum seeker named Israfil Shiri entered the offices of Refugee Action in Manchester doused in flammable liquid and calmly set fire to himself in front of the horrified workers. Shiri had been in the United Kingdom for two years, and his appeal for asylum had recently been turned down. Having lost his income support, he was living on the street in a trash bin, despite suffering from a medical condition that left him unable to eat without bleeding and vomiting. He died five days later. On April 30, 2011, a seventeen-year-old Afghan asylum seeker in France named Aminullah Mohamadi hanged himself in Vilette

Park in Paris because he believed that his social assistance payments would be cut off on his eighteenth birthday and that he would be deported back to Afghanistan.

Such deaths are also casualties of the border, victims of a "fight" against illegal immigration that is often steeped in the rhetoric of war and invasion. In June 2003 Umberto Bossi, the leader of Italy's xenophobic Northern League, responded to news of a mass drowning of migrants in the Mediterranean with the recommendation that the Italian navy should fire warning shots at incoming migrant boats. If these warnings had no impact, Bossi told his interviewer, "after the second or third warning, boom . . . the cannon roars. Without any beating about the bush. The cannon that blows everyone out of the water. Otherwise this business will never end."[2] In a 2006 article in the *Sunday Times* Rear Admiral Chris Parry, one of the British Ministry of Defence's most prominent strategic thinkers, argued that Europe faced a form of "reverse colonisation" by Third World immigrants, which he compared to "the 5th century Roman empire facing the Goths and the Vandals."[3]

Most governments tend to avoid such intemperate language, but there have been moments when the struggle to seal Europe's borders against its unwanted immigrants has resembled a military confrontation, albeit of a kind that no one has seen before. On April 28, 2008, according to the Spanish newspaper *El País*, a Moroccan naval patrol boat in the Mediterranean slashed a dinghy carrying thirty African migrants, all of whom drowned. On September 12, 2010, in the days when Muammar Gaddafi's political romance with the European Union was still in full bloom, a Libyan patrol boat opened fire on an Italian fishing boat in the Mediterranean, riddling it with bullets. There were no deaths or injuries, but Italy's Northern League interior minister, Roberto Maroni, offered the sympathetic explanation that the Libyans "perhaps . . . mistook the boat for a boat with illegal migrants."

Such incidents are part of a "war" on irregular immigration that often echoes the equally phantasmal "war on terror" in its ability to generate legally ambiguous spaces where abuses of state power are removed from democratic scrutiny and accountability and where transparency is murky or nonexistent. Consider the scene that unfolded on flight TE453 from London's Gatwick Airport to the Lithuanian capital, Vilnius, on April 24, 2004. Jessica Hurd, an English photographer who was flying on the plane, later told the Medical Foundation for Victims of Torture how three Lithuanian women with three children were brought on board for deportation, accompanied by uniformed immigration officers.

According to Hurd, the deportees were screaming and crying as they were led to the back of the plane. One of them was an adolescent girl, whose accompanying official held her tightly by the neck. Another woman "had handcuffs on and was only wearing her underwear: bra and pants." When Hurd complained about this treatment, one of the officers ordered her not to interfere with "government business." She continued to protest until the escorts eventually marched all six deportees off the plane.[4]

Such events are another consequence of the remorseless and often pitiless struggle by European governments to "secure" and "protect" their borders. This book is an analysis of Europe's "hard" borders, based on a series of personal journeys to some of the places where this hardening process is most apparent. It is a book about physical and bureaucratic barriers and the political and human consequences of these barriers, about the "illegal immigrants" who cross borders and the officials and institutions that try to stop them. It is also a book about the political forces that have made these borders possible. Borders are not just political boundaries or lines on a map: they are also an expression of the fears, phobias, and expectations of the societies that enforce them.

The project of European integration was a response to the darkest period of European history, which had spawned the Nazi and Soviet dictatorships, fascism, two world wars, and genocide. The founders of the European Union aspired to build a different kind of Europe, defined in Article 2 of the 2008 Lisbon Treaty, which states, "The Union is founded on the values of respect for human dignity, freedom, democracy, the rule of law and respect for human rights, including the rights of persons belonging to minorities." These commitments are enshrined in various European treaties and conventions, in addition to the adherence of EU member states to international human rights treaties and agreements such as the Geneva Convention on the Status of Refugees, the Convention on the Rights of the Child, the Convention Against Torture and Inhuman and Degrading Treatment, and the UN Charter.

These principles are often glaringly at odds with a repressive and punitive response to irregular migration whose consequences are often invisible to the general public or obfuscated by official denials and a rhetorical insistence on the intrinsic humanity of Europe's border enforcement policies and objectives. This book is an attempt to address that discrepancy, but its perspective is not confined to Europe alone. According to the 2009 UN Human Development Report, 214 million people are currently living outside their national borders—a figure that includes some 50 million undocumented migrants and 14 million refugees, and does not include 26 million internally displaced persons who remain inside their national borders and therefore are not classified as refugees. Across the world governments have responded to these developments by attempting to transform their borders into militarized instruments of exclusion and repression.

At no time in history have so many people attempted to cross international borders without authorization, and at no time have so many governments gone to such lengths to try to stop them. All this raises crucial questions about human rights and global inequality, about security, migration, and the obligations of governments to refugees and noncitizens in a century that is likely to be dominated by the new global mobility. To some extent therefore, the confrontation between Europe and its unwanted intruders is specific to Europe, but it is also a reflection of a much wider phenomenon.

There is much about Europe's borders that is disturbing and horrific. But these borders also contain other stories: of the tenacity, resilience, and desire of the migrants who cross these borders; of ordinary Europeans from many different countries who have gone to extraordinary lengths to help them; of border zones that often contradict and subvert the expectations placed upon them. In these interactions, I would like to hope, Europe's borders may point the way toward a different kind of Europe—and a different kind of world—than the one that is presently under construction.

PART ONE

Hard Borders

Without consideration, without pity, without shame
they have built great and high walls around me.
And now I sit here and despair.
I think of nothing else: this fate gnaws at my mind;
for I had many things to do outside.
Ah why did I not pay attention when they were building the walls.
But I never heard any noise or sound of builders.
Imperceptibly they shut me from the outside world.

—CONSTANTINE CAVAFY, "WALLS" (1896)

1

A Gated Continent

National borders are hugely symbolic. They define the territory over which a state exercises sovereignty; they are an integral part of its identity; and they traditionally represent the point at which a person seeking to enter the country must demonstrate their admissibility.

—Proposals for a new European Border Guard,
House of Lords, United Kingdom, 2003–4

At first sight Europe's new borders present something of a paradox. For nearly half a century, western Europeans regarded the Berlin Wall as the incarnation of Communist tyranny, whose "closed" borders were guarded by concrete barriers, watchtowers, and armed guards. In June 1987 Ronald Reagan famously urged the Soviet president Mikhail Gorbachev to "tear down this wall" as proof of his commitment to perestroika. Twenty-nine months later an astonished world watched as crowds hacked their way through the wall during the tumultuous autumn of 1989.

In the euphoric atmosphere that prevailed in many Western capitals, the more visionary proponents of globalization hailed the advent of a new "borderless" world in which such barriers would become obsolete. In *The Borderless World: Power and Strategy in the Global Marketplace* (1990), the influential business strategist and management guru Kenichi Ohmae argued that national borders were no longer relevant to a global economy connected by twenty-four-hour interdependent cycles of production and consumption that encompassed even the most distant countries.

Economists, politicians, and corporate CEOs all echoed the same theme. More than two decades after the fall of the Berlin Wall, some of these expectations have been fulfilled. Today we inhabit a world in which commodities, capital, and information effortlessly permeate national frontiers, and vast sums of invisible money are ghosted back and forth across the world at the click of a computer keyboard in "cross-border equities" and "cross-border portfolio transactions." It is a world that seems closer than ever to bearing out Marshall McLuhan's prediction of a global village where technology has "extended our central nervous system in a global embrace, abolishing both space and time,"[1] where Facebook, Twitter, and MySpace link millions of people in transnational virtual communities, where dozens of twenty-four-hour digital news channels with global reach now emulate CNN's ability to "go beyond borders," and a ubiquitous and seemingly irresistible McWorld of Starbucks and Zara, Hannah Montana and Rihanna, Benetton sweaters and the Nike swoosh extends from Paris to Shanghai.

It is a world in which many countries have dispensed with some of the traditional tenets of national sovereignty. In Europe, South America, Asia, and the Americas, governments have established regional economic frameworks and free trade zones and dismantled customs barriers and regulations that once limited foreign trade and investment.

Yet this same period has also been marked by a new global emphasis on borders. Across the world governments have reinforced their national frontiers with fences, walls, and other technological barriers. This process of "re-bordering," as the American political scientist Peter Andreas puts it, is not limited to the nation-state. From Cape Town and Manila to São Paulo and Los Angeles, moneyed urban communities have retreated into gated blocks of flats or walled-off neighborhoods, monitored by closed-circuit cameras and private twenty-four-hour security guards. In other countries town councils and municipal authorities have built walls to keep dangerous or harmful people out—or keep them in.

In 2010 the town council of Ostrovany in eastern Slovakia built a wall to separate the local Roma settlement from the surrounding community. In 2009 government officials in Rio de Janeiro began the construction of a series of "environmental walls" around some of the largest slums or *favelas* in preparation for the 2016 Olympic Games, walls that critics alleged were intended to keep their inhabitants out of sight. At the height of the Iraq insurgency in Baghdad, the U.S. military built a series of blastproof twelve-foot concrete barriers around markets and Sunni and Shia neighborhoods. In

2010 the Iraqi government announced its intention to enclose Baghdad itself within these "protective security walls."

All these walls and barriers have their own rationalizations and objectives, from security and crime prevention to lifestyle protection, but all of them share a common determination to limit and control the movements of unwanted and potentially dangerous people. While cities and gated communities seek to acquire the powers of inclusion and exclusion that traditionally belonged to the state, states across the world have increasingly sought to become gated nations and transform their borders into impregnable walls.

These tendencies have been particularly striking—and anomalous— among the liberal democracies that "won" the Cold War. In Europe, the United States, and Australia, national borders have acquired a political importance that was entirely absent throughout their global confrontation with the Soviet Union. And before we can consider the very particular trajectory that these tendencies have taken in Europe, we need to consider the broad historical trajectory of the barriers that Ohmae and so many others believed were destined for obsolescence.

A Brief History of Borders

What are borders for? Most dictionary definitions of *border* contain the notion of an edge, limit, or periphery that distinguishes one area from another. The *Oxford English Dictionary* is more specific in defining it as "a boundary between two countries or other areas." These boundaries may consist of manmade barriers, such as walls, fences, dikes, and ditches, or they may consist of rivers, mountains, and other natural obstacles that constitute borderlands, marches, and frontier zones of indeterminate status that act as buffers between rulers or rival centers of power, such as the "debatable lands" that separated England from Scotland in the fifteenth and sixteenth centuries.

Borders may be agreed upon through custom and negotiation, or they may be contentious and provisional, the result of changing geopolitical alignments, military defeats, or unilateral attempts by one state to absorb the territory of another. From Hadrian's Wall and the Great Wall of China to the Maginot Line, states have fortified their frontiers as a barrier against potential aggressors or invaders. In the course of history such barriers have often been imbued with symbolic meanings and connotations. In classical times the fortified frontiers or *limes* (limits) of the Roman Empire were often imagined as a fragile dividing line between Roman civilization and the barbarian world beyond. In the sixteenth and seventeenth centuries, Hapsburg military victories over the Ottomans in Hungary were followed by the establishment of chains of fortresses that marked Europe's eastern frontier between Christendom and Islam.

Other borders have acquired their own imaginative distinctions—between civilization and barbarism, East and West, tyranny and freedom—and these associations have sometimes been dramatized by evocative sobriquets, from Churchill's "Iron Curtain" to the "green line" of civil war Beirut or the "bloody borders" that the late political scientist Samuel Huntington once identified as a specific characteristic of Islam.

In theory, borders mark the point where one state ends and another begins, but national borders are a relatively recent historical innovation. In medieval and early modern Europe the local boundaries of lordships, parishes, and city-states were at least as significant as national frontiers or the changing boundaries imposed by kings and emperors. As states extended their political control over wider territorial areas and larger groups of people, it became increasingly important for their rulers to know the limits of their authority and to determine clear boundaries between themselves and their neighbors and rivals—an objective that was made possible through the advent of scientific methods of land surveying and cartography.

It was not until the early seventeenth century that European maps began to show state borders for the first time. In 1604 the Dutch geographer Mattheus Quadt published an atlas of Europe that marked state borders with dots and color washes rather than lines to indicate their tentative or disputed status. These borders were not necessarily accepted by neighboring states—or by those who lived inside them. It would take more than three hundred years of slow political evolution and often violent conflict before the notion of the modern state with exclusive jurisdiction over sovereign borders was fully accepted in Europe.

This transformation was dependent on various factors: the growth of centralized state bureaucracies with authority over taxation and military recruitment, the spread of secular nationalism, the advent of capitalism, and the gradual absorption of localities and regions into national economies with distinct currencies, tariffs, industries, and markets. The consolidation and advance of the European state system was paralleled by the imperialist mapping of the world, in which European colonial powers established borders and boundaries to demarcate their empires and spheres of influence. By the

early twentieth century the territorial nation-state had become the cornerstone of the international system, and the bordering of the modern world
was completed during the period of decolonization and the formation of
dozens of new states in the aftermath of World War II.

Defining Boundaries

Borders are often described as an essential component of international stability, in an extrapolation of the principle that "good fences make good
neighbors." But they have often been a cause of violence, both between states
and within them. This is not merely a question of boundary disputes over
territory and resources. National borders are not just political divisions between states. They also seek to confirm or inculcate a shared sense of identity
and belonging and an exclusive set of national rights and privileges among
the people who live inside them. To the nineteenth-century German geographer Friedrich Ratzel, the frontiers were the "skin" that surrounded the
living organism of the nation-state.[2]

Whether these identities are imagined in terms of a shared national history, language, ethnicity, or ideology, they are often dependent on the state's
ability not just to know where one national community ends and another
begins but also to decide who has the right to live inside them. In ancient
Greece expulsion from the political community or polis was one of the worst
punishments that could be inflicted on those who broke its rules. In Sopho-
cles' *Antigone*, the tyrant Creon describes such a transgressor as "a person
without a city, beyond human boundary, a horror to be avoided."

History is filled with examples in which unwanted people have been driven
"beyond human boundary" in an attempt to preserve or confirm the character
of the state or the collective identities of those who live inside their borders.
In some cases states have sought to achieve these objectives by closing their
borders to prevent their populations from leaving—and also by preventing
unwanted or extraneous people from entering. In the Middle Ages, the gates
in the fortified walls of city-states constituted the primary border checkpoints, where undesirable people could be excluded or prevented from entering. This group included heretics, vagrants, beggars, prostitutes, "masterless
women," lepers, Gypsies, Jews, and the "wandering poor."

Modern states have pursued the same powers of exclusion, but it was not
until the nineteenth century that the territorial border became the point

where potential intruders were scrutinized and denied entry. In 1561 the English Privy Council became anxious at the potential impact of continental immigration on religious stability and ordered the local authorities across London "to searche out & learne the holl number of Alyens & Strangers" in the city.[3] In 1601 the Tudor institution known as the Bridewell Court—a premodern combination of workhouse and correctional facility for "disorderly" paupers—expressed its alarm at the "great numbers of negars and Blackamoores which . . . are crept into this realm," and Queen Elizabeth subsequently issued a royal proclamation ordering their removal.[4]

These ordinances were themselves a testament to the permeability of state borders. Aristocrats and merchants might carry royal permits or letters of safe conduct, but such documentation was not always obligatory or necessary, and even travelers who were less well-heeled were able to cross European frontiers without being checked on entry. As late as the eighteenth century, European travelers were generally monitored by town and local authorities rather than by officials at state frontiers.

During the nineteenth century, screening procedures at the border became more common, from registers of incoming ships at ports and harbors to designated officials with the ability to impose quarantine, inspect cargoes, and check lists of passengers. Some European countries also mandated internal passports and documentation to control the movements of people inside their borders, from the work record or *Wander-Buch* (wandering book) that apprentice journeymen were obliged to carry with them in preunification Germany to the internal passports that tsarist rulers imposed on their subjects.

For much of the nineteenth century and the first decade of the twentieth, however, control over state borders was generally weak and sporadic, and this at a time when more people were emigrating than at any previous point in human history. Between 1840 and 1914, some 50 million Europeans emigrated to the Americas and the colonies, and some 20 million indentured Indian and Chinese workers were recruited as indentured "coolie" laborers in South Africa, the Caribbean, and the Pacific Rim. There were also large-scale migratory movements within Europe itself, from Italian construction and factory workers in France and Switzerland and Polish agricultural laborers in Bismarck's Germany to the Irish navvies in Victorian Britain.

Many of these journeys were made with little or no documentation. During the French Revolution and the subsequent revolutionary wars, both France and Britain introduced restrictions on aliens, aimed at vetting foreigners with dissident political views, but these restrictions fell into disuse following the Napoleonic Wars. For much of the nineteenth and early twentieth centuries, however, passports and visas were discretionary and often were not required at all.[5] Writing from exile in 1941, Stefan Zweig nostalgically recalled his globetrotting years before World War I, when "everyone could go where he wanted and stay there as long as he liked. No permits or visas were necessary, and I am always enchanted by the amazement of young people when I tell them that before 1914 I travelled to India and America without a passport. Indeed I had never set eyes on a passport."[6]

"Paper Walls" and the Creation of Illegality

These barriers were not entirely absent, and the freedom granted to a middle-class Austrian writer was not universal. For many nineteenth-century governments, migration was a positive and even essential phenomenon, one that provided a source of labor and population growth in their own countries and their colonial territories overseas, as well as a safety valve in economically depressed regions whose populations might otherwise have turned against their rulers.

In the last decades of the century, however, a number of governments began to introduce immigration restrictions for the first time against specific racial or national categories of immigrants. In 1882 the U.S. government passed the Chinese Exclusion Act, following a racist "yellow peril" campaign by California politicians; the ban remained in place until 1943. In 1897 the British colony of Natal introduced a language test, barring entry to anyone who could not fill out an application form in English—a test that was specifically intended to eliminate "coolie" labor from India. The "Natal formula" was introduced in Australia in an attempt to limit the entry of Chinese migrants, and was subsequently adapted to other nationalities.

A number of governments began to introduce immigration restrictions in Europe in the same period. These efforts were partly intended to protect the indigenous labor force from competition following the global recession of the last two decades of the century, but then, as now, certain categories of immigrants were also depicted as inimical to the identity of the state. In 1885 the German chancellor Otto von Bismarck ordered the expulsion of forty thousand Polish workers from Germany to prevent "the Polonization of a large segment of the Prussian population." In 1912 the French government obliged all "nomads"—a denomination that generally referred to the country's 4 million Italian immigrants—to carry documents with their fingerprints and photographs. Even in laissez-faire Britain, Parliament approved the Aliens Act of 1905, which limited the entry of "destitute foreigners"—a category that was generally understood to mean Jews fleeing poverty and persecution in tsarist Russia.

These restrictions were often driven by the scientific racism and eugenicist doctrines of the period, which depicted immigration by those of "inferior" or "degraded" racial or national groups as a threat to purity of the national "stock." In 1893 Justice Milieus de Villiers of the Orange Free State justified the exclusion of Asians on the grounds that "every European nation or nation of European origin has an absolute right to exclude alien elements which it considers to be dangerous to its development and existence."[7] In *Efficiency and Empire* (1901), the anti-immigrant lobbyist Arnold White warned that "rule by foreign Jews" threatened "the best forms of our national life."

Before World War I such restrictions were not easily enforced and borders were often porous. In the United States, the Mexican border was virtually an open frontier until the creation of the U.S. Border Patrol in the early 1920s, and Chinese migrants routinely avoided the increasingly rigorous identity and documentation checks at Angel Island in San Francisco by crossing the land frontier from Mexico. In Germany Poles were often able to avoid expulsion or slipped back across the border after being expelled, while Italian immigrants continued to live and work in France without the documentation they were theoretically obliged to obtain.

Such evasions became more difficult during World War I, when governments introduced tighter visa restrictions and began to demand proof of identity at ports and border entry points. By the end of the war, the presentation of passports, visas, and travel documents at the border had become a more or less universal obligation, and the same requirements were continued into the security-obsessed postwar years. Looking back on the period between the two world wars, Stefan Zweig described a general phenomenon in which "all the humiliations previously devised solely for criminals were now inflicted on every traveler before and during a journey. You had to be photographed from right and left, in profile and full face, hair cut short enough to show your ears; you had to have your fingerprints taken—first just your thumbs, then all ten digits; you had to be able to show certificates of general health and inoculations, plus papers issued by the police certifying that you had no criminal record; you had to be able to produce documentary proof of recommendations and invitations, with addresses of relatives; you had to have other documents guaranteeing that you were of good moral and financial repute; you had to fill in and sign forms in triplicate or quadruplicate; and if just one of this great stack of pieces of paper was missing, you were done for."[8]

In a compartmentalized international system where rights and protection abroad were contingent on the possession of a passport and visa, travelers who attempted to cross national borders without the required documentation were not only illegal trespassers in someone else's territory but also stateless nonpeople to whom governments owed no obligations. In the first half of the twentieth century, however, this new world of bordered states and "paper walls" came under unexpected pressure, as a new category of illegal traveler appeared on the international stage.

Refugees

Enforced exile and population displacements were not a historical novelty in twentieth-century Europe. But the massive population displacements that took place in the aftermath of World War I were unprecedented in both their scale and their repercussions. Millions of people were driven out of their countries during the violent redrawing of national boundaries that followed the collapse of the Hapsburg, Russian, and Ottoman empires, and many of them became permanently stateless when their governments revoked their citizenship for ideological reasons.

These refugees not only constituted a series of potentially destabilizing humanitarian crises for neighboring states but also raised the question of who was responsible for actually dealing with them. For the first time in history, governments were obliged to look for collective solutions to deal with a stateless population that challenged the concept of a world system in which rights and protection were dependent on membership in a particular state or nationality.

In 1922 the League of Nations issued special passports, known as "Nansen passports" after its High Commissioner for Refugees, the explorer Fridtjof Nansen, to refugees from the Soviet Union, which enabled their holders to cross (some) international borders legally with limited consular protection. This improvised expedient was partly successful because of the willingness of countries such as France to accept large numbers of Russian refugees after World War I, which eventually made it possible to resolve the postwar refugee crises.[9]

The international response to these crises nevertheless established the refugee as a deserving category of illegal migrant, with special claims on the world's conscience that could—in certain circumstances—override the principle of state sovereignty over national borders. But such acceptance was not unconditional, and the generosity shown toward refugees from Soviet Russia was not extended to Jews fleeing Nazi persecution in Germany and Austria in the 1930s, where the prevailing international consensus was notoriously embodied by the 1938 League of Nations conference at the French town of Evian-les-Bains to consider the international response to the persecution of Jews under Hitler.

Though governments agreed in principle to provide protection to Jewish refugees, a number of delegates argued that their countries were already "saturated" with Jews and that a further influx would exacerbate racial tensions and create a "Jewish problem." Various countries had already introduced tight quotas on Jewish immigration, and because the Nazis identified Jewish émigrés as Jews in their passports, many were able to find a safe haven only through complicated and unauthorized border crossings or by using forged documentation. Escape became even more difficult when war broke out and Jews found themselves trapped in occupied Europe when Nazi plans changed from expulsion to extermination.

It was partly in response to these failings that the newly formed United Nations adopted the Geneva Convention on Refugees in 1951, subsequently extended with the Protocol Relating to the Status of Refugees in 1967, in which states agree to provide protection to refugees who leave their countries "owing to a well-founded fear of being persecuted for reasons of race, religion, nationality, membership of a particular social group or political opinion."

This definition left various questions answered. Who decided whether the fear of persecution was "well-founded"—governments, the Office of the United Nations High Commissioner for Refugees (UNHCR), or refugees themselves? How could refugees prove their persecution? What happened when such proof was not available and their claims were rejected? The convention was enacted in the aftermath of World War II, when the resettlement of Europe's displaced populations was seen as essential to the continent's political and economic stability. In 1948, Article 13(2) of the Universal Declaration of Human Rights declared, "Everyone has the right to leave any country, including his own, and to return to his country." This principle was drawn up in response to the closed borders of the European dictatorships of the 1930s and their Communist successors in the immediate postwar period, which were primarily intended to prevent their citizens from leaving their countries rather than entering them. It was not accompanied by any corresponding obligation on the part of states to accept people who try to cross their borders without authorization.

With the onset of the Cold War, the obligation to provide refugee protection—and allow potential refugees to leave their countries—was politically expedient for many Western governments, and a safe haven in Western Europe was generally available to all who escaped from the Communist bloc, regardless of whether their motives were "economic" or "political." Less than half a century later, however, European governments were beginning to seek ways of evading these obligations in an attempt to limit or prevent the entry of refugees from an unexpected and less desirable source.

The Coming of Fortress Europe

For much of the nineteenth and early twentieth centuries, the great migratory movements that shaped European history were directed outward to the Americas and the colonial world, or took place within the continent itself. In the years that followed World War II, this historic pattern was reversed, as a number of European countries tolerated or actively encouraged immigration from the Third World and their former colonies in order to make up for the postwar shortage in unskilled labor.

North Africans in France, Belgium, and the Netherlands; Turkish *Gastarbeiters* (guest workers) in Germany; Indians, Pakistanis, and West Indians in Britain—all formed part of a new migratory phenomenon that was initially regarded by the governments concerned as a pragmatic and short-term expedient. Instead, many of these migrant workers began to establish themselves in their adopted countries and brought their families with them. For the first time in their history, white European societies found themselves faced with the permanent presence of significant nonwhite populations within their territories. This transition was often achieved in the face of bitter and sometimes explicitly racist opposition, emanating primarily from the conservative and far-right parts of the political spectrum.

As early as the 1960s, however, even left-of-center governments such as the British Labour Party had begun to impose new visa requirements and entry restrictions that were specifically designed to curtail Third World immigration, and these efforts intensified during the global recession that followed the 1973 oil crisis. By the mid-1980s the legal avenues for unskilled Third World migration into Europe had been drastically curtailed across the continent, and many European governments—and the European Union as a whole—were becoming increasingly concerned with the phenomenon of illegal immigration.

These concerns coincided with an increase in the global refugee population, much of which was due to wars, civil wars, and political conflicts in the Third World. Most of the world's refugees remained inside their own borders or close to the countries they were forced to leave. From the mid-1980s onward, however, there was a significant increase in the numbers of refugees seeking protection in the West, and these numbers surged to new heights during the Balkan wars of the 1990s. Where European governments had once welcomed refugees from Eastern Europe during the Cold War, they were less well-disposed toward Iranian or Turkish Kurds, Sri Lankans, and other Third World refugees, who were increasingly portrayed by politicians and the media as "economic migrants" seeking to evade the continent's immigration restrictions.

By the end of the Cold War "asylum seeker" was firmly enshrined in European political and media discourse as a subcategory of refugee whose legitimacy had yet to be proven and whose claims were frequently assumed to be suspect. These suspicions were often steeped in racialized assumptions, as "asylum seeker" became code for Third World immigrants in general. But they were also fueled by the belief that Europe's immigration restrictions were being violated on a massive scale. To many Europeans the refugees from the Balkan wars, the African "boat people" arriving on Mediterranean beaches, and the impoverished Albanians who arrived on commandeered hulks at the ports of Brindisi and Bari were the most visible expression of an invisible and potentially limitless tide of impoverished and desperate migrants that threatened to engulf the continent.

These "invasion" narratives were often based on hypotheses and fantasies rather than actual numbers. In 2004, the European Commission statistics office, Eurostat, estimated that the total number of non-EU nationals living in Europe's fifteen member states was 25 million, or 5 percent of the total population. Within individual countries, the percentage was sometimes higher. But even in Germany, which had more non-EU immigrants than any other country in Europe, UN statistics listed 10,758,061 people as immigrants in 2010, which amounted to only 13 percent of the overall population.

Such statistics were often ignored or inflated in the xenophobic anti-immigrant climate that spread through many European countries in the last decade of the century, and which was reflected in the savage neo-Nazi campaign against *Uberfremdung* or "over-foreignization" that accompanied the unification of Germany, in the electoral rise of the traditional far right and new populist parties across Europe with an anti-immigrant agenda, and in political tensions with Europe's Muslim communities. All these developments reinforced the determination of European governments to enforce the continent's immigration restrictions and prevent unauthorized entry at the border.

Today responsibility for monitoring Europe's borders is shared between national governments, police forces, and immigration officials and some 400,000 border guards in different countries. It also includes the new security architecture of the European Union itself, whose bewildering array of Euro-acronyms includes the new European border agency Frontex, the Rapid Border Intervention Teams (RABIT), and the police and judicial cooperation in criminal matters (PJC) agencies Europol, the European Police College (CEPOL), and Eurojust. Satellite surveillance, naval patrols on the high seas, a proliferation of immigration detention centers that extends across the continent and beyond, "offshore" border controls, and neighborhood partnerships aimed at monitoring and trapping unwanted travelers before they even reach European territory—all these checks and barriers have formed part of a sustained and far-reaching border enforcement program that has transformed the traditional notion of the border as a territorial dividing line.

These developments have not been confined to Europe. In the United States and Australia, the post–Cold War period was accompanied by an upsurge in nativism, xenophobia, and anti-immigrant hostility—and also by a new political emphasis on borders and border security. In the early 1990s, the U.S. government began to bolster the U.S.-Mexico border with new barriers and fences, surveillance technologies, Border Patrol personnel, and periodic deployments of the National Guard and the army, in an attempt to prevent irregular migration from Mexico and Latin America. In the late 1990s Australia deployed its navy and air force in the Pacific in response to relatively low numbers of asylum seekers seeking to reach Australian territory.

The drift toward militarized borders by the world's leading liberal democracies was accelerated by the 9/11 attacks and the global state of emergency that followed, but security considerations do not in themselves explain the new political significance of border enforcement. In 2003 the International Organization for Migration (IOM) described a "migration governability crisis" in which "states feel they have lost the sovereign right to determine who enters and remains in their territories."[10] The restoration of this "sovereign right" has been a key objective in the militarization of Europe's borders. Today European politicians routinely talk of their determination to become "masters of our borders" or "reclaim our borders," as David Cameron recently expressed it.

American and Australian politicians are prone to similar statements. In Europe, however, these developments have coincided with a unique and in many ways remarkably successful experiment in which twenty-seven countries have voluntarily abolished their mutual border controls to allow Europeans unlimited freedom of movement within the continent, in ways that would have been inconceivable in the security-obsessed interwar years that Stefan Zweig lived through. Europe is also exceptional in that its territorial limits have yet to be conclusively defined. Since the signing of the Maastricht Treaty in 1993, the European Union has undergone three enlargements, and the process of expansion may not have run its course.

The prospect of further enlargements into the Balkans, and potentially at least to Turkey and Ukraine, could eventually extend the EU's political boundaries to within a few hundred miles of Moscow and across the Black Sea, adding Iraq, Iran, Azerbaijan, Syria, and Georgia to the list of EU neighboring countries. In effect, Europe's borders are provisional and transitional boundaries in a political space that is still under construction. But throughout each of the EU's successive enlargements, the incorporation of new member states into the new borderless European space has been dependent on a persistent hardening of Europe's "external" frontiers in a symbiotic dynamic between "soft" and "hard" borders whose origins can be traced back to a meeting on a river in the heart of Europe more than three decades ago.

2

Postcards from Schengenland

It is not a question of eliminating ethnic and political borders. They are a historical given: we do not pretend to correct history, or to invent a rationalized and managed geography. What we want is to take away from borders their rigidity and what I call their intransigent hostility.

—ROBERT SCHUMAN, 1963

With its low forested hills and vineyards and a picturesque location on the edge of the Moselle River, the village of Schengen in southern Luxembourg is a pleasant stopover on the Luxembourgish wine-growing itinerary, with a few quirks from European history to appeal to the more discerning tourist. In 1793 Goethe paused here on his way back from the French revolutionary wars to paint a watercolor of a liberty pole on the banks of the Moselle. Victor Hugo, the republican exile who once dreamed of a "United States of Europe," left a sketch in coffee grounds of Schengen Castle, whose remaining conical tower still constitutes the most striking architectural feature of the village. A few miles away, in the spa town of Mondorf-les-Bains, Herman Goering and other high-ranking Nazis were held by the American army before their trial at Nuremburg.

What makes Schengen unique is its geographical location. Cross the bridge that leads from the center of the village and turn left, and you enter the Saarland region of Germany. A few hundred yards to the right and you find yourself in the French province of Lorraine. On the balmy afternoon of June 14, 1985, officials from the foreign ministries of France, Germany, and the Benelux countries (Belgium, Netherlands, and Luxembourg) gathered aboard the riverboat *Princesse Marie-Astrid* alongside the bridge for a historic meeting that would transform Schengen into an iconic symbol of the new Europe. After a leisurely lunch the assembled dignitaries signed a treaty that committed their five countries to the "gradual abolition of checks at the common border" and the replacement of passport controls with the "simple visual surveillance of private vehicles crossing the common border at reduced speed, without requiring such vehicles to stop," for drivers who carried an identifying badge with a green dot attached to their windshield.

To some extent these seemingly innocuous arrangements confirmed what had already been a de facto practice in the Benelux countries for many years, but the participation of France and Germany had far wider implications. By establishing a borderless zone in the heart of Europe, the agreement effectively constituted a fait accompli intended to set in motion an irresistible process of political and economic unification that the rest of the continent would be obliged to follow. Its significance was not lost on its signatories. As the host country, Luxembourg chose to stage the signing ceremony at the exact point on the Moselle River where the political borders between the three countries merged, to highlight the agreement's symbolic message of unity and convergence.

The Schengen Agreement was ratified in the same place five years later in the 1990 Schengen Convention. By the time it came into force in 1995 Spain, Italy, and Portugal were also members of what was now known as the Schengen area. These arrangements remained outside the legal framework of the European Union until 1997, when the Schengen laws or *acquis* were formally incorporated into the Treaty of Amsterdam. Today the Schengen area consists of twenty-five states with a combined population of more than 450 million people, who are able to move freely across a political space of 1,664,911 square miles, within a common external frontier made up of 26,515 miles of land borders and 5,484 miles of coastline.

Not all the countries in the Schengen area are members of the EU and not all members of the EU belong to Schengen, but this obscure village of five hundred inhabitants is now a household name, familiar to millions of travelers through the separate entry points at European airports that distinguish between Schengen and non-Schengen travelers. Today the avuncular mayor of Schengen, Roger Weber, likes to tell the story of how he once drove past the *Princesse Marie-Astrid* on the day the agreement was signed with no idea of what was taking place on board. As a result of that meeting, Weber has become something of an international statesman. In 2007 he was invited to Bratislava to celebrate Slovakia's accession to the Schengen area, and he was guest of honor at a special Schengen day at the Shanghai World Expo in 2010. Schengen has also become a place of pilgrimage both for eastern European politicians whose countries have joined the Schengen area and for non-European tourists curious to see the origins of the name that appears on the three-month visas that allow them to travel freely across much of the continent.

Schengen has astutely taken advantage of its unexpected preeminence. Next to the bridge, in the now renamed Europe Promenade, three rectangular pillars commemorate the three signatories to the agreement, directly opposite the place where the *Princesse Marie-Astrid* was moored. Farther down the bank, a slab from the Berlin Wall stands as a monument to the barriers that Schengen was intended to erase. Schengen now hosts a European Museum, opened in 2010, whose exhibits include items seized by customs, Luxembourg border police uniforms, old boundary stones, and discontinued European passports like anachronistic relics from a vanished world. In a continuous video, smiling citizens from each Schengen member state and from some non-European countries intone the single word "Schengen" like a mantra, in an expression of what the museum calls the "collective 'we-feeling'" of the Schengen area.

The museum also contains video interviews with the original diplomats who signed the agreement. Catherine Lalumière, the emissary of François Mitterand, remembers the meeting as an "outing in the country" that she attended despite opposition from Interior Ministry officials. Lalumière, like her co-signatories, looks back fondly at a treaty that she regards as a positive and benign achievement, qualified briefly by a note of regret at "the instrument of fortification that Schengen would become. That wasn't our intention."

These fortress-like components of Schengen may not have been intended, but the long delay between the signing of the 1985 agreement and its actual implementation ten years later was partly due to the fears of various interior ministries, including her own, that the absence of border controls would make it more difficult to prevent illegal immigration and might jeopardize their national security. To dispel these anxieties and address the "security deficit" engendered by the new dispensation, the implementation of Schengen has always been contingent on the concept of reinforced or "compensatory" controls at Europe's external borders. In effect the countries that made up the Schengen area's outer perimeter were obliged to assume responsibility not only for sealing their own borders against unwanted or undesirable visitors but also for enforcing the immigration restrictions of all the European Union's member states.

To join Schengen, prospective "border countries" were required to monitor and secure their borders in accordance with the three thousand pages of Schengen rules or *acquis*. In addition, European governments developed a range of instruments to control the movements of non-EU citizens or "third-country nationals" *inside* Europe's borders. These included the Eurodac database, where fingerprints of all asylum claimants in any European country are recorded, and the Schengen Information System (SIS), a vast computerized database containing photographs, biometric data, and millions of names of people and objects of interest, from stolen cars, wanted criminals, and suspected terrorists to "aliens" who have been refused entry or asylum seekers whose claims have been rejected. Directed from a central location in Strasbourg, the SIS can be accessed by police forces across the continent and at all the border checkpoints of Schengen member states, and is due to be replaced by a more advanced version, SIS II, currently scheduled to become operative in 2013 with an anticipated operating capacity of 100 million alerts.

All these developments have given Schengen a dual and contradictory character. On one hand, its aims were laudable, even idealistic: to transform the European Union into a common "area of freedom, security and justice" and bring the union closer to all its citizens by allowing Europeans the opportunity to live, work and travel anywhere in the continent. For non-European travelers, Schengen has made travel across the continent less complicated by removing the need to make multiple visa applications.

For travelers without passports or visas, however, Schengen has had very different repercussions. The diplomats who enjoyed their leisurely lunch aboard the *Princesse Marie-Astrid* on that balmy June day in 1985 undoubtedly did not foresee that men, women, and children would one day be drowning in the Mediterranean, shot trying to cross border fences, mutilating themselves in detention centers, or reduced to destitution in the heart of some of Europe's great cities. But all these events have been consequences of the Schengen "compensatory" borders, and it is to these borders that we must now turn.

Facing East

It takes about seven hours by train from Warsaw to reach the town of Terespol on Poland's eastern border with the Belarussian fiefdom of "Europe's last dictator," Alexander Lukashenko. On the other side of the border lies the city of Brest, where the beleaguered Bolsheviks once signed the humiliating Treaty of Brest-Litovsk in 1918, which (temporarily) ceded a quarter of the Russian Empire to Germany and the Central Powers. Today this remote town of six thousand inhabitants is the busiest border crossing point in Poland, and the EU and Polish national flags testify to its new role as an outpost of Europe and Schengen that began in December 2007 with Poland's accession to the Schengen area and the formal dissolution of the Germany-Poland border.

The monitoring and control of Poland's 795-mile border with Lithuania, Kaliningrad, Belarus, and Ukraine that is now part of Europe's eastern frontier has shifted to the Straz Graniczna (Polish Border Guard). A former unit of the Polish army before World War II, the Straz Graniczna's uniforms, training, and equipment are a testament to its dual role as a border police force and a militarized guardian of Polish national sovereignty. In a country whose frontiers have been forcibly rearranged by invasions and occupations by its more powerful neighbors and which has twice been erased from the map of Europe, it is perhaps not surprising that Poland takes the security of its borders very seriously. But the Straz Graniczna's current role in Europe's border security arrangements reflects the priorities of Schengen and the European Union rather than Polish anxieties about invasion or occupation.

"We were ready before Schengen," says Captain Artur Barej, the amiable commander of the Terespol Border Guard. "We knew we would be protecting the EU border and we were already prepared for it." Barej exudes confidence, and with good reason. His 350 officers control a border area that encompasses three separate crossing points for road traffic, trucks, and rail transport, a number of internal "community roads," and some fifty-odd miles of "green border" that includes the Bug River and the largest remaining prehistoric forest in Europe. Thanks to Schengen, his officers have a panoply of cutting-edge technologies that few border forces, with the exception of the U.S. Border Patrol, can emulate. These include a thermic camera with a range of four and a half miles mounted on a tower at the Border Guard headquarters, four mobile vans with infrared cameras, a mobile office known as the "Schengen bus," a patrol boat to monitor the nearby Bug

River, two quad bikes, and a scrambler to patrol the more inaccessible forested areas along the border. There are also eight dogs with the ability to sniff out cigarettes, radioactive materials, explosives, narcotics, and people, and a shooting range where his officers train with revolvers, shotguns, and machine guns.

At the road crossing point, a queue of cars stretches back about half a mile from the new glass booths and awning, co-financed by Norway, waiting for inspection by guards and also by radiometric gates that can detect radioactive materials in vehicles. A few miles away a gleaming new glass facility for border guards and customs officers is close to completion at the Terespol train crossing, also built with Schengen funds. Outside the dilapidated former railway station on the other side of the tracks, border guards in stiff green uniforms and peaked hats check passenger documents with mobile handheld computers connected to a national database and the Schengen Information System.

An average of twenty-five freight trains and fifteen to twenty passenger trains pass daily through what was once an obscure provincial railway station, including local trains from inside Poland, the Moscow–Warsaw–Berlin passenger train, and a succession of freight trains carrying coal, timber, and other supplies from Belarus and the Russian Federation. A mile away a stream of trucks moves in and out of the customs compound through a three-mile road fenced in on both sides and flanked by 130 cameras. On weekends this compound sees between 1,500 and 1,800 trucks passing through, some of which are obliged to pass through the giant Heimann X-ray that encloses trucks like a car wash and can detect radioactive materials, explosives, people, and smuggled cigarettes.

The truck crossing also boasts a gleaming new glass customs facility, one side of which was reserved for Belarus officials. Relationships between the EU and Belarus have been fraught since Lukashenko's violent repression of the protests that followed the manipulated 2010 elections, and Belarus has refused to take up these new quarters, which are now filled with plants and flowers instead, giving them the somewhat incongruous feel of a frontier greenhouse. Captain Barej insists that these tensions have not affected the relationship with his counterparts on the other side of the border. "We shouldn't confuse our cooperation as border guards with the political situation," he says. "We have a shared aim to protect the border on both sides."

Much of this "protection" is aimed at preventing smuggling, particularly cigarettes. But the Terespol border is also a significant entry point for irregular migration. There are some half a million undocumented migrants in

Poland, a figure that includes some 300,000 Ukrainians and 50,000 Viet-namese, and Poland is also a transit country for migrants and asylum seekers heading for Germany and western Europe. In 2010 between 360 and 367 migrants were caught trying to cross the border here. The majority come from Belarus and the Russian Federation, but migrants from Chechnya, Georgia, and even Africa and Asia have also tried to slip across the land border at night, by walking across over the Bug River when it freezes over, by jumping from trains when they slow down to enter the station, or by using forged documents or visas on the train from Moscow via Minsk.

Terespol is one of the main entry points for refugees and asylum seekers coming to Poland. According to Lieutenant Ana Holowacz, the head of the "second line" of border control that processes asylum appeals at the border, the number of asylum seekers coming through Terespol in 2010 averaged between fifty and seventy a week. Following their initial assessment by Ho-lowacz's team, asylum seekers are transferred to an open reception center twenty-five miles away in Biala Podlaska, the closest city of any significance and a hub of cross-border trade between Poland and Belarus.

Situated in a featureless industrial suburb on the edge of the town, the center consists of a block of flats directly opposite one of the four "closed" or "guarded" immigrant detention centers that have been constructed along the Polish border with EU co-funding as a result of Poland's membership in the Schengen area. I was not allowed to visit the open center, but I was given a tour of the Biala Podlaska detention center on condition that I did not at-tempt to speak to any of the detainees. Built in a refurbished military bar-racks, the center is typical of the new generation of Schengen immigrant jails, with its fifteen-foot zinc walls, rolls of barbed wire, closed-circuit cameras, and barred windows on the upper floors.

According to its commanding officer, Captain Rogowski, the center, which has a capacity of 170, housed ninety-one detainees from Georgia, Chechnya, and other countries "all over the world," including both undocu-mented migrant workers and rejected asylum seekers from Poland and other European countries. Its facilities were clean, modern, and well-equipped, with a library, a medical room with a nurse and doctor, a family unit, a soc-cer field, and a children's playground, and each section was separated by metal doors and grilles and subjected to the permanent panoptic gaze of closed-circuit cameras.

When a group of adult detainees appeared outside the canteen, I was hur-riedly whisked away to a children's playroom, where five Chechen children were playing with two local primary school teachers. One boy who looked about five cheerfully said hello to me in Polish and did not seem overawed by the uniformed guards gazing solemnly down at him. All these children, like their parents and the other detainees in the center, were awaiting deportation, and some of them had been there for more than a year.

A number of them were asylum seekers whose appeals had been rejected in Poland itself; others had been returned to Poland under the terms of the 1990 Dublin Convention and its 2003 successor, Dublin II, which stipulates that asylum claims must be limited to a single EU member state. These requirements were theoretically designed to eliminate the practice of "asylum shopping," whereby asylum seekers whose appeals were rejected in one country could try again in another. To ensure enforcement of this requirement, all asylum applicants have their fingerprints entered into the Eurodac database, and fingerprinted "Dubliners" who are caught in other European countries are sent back to the place where they made their original claim.

Intended to "harmonize" the EU's asylum procedures among member states, the Dublin Convention has in practice shifted responsibility for screening asylum claims onto outlying "border countries" such as Poland, which are not necessarily noted for their generosity in granting refugee protection. Out of 6,534 asylum applications in Poland recorded by UNHCR in 2010, only 82 were given refugee recognition, and another 439 received some form of temporary "subsidiary protection." Eastern Europe was at the center of many of Europe's great refugee crises during the first half of the twentieth century, and also in the 1990s as a result of the wars in the Balkans and the Caucasus. To some extent the formidable array of equipment and personnel along the Polish border is a preemptive response to any future migratory "invasions" from the East, but it was also intended to make it more difficult for migrants—or refugees—to cross an eastern frontier that has always been considered particularly problematic in security terms.

The Friendly Border

For more than a decade after the collapse of Communism, the European Union's eastern frontier consisted of the postwar Oder-Neisse line between Poland and the newly unified Germany, and the border between Germany and the Czech Republic. As a result of the 2004 EU enlargement and the subsequent accession of Poland, Slovakia, Hungary, Slovenia, Estonia, Latvia, and Lithuania three years later, Europe's eastern borders shifted hundreds of miles eastward, forming a ragged and complicated frontier that begins at the twinned towns of Narva and Ivangorod on the Estonia-Russia border and descends more than two thousand miles to the Slovene coast in the Gulf of Venice.

These boundaries currently adjoin the Russian Federation, Belarus, and Ukraine, but they also enclose the Baltic exclave of Kaliningrad, which is politically part of the Russian Federation even though it is geographically located some 185 miles inside the European Union. The eastern border countries also include Romania and Bulgaria, which are members of the European Union but whose border security arrangements have yet to fulfill the requirements of the Schengen Borders Code. Romania adjoins Moldova, the poorest country in Europe, which is further divided into the breakaway pseudo-state of Russian-speaking Transnistria, whose borders are not recognized by any state in the world. Six Balkan states are also potential candidates for EU membership.

Throughout these enlargements, the evolution of the eastern frontier has been shaped by contradictory aspirations. On one hand, governments in eastern and western Europe have sought to consolidate the reintegration of the former Communist bloc into the European mainstream both politically and economically—an objective to which the free movement of goods and people was seen as crucial. At the same time Europe's eastern frontier was regarded by western European governments as a vulnerable barrier against a range of security threats that include terrorism (including the prospect of weapons of mass destruction from the former Soviet nuclear arsenal), ethnic conflict, political instability, organized crime, and irregular migration (whether in the form of refugee emergencies or economic migration).

Last but not least, the EU has been keen to avoid transforming its eastern border into a new "iron curtain" that would damage relations between Europe and its neighbors and undermine or override local relationships between its eastern border countries and Ukraine, Belarus, and Russia. The balance between these security and immigration priorities and the EU's promotion of a "friendly Schengen border" in the east has not always been easy to maintain.

Much of what is now western Ukraine was once part of Poland, and communities on both sides of the border often have relatives and family connections on the other side. During the 1990s millions of Russians, Ukrainians, and Belarussians entered Poland each year to work or do business as a result of the relaxation of the tight border controls of the Communist era. In the immediate aftermath of Poland's incorporation into the Schengen area, this new openness was drastically restricted as a new visa regime was introduced for Belarussians and Ukrainians in accordance with the Schengen rules. These arrangements generated chaos at the Poland-Ukraine border, as trucks and vehicles were stranded at border crossing points for hours and even days and thousands of Ukrainians were turned back at the border because they had the wrong papers or had not understood the new restrictions.

These requirements have since been relaxed somewhat as part of the on-going attempt to promote the "friendly border." Today Ukrainian and Belarussians living close to the border can enter Poland with three-month tourist visas that are limited to one every six months, on condition that they remain within an eighteen-mile radius of the border, while Polish citizens do not need visas to enter Ukraine.

The Poland-Ukraine border nevertheless remains subject to extraordinary levels of monitoring and control, largely in an attempt to detect and prevent the entry of Ukrainian migrant workers. You cannot go very far along the border without encountering the Border Patrol in their green military uni-forms, police cars, and checkpoints, while teams of blue-uniformed railway police are a constant presence at railway stations or on trains between the border and Warsaw, checking papers and looking out for smugglers or for-eigners whose papers are not in order.

Take the busy 222-mile road that runs southward parallel to the Bug River from Terespol to the city of Chelm and you pass through a sweeping cultivated plain broken by great stretches of pristine birch forest and bayou-like marshland. In the late spring of 2011 there were still patches of snow among the pines and birch trees as we drove south from Terespol to the border checkpoint of Dorohusk, past a succession of nondescript bor-der towns and villages each with its single church and school. The crosses and statues of the Virgin Mary that dotted the roadside and the wooden barns, farmhouses, and occasional horse-drawn cart evoked the Catholic, peasant-based societies of the eastern borderland that Poles call the *kresy,* while a sign indicating the Nazi death camp of Sobibor provides a somber reminder of the darker episodes that once took place amid these pastoral surroundings.

In the course of history countless armies and invaders have marched back and forth across these vast plains: Mongols, Tatars, Russians, Germans,

French, and Poles. Dorohusk is the main crossing point between Poland and Ukraine across the Bug River, along the road from Warsaw to Kiev that once constituted the main supply route for Hitler's armies during Operation Barbarossa. More than 2 million people and 1 million vehicles cross the bridge at this isolated rural hamlet every year. In January 2008 Dorohusk became a symbol of post-Schengen border chaos when three thousand trucks were marooned on the Ukrainian side of the border. Today things have improved somewhat, but Dorohusk remains a notorious traffic bottleneck. When I was there a queue of trucks stretched back more than a mile on the Polish side. During the week the average waiting time is three hours, and on weekends drivers can sometimes wait for an astonishing ten hours or more.

These delays are due not just to the volume of traffic but also to the rigorous document checks and customs searches that take place on both sides of the bridge. All vehicles pass through radiometric detection gates, and trucks and vans may also pass through giant X-ray machines. In 2010 Dorohusk was visited by agents from the U.S. Border Patrol, which has promised to upgrade the crossing's radiometric detection devices, in another indication of the involvement of American border authorities in Europe's eastern border security that includes training programs for Ukrainian border guards and the secondment to nearby Moldova of Native American trackers known as "Shadow Wolves" used by the U.S. Border Patrol to trace undocumented migrants at the Arizona border.

The prospect of weapons of mass destruction or smuggled nuclear materials from the former Soviet Union has been a security preoccupation of the United States since the early post–Cold War period, and these anxieties have since intensified as a result of the 9/11 fixation with terrorist "dirty bombs." "Terrorism affects us all," says Second Lieutenant Joanna Ćwikła-Sztembis, second in command of the Dorohusk checkpoint, in the excellent English (which she calls "Schenglish") that is a result of the numerous training programs she has participated in since Poland joined Schengen. But the main priority at Dorohusk, Ćwikła-Sztembis insists, is "illegal immigration," most of which consists of migrant workers from Ukraine and Moldova. Each year thousands of Ukrainians, Russians, and Moldovans come through the checkpoint with tourist visas or forged papers in search of work in Poland or western Europe.

In 2010, 203 people were refused entry in Dorohusk and another 421 were sent back into Ukraine because they had been caught working illegally or had overstayed their visas. Few people try to cross the "green border" away from the checkpoint. In an exposed plain divided by the Bug River, such crossings are difficult if not impossible, and it is hard to get anywhere near the border without being detected. Nor do many asylum seekers pass through Dorohusk: in 2010 the numbers did not reach double digits. For the last few years, most asylum seekers attempting to cross the Schengen "friendly border" have taken routes farther south, in Slovakia and Hungary.

The Corner of Europe

If Poland was prepared to play the role of European border policeman before joining the EU, the same could not be said of the Slovak Republic. Before Slovakia's 1993 "divorce" from the Czech Republic, few Slovaks even expected to be citizens of an independent state in the European Union, let alone that their country would become a transit point for irregular migration from the former Soviet Union and beyond. From the late 1990s onward, however, migrants and asylum seekers from as far afield as Afghanistan, Iraq, India, and the Horn of Africa have attempted to pass through Slovakia and reach Austria, Germany, Italy, and other countries in western Europe.

As in Poland, many asylum seekers found themselves obliged to make their appeals in Slovakia as a result of the vagaries of the Dublin system. As a result, asylum claims rose steadily from 1,320 in 1999 to a peak of 11,395 in 2004, the year Slovakia joined the European Union. Out of 56,072 applications for asylum made between 1993 and February 2011 only 573 people were granted refugee status, with another 312 given temporary protection.[1] In Bratislava I asked Bernard Priecel, director of the Migration Office at the Slovak Ministry of Interior, about the reason for these strikingly low figures. "For us the main document is the Geneva Convention, and most migrants are economic migrants," he said. "The fact is that the economic situation in Slovakia is not good enough to grant asylum for humanitarian reasons in large numbers."

In a poor country that is still in the throes of what Priecel calls "hard capitalism," there is no doubt that Slovakia's transformation into a transit point for migration has put a strain on its resources. In 2001 the Slovak Migration Office had only 171 employees to deal with more than eight thousand asylum appeals. But Slovakia's asylum system has also been criticized by UNHCR for its "arbitrary and inconsistent decisions" and for what Pierfrancesco Maria Natta, the head of UNHCR's Bratislava office in 2004, described as a failure to distinguish "refugees, those who are fleeing persecution and entitled to protection, and those who are economic migrants."[2]

Priecel rejects these charges and insists that his country has done the best it can in difficult circumstances, but Slovakia's role as an EU border country has not been entirely unwelcome. In addition to participating in international border enforcement operations in the Mediterranean, Slovakia has received financial and logistical assistance from the European Union in reinforcing its own borders, and to some extent has used border enforcement to its diplomatic advantage. As Priecel puts it, "Slovakia is gaining credits within the EU and in the world because of the asylum agenda. It's becoming more known, gaining positive reviews from the outside."

Much of this attention has been focused on Slovakia's remote eastern border with Ukraine, which lies some 318 miles from Bratislava in the most underdeveloped region of the country. A train from the capital passes through the stunning alpine landscape of central Slovakia, with its lakes, rivers, and pristine forests, past dilapidated railway stations, featureless industrial towns, and pretty villages with sloped tile roofs and archaic dust-caked factories, to Slovakia's second city, Kosice. From here you catch a combination of buses to the border. Eastern Slovakia is home to much of the country's Roma population, whose poverty and marginalization are consistently visible in the run-down urban ghettos and shacks dotted across the region and the frequent presence of Gypsy beggars in many towns.

The border itself is located in the area variously known as Subcarpathia, Transcarpathia, and its older designation Ruthenian Carpathia, and runs for 61 miles from the Tatra Mountains of Poland to the north and the Great Hungarian Plain. Together with the Hungary-Ukraine border, this narrow corridor has been the main entry point for undocumented migration at the EU's eastern frontier for the best part of a decade. Most attempts to cross the border take place along the flatter southern plain beyond Sobrance, the easternmost town in Slovakia.

A former spa town during the Austro-Hungarian Empire, Sobrance epitomizes the shifting national jurisdictions of Europe's eastern borderlands. Before World War I, it was known by its Hungarian name, Sobranzce, as a popular resort in the Hungarian county of Ung. In 1920 Ung County became part of the newly created Czechoslovakia; in 1938–39 the region was reannexed by Hungary following the Nazi occupation of Czechoslovakia, before it was divided once again between Czechoslovakia and the Soviet Union in 1945.

Today this border has been comprehensively Schengenized. When Slovakia joined the European Union in 2004 the Slovak Border Guard had 293 officers deployed along the eastern border. It now has 890 officers and a new operational headquarters in Sobrance, equipped with fixed infrared cameras and mobile and handheld cameras for the more mountainous sections farther north, in addition to an array of jeeps, patrol cars, boats, snowmobiles and snow clearance vehicles, and truck and train X-ray devices.

As in Poland, the territorial frontier is only one component in a tiered model of border enforcement that extends some nine miles into Slovakia and includes Border Guard and police checks along minor and major roads. At the Border Guard headquarters in Sobrance, Lieutenant Colonel Jan Vinc showed me a PowerPoint presentation with lines of police, dogs, jeeps, and vehicles drawn up along the border like an eighteenth-century army in defensive formation. Most of this has been financed by the EU. "You can't compare before Schengen and now," says Vinc. "Before Schengen this border was the Slovak border. Now we are responsible for the protection of all people in the European Union."

These efforts are mainly concerned with immigration enforcement. At the spanking new Schengen-financed border checkpoint in the tiny hamlet of Vyšné Nemecké, the blue awning with the Slovak and EU flags rises incongruously from the cultivated and mostly unpopulated plain, and a queue of trucks and cars stretches back along the potholed road toward Sobrance. In 2006, 2,356 migrants were intercepted in this immediate vicinity. Now a thousand feet of the border on either side of the checkpoint is sealed off by a two-tiered fence under permanent camera surveillance, and few people get across.

On a computer screen in his office the checkpoint's commanding officer showed me camera footage of a group of migrants who had been recently caught trying to cross the fence. Their faceless illuminated figures looked like images from an exposed photographic negative as they hurried across the narrow strip, seemingly unaware that their progress was being monitored. Afghans, Chechens, Ukrainians, Moldovans, Iraqis, Bangladeshis, and Somalis have all attempted to cross the border here, rather than the more remote but inaccessible mountains farther north, where border crossings have sometimes ended tragically in temperatures that can reach –20 to –25° F in winter. Three years ago, two Bangladeshis froze to death when they crossed the mountains in deep snow in ordinary summer clothing, without water or food. In September 2010 two African women were found dead in two separate locations near the Starina reservoir in Poloniny National Park along the border without any identification documents.

Since 2007 the number of migrants intercepted at the border has fallen to a total of 495 in 2010, but people are still trying. Three Somalis had been caught early that morning, the checkpoint commander said, and it had not yet been determined whether they were refugees or economic migrants. In theory any migrant who asks for asylum is given an initial interview before being transferred to the asylum reception center in the city of Hummene to have his or her claim assessed. But the Slovak Border Guard has been accused by human rights groups, NGOs, and migrants of disregarding these procedures and summarily deporting would-be refugees across the border into Ukraine without giving them the opportunity to apply for asylum despite their appeals.

The officers at Vyšné Nemecké insist that anyone who wants to apply for asylum can get it, though one officer suggested that Somalis did not always speak good enough English to make themselves understood. I had met many Somalis who spoke perfectly good English, and even those who didn't were more than likely to know the word "asylum," which should at least have granted them access to an interpreter. But the EU and Slovakia have signed readmission agreements with Ukraine that allow them to return migrants caught crossing the border from Ukrainian territory, a trajectory that can be established through camera footage, footprints, bus and train tickets, or other documents. These arrangements certainly allow for the possibility that border guards might hear what they want to hear. There have also been allegations from migrants and human rights groups that Slovak and Hungarian border guards have paid their Ukrainian counterparts bribes to take migrants back without giving them the opportunity to seek asylum.

When I asked the checkpoint commander and his officers why they thought people were prepared to go to such lengths to get into Europe, one officer replied that this was a "philosophical question," while another suggested that it was due to the economic situation in the countries that migrants come from, and insisted that "if they really need help, then it's possible to get it, but there are other organizations to do this. It's not our job."

Much of the work of the border guards at Vyšné Nemecké consists of the same repetitive and laborious tasks: checking documents and confirming identities, searching vehicles for smuggled cigarettes, and checking license plates against databases of stolen vehicles. In addition to a range of Slovak and European police databases containing names of wanted or proscribed people, the checkpoint is equipped with sophisticated devices for analyzing forged documents. One officer demonstrated the VSC-4 Plus microscope cum computer, which uses filters, ultraviolet light, and a database of passports from every country in the world to detect even the most minute deviations, from different design patterns and color tints invisible to the naked eye to blurred edges of letters and spacing between numbers.

Every year hundreds and sometimes thousands of travelers are refused entry because their documents are fraudulent or inadequate, because their reasons for entering Slovakia are considered suspect, or because their names appear on the Schengen Information System blacklist—a list that includes not only criminals but "third-country nationals" deemed in Article 94 (1) of the Schengen Convention to pose "a threat to public policy or public security or to national security." This category clearly allows for wide latitude in interpretation, and whether Slovak border guards were making these decisions for themselves was not clear. But whatever the reasons for sending people back, these decisions could not be taken without the cooperation of their counterparts on the other side of the border.

Uzhgorod

Since the late 1990s the European Union has consistently sought to involve neighboring countries in its attempts to prevent irregular migration, and Ukraine's participation in these "externalized" border controls has been a key factor in the fall in the number of migrants in Slovakia and Hungary in the last few years. In 2004 Ukraine agreed to the EU's European Neighbourhood Policy, and since then it has become increasingly proactive in preventing its own citizens from entering Europe without authorization and also in stopping migrants attempting to transit to Europe through Ukrainian territory.

The EU, the International Organization for Migration, and even the U.S. State Department have all provided technological and financial assistance, training, and capacity-building programs to the Ukraine State Border Guard Service, which includes visits by Ukrainian border guard officials to the U.S.-Mexico border. Europe has also helped Ukraine upgrade its immigration detention facilities or "vagabond centers" and funded the construction of new centers.

The rights and welfare of migrants have not been a high priority in this cooperation. In 2005 Human Rights Watch reported that migrants and asylum seekers in Ukraine were "routinely detained in appalling conditions; subjected to violence, robbery, and extortion; denied legal assistance; and in some cases sent back to countries where they face persecution and torture."[3] The report also noted that migrants were being routinely shunted back into Ukraine across the Slovak and Hungarian borders, in what its authors described as a wider tendency to use Europe's readmission agreements with neighboring countries as "tools to transfer migrants and asylum seekers out of EU territory in violation of their basic rights."

Most migrants and asylum seekers heading for Slovakia pass through the city of Uzhgorod, just a mile on the other side of the border. The administrative capital of Ukrainian Transcarpathia, Uzhgorod still evokes some of its former provincial splendor as Ungar, the Hungarian capital of what was once known as Ruthenian Carpathia, with its tree-lined river walkway, its mixture of Catholic and onion-domed Orthodox churches, and its elegant but slightly dilapidated nineteenth-century facades. When I was there it rained almost every day, and it was easy to imagine the horse-drawn carriages of Austrian and Hungarian landowners among the run-down cars that splashed their way through the pools of water in the potholed cobblestone streets.

The presence of women and children selling sprigs of herbs and bags of yogurt on the pavement and the sight of people rummaging through trash bins near the railway station was a reminder of Ukraine's twenty-first-century poverty. Like Sobrance, Uzhgorod has changed nationality various times, and its multiethnic population includes Hungarians, Russians, Ukrainians, and Roma. In recent years this city of 124,000 has acquired a new population of transient migrants that includes Pakistanis, Palestinians, Sri Lankans, Somalis, Iraqis, and Afghans.

One of them was Ajaab, a twenty-one-year-old Somali student from Mogadishu, who left Somalia in 2007, when his father was killed by the extremist Islamist militia al-Shabaab after defying an order to close his cigarette shop on the grounds that selling cigarettes was "against Islam." That same year his mother was shot dead in her house during the fighting between militias and the Ethiopian-backed Transitional Federal Government, and his sister and some of her friends were executed by al-Shabaab because they had boyfriends and were accused of prostitution. Ajaab sold his parents' house and shop for $8,000 and paid a smuggler to fly him from Dubai to Moscow, where another contact promised to take him to Europe for $3,000.

Together with a group of Somalis, he came to Uzhgorod and tried to cross the Hungarian border, only to be caught by Hungarian border guards. Ajaab says that he asked for asylum, but this request was ignored and he was sent back to Ukraine the following day. "Usually they interview you, and ask you where you crossed from," he told me, "and if you say you came from Ukraine, they just communicate with the Ukrainians, and sometimes they pay them money to deport you back to Ukraine." On his return to Ukraine he was beaten up by Ukrainian border guards in an attempt to find out who helped him cross, before being taken to a detention center where he was held for six months.

In 2010 he tried to enter Hungary again, only to be caught once again by Ukrainian border guards and placed in detention for another six months. When I met him he was marooned in Uzhgorod and sharing a flat with seven other Somalis, all of whom were hoping to get to Europe. Life as a migrant in Ukraine is precarious and difficult.

Abdulkhani is a slim and soft-spoken nineteen-year-old from the city of Luuq in southwest Somalia, and a member of the marginalized and often persecuted Tumaal ethnic minority. In 2009 al-Shabaab militants came to the photographic shop where he worked, told him that photographs and cameras were "not allowed by Islam," and ordered him to go to Mogadishu to fight the Transitional Federal Government and African Union troops. Abdulkhani had no interest in fighting in the war and raised the money to pay for a forged passport, which got him to Dubai and Moscow. Unable to find work, he came to Uzhgorod and tried to cross the Hungarian border on August 31, 2010. He was arrested by Ukrainian border guards and taken to the detention center in the border city of Chop, where Ukrainian immigration officials rejected his appeal for asylum on the grounds that he had no documents to prove that he came from Somalia.

With the help of a local lawyer, he eventually received a green card granting him permission to live temporarily in Ukraine. But this document does not give permission to work and has to be renewed at police discretion every week or sometimes every few days, and every few months Abdulkhani has to go to court for a further renewal. Ukrainian police and border guards are notoriously corrupt, and there have been cases of police extorting bribes from migrants in exchange for these renewals.

The two men share a flat wih other Somalis that costs $200 a month, a sum they manage to raise with help from friends and relatives abroad. At least once a week and sometimes more, the flat is raided by police in the early hours of the morning to check documents, inspect their mobile phones, or see if any new people have arrived. The local police routinely pick up migrants in the street and hold them for up to eight or nine hours, for no apparent purpose except to harass them. As a result, most of the Somalis rarely go out unless they have to, while Somali women living in another flat only use taxis. According to Abdulkhani, police are not the only threat to migrants in a country where the presence of black people is still a historical novelty: "If you have money and documents, Ukraine is a good country. But if you're a person like me, really it's a very hard situation. Ukraine isn't a friendly country. If someone is an immigrant they don't like you really, and if the person is black they totally don't like you. Ninety percent of the people are racist. Some of them when they see you buying something they just come up and laugh at you. They're just checking you out. And if you ask them why are you laughing and speak Russian to them, they start abusing you. Even when we go to shops to buy something they're not happy to sell you something. They shout at us when we don't know the language and point at things, and throw you out of the shop."

No one knows how many migrants are trapped in this situation in Uzhgorod at any one time, and no government seems to be in any hurry to find out. The Ukrainian government's willingness to accept readmitted migrants— whether officially or unofficially—has sometimes resulted in "chain deportations" in which refugees from Chechnya and other conflict zones in the Russian Federation have been sent back to Ukraine from the EU and handed over to Russian authorities, who regard them as rebels and terrorists.

It is difficult to see what Ukraine gets from these arrangements, except for financial assistance to control its borders and set up detention centers—and the possibility, however remote, of EU membership. They have certainly not brought many benefits to ordinary Ukrainians who routinely cross the border. When I returned to Slovakia on a Sunday morning, it took a numbingly tedious four and a half hours to get from the Ukrainian crossing point, with its astrakhan-hatted guards and its heroic Soviet-era statue of a Red Army soldier pointing toward Europe, to the Slovak side of the border—a distance of little more than a third of a mile. Each car was meticulously searched by Ukrainian officials and the documents of their occupants were inspected, and then the identical search was repeated by their Slovak counterparts. It was not the greatest advertisement for the eastern "friendly border," but at least these travelers were allowed to cross, unlike the Somalis and other "third-country nationals" I had left behind in Uzhgorod, for whom entry into Europe would always be prohibited.

3

Policing the Spanish Frontier

The nine miles from Tangier to Algeciras have become like
The 5,000 miles from Kinshasa to Brussels
God, Our Father in Heaven, it is now your problem.

—Congolese migrant singer El Pacha Docha

On September 2, 2000, the Spanish photojournalist Javier Bauluz published a shocking and seemingly incredible photograph in the Spanish newspaper *La Vanguardia*. In it a Spanish couple are sitting under a flowery umbrella on a beach near Tarifa in southern Spain, staring at the corpse of an African migrant lying facedown near the edge of the sea a few yards away. The man is wearing sunglasses and swimming trunks, the woman a fashionable bikini. What makes the photograph disturbing is not just its jarring juxtaposition of leisure and tragedy, wealth and poverty, but the fact that the couple appear to be so completely unaffected by the presence of the body in the jeans and yellow sweatshirt that they remain seated alongside their cooler and drinks.

This photograph was widely circulated internationally with captions such as "Death at the door of paradise" and "The indifference of the West" and aroused such anger and disbelief that some commentators alleged that it had been faked. To refute these allegations Bauluz wrote an article describing how he was called out on assignment to a beach near Tarifa. On arriving at the scene he was appalled to find that the presence of the body lying in the sand appeared to have produced virtually no response from the holidaymakers present:

People got on with their day at the beach. They swam and sunbathed. Kids splashed water along the shoreline. Just a few of the swimmers, five or six in a tight circle, commented on the tragedy. It seemed like a lack of respect to me and I was outraged. Whether black or white, he was dead. Unfortunately, I was not at all surprised. This is the same indifference I have seen on so many other days when the fate of immigrants has been involved.[1]

This anonymous migrant was one of thousands who have drowned in the last two decades trying to cross the "southern maritime borders" of the Schengen area. With its proximity to the Middle East and North Africa and a combined coastline of 21,199 miles that includes Spain, Italy, Malta, and Greece and extends across the Mediterranean, the Aegean, the Adriatic, and the South Atlantic, southern Europe has been the most visible route for irregular migration ever since the early 1990s, and until recently these pressures were primarily concentrated on Spain.

Spain has historically been associated more with emigration than with immigration, and it was not until after Spain's accession to the Schengen area in 1991 that undocumented migrants first began to cross the Mediterranean from North Africa in the rickety boats and dinghies known as *pateras*. Many were heading north to other European countries in search of work, but rising economic prosperity also fueled a demand for migrant labor inside Spain itself. Initially most irregular migrants were Moroccans, seeking to evade the tighter visa restrictions imposed by the Spanish government on Moroccan nationals as a result of Spain's accession to Schengen.

As the decade wore on, migrants from sub-Saharan Africa and other countries farther afield also attempted to reach the Spanish coast, and a once impoverished country that only a few years before had provided a steady flow of Spanish migrant workers to factories in Belgium, Germany, and Yugoslavia became the indispensable guardian of the "southern maritime borders" at the closest point between Europe and its unwanted intruders from the global South.

"Europe's Rio Grande"

With only eighteen miles separating Spain from Morocco at its narrowest point near Tarifa, the Strait of Gibraltar was until recently the main entrance into Europe for thousands of North African and sub-Saharan migrants. For years thousands of *harraga*—"those who burn," as Moroccans call undocumented migrants from North Africa—and sub-Saharan Africans regularly set out across this narrow and treacherous strip of water on moonless nights in *pateras*, in dinghies, and even on children's flotation devices—a spectacularly dangerous method of transport in a narrow maritime channel whose risks stem not just from strong currents and waves but also from the ships and tankers that ply this busy maritime corridor between the Mediterranean and the Atlantic.

Between 1997 and 2001 alone, there were 3,285 known deaths in the Strait, and the real number may well be higher. Some were hit by passing ships or poisoned by toxic gases produced by the interaction of fuel and seawater. Most drowned, sometimes within yards of reaching the shore because they could not swim, or because the smugglers who brought them were unwilling to risk arrest by taking them ashore and ordered them out.

In the last few years these journeys have become increasingly rare, and few migrants "burn the Strait" on moonless nights or land on crowded beaches during the summer "migration season." One of the reasons for this decline can be found at the port of Algeciras in southern Spain. At the headquarters of the Algeciras Civil Guard, a large radar screen tracks even the smallest vessels in the busy maritime highway that connects the Mediterranean to the Atlantic Ocean.

Uniformed officers pore over rows of computer screens that provide live camera footage of the Strait twenty-four hours a day. This office is the nerve center of the Sistema Integrado de Vigilancia Exterior (Integrated Exterior Vigilance System) or SIVE, the jewel in the crown of the surveillance technologies that the European Union has put in place in the western Mediterranean over the last decade. Initially installed with co-funding from the European Union in 2000, SIVE is a sophisticated system of cameras and radar stretching from Málaga to Tarifa, enabling Civil Guard technicians in Algeciras to permanently monitor the Strait of Gibraltar.

The main purpose of SIVE is the detection and interception of irregular migration. Before its construction, the Civil Guard relied mainly on binoculars to detect migrant crossings in the Strait. Now Civil Guard officers can detect any suspicious or extraneous movements on the radar screen and zoom SIVE's powerful revolving cameras toward them, enabling them to direct interceptions or search-and-rescue operations. To demonstrate the system's efficiency, officers at Algeciras showed me archive footage of a boat-load of migrants being intercepted by Civil Guard officers on a beach near Tarifa.

The grainy pictures were taken from a distance, so both migrants and their pursuers were reduced to tiny Pac-Man-like dots chasing each other. Watching the astonishingly large number of dots pour out of their tiny boat and scatter across the white sand trying to evade their pursuers, I thought of the *torres vigias* (watchtowers) built by Spanish rulers during the sixteenth century in a mostly ineffectual attempt to protect Spain's vulnerable coast-line from Muslim corsairs, Protestant privateers, and putative Turkish in-vaders. SIVE is a high-tech watchtower overlooking Europe's equivalent of the Rio Grande—a narrow moat between the Third and First Worlds, be-tween the largest trading bloc in the world and a continent whose poverty, wars, and youthful population are perceived by the EU as a threat to its pros-perity, stability, and security, and which also acts as a maritime cordon sani-taire against a new "invasion" from the Muslim Maghreb, just as it once did in the days of Philip II.

The Civil Guard officers who operate this system were at pains to empha-size its effectiveness in facilitating search-and-rescue operations, but the overriding purpose of SIVE is deterrence and prevention. Critics of the system, such as the Andalucian Human Rights Association (APDHA), have argued that SIVE may even have increased the numbers of deaths at sea by forcing migrants to take longer and more circuitous routes to avoid detec-tion. There is some truth in these accusations. In the wake of its installation, smugglers initially shifted their routes away from the Strait toward Almeria in the north and southward toward Cádiz. As Spain and Morocco intensi-fied their vigilance in the western Mediterranean, migratory routes shifted farther south into the Atlantic, and migrants began to arrive in the Canary Islands from West Africa in the larger fiberglass dinghies and fishing boats known as *cayucos*.

These journeys took longer and were made in rougher seas. Between 2001 and 2006 as many as seven thousand people may have drowned following the "*cayuco* route," according to APDHA. By 2008, 89,851 people had ar-rived in the Canary Islands across the South Atlantic, with a peak of 36,678 in 2006. Since then these routes have also been closed. In 2001, SIVE was installed on Fuerteventura, using radar technology from the 2001–2 Afghan war, and it has since been extended to the other Canary Islands as part of Operation Seahorse, a joint Spanish-EU network of observation satellites, and helicopter, aerial, and naval patrols stretching from West Africa to Portugal.

In 2007 Spain and other EU member states acting under the direction of the European border agency Frontex began a series of joint naval operations in the South Atlantic in collaboration with various West African governments, with the aim of intercepting migrant boats before they left West African territorial waters. The following year nearly six thousand migrants were "convinced to return to safety" or "escorted back to the closest shore" with the cooperation of a number of West African governments. These efforts had a dramatic impact, with a 64 percent fall in the number of boat arrivals on the Canary Islands the following year.

The closing of the *cayuco* route was undoubtedly a positive development, given the hardships and risks that these journeys entailed, but as in the Mediterranean, humanitarian rescue was a by-product rather than a primary objective of enforcement operations that were intended to stop migrants setting out for Europe and send them back. In effect, Spain and the EU extended Europe's borders into West African territorial waters and even into West Africa itself, where Civil Guard officers now provide training and capacity-building programs to help police and coast guards from various countries to prevent migrants from embarking on these journeys.

In 2010, few migrants were coming to Spain by sea. In the first three months of the year there were no *patera* crossings in the Strait, according to the Algeciras Civil Guard, and the few cases of unauthorized entry consisted of individuals smuggled in cars and vehicles on ferries. This reduction was partly due to the contraction of the Spanish economy since 2008, which has resulted in many Moroccan workers returning home. But another explanation lies in the barriers that Spain and the EU have put in place on the other side of the Strait.

The Colonial Border

The Spanish exclave of Melilla is a long way from the vineyards and châteaus of the Moselle valley, and it is separated from its Moroccan neighbor by the most formidable and physically imposing of all the Schengen borders. Visitors from Morocco pass through the dusty border town of Beni Enzar, with its Berber and Arabic shops and street signs, cracked pavements, and women in hijabs and kaftans, past touts waving immigration forms, to the dilapidated concrete border posts where Moroccan police officers morosely inspect passports and travel documents. From there a caged tunnel leads toward the modern blue awning topped with Spanish and EU flags, with its twenty-foot-high fence snaking off in both directions.

This fence separates one of the poorest provinces in Morocco from an outpost of Spanish and European affluence, replete with Spanish street names, elegant modernist buildings, marinas, water parks, familiar brand names, and a profusion of four-wheel-drive vehicles that in an almost entirely urbanized territory of just over eight square miles have no obvious purpose except to demonstrate the wealth and status of their owners. This world of designer shops, Rolex watches, and twenty-first-century Euro-consumerism coexists with relics of the colonial past, from Franco-era monuments and statues of the Virgin of Africa to streets and squares that are named after generals, legionnaires, and forgotten African battles and read like an index from some of the more reactionary chapters in Spanish history.

Melilla is the oldest of Spain's two African colonies. It was conquered by a Spanish expeditionary force in 1497, during the abortive attempt by Ferdinand and Isabella to follow the completion of the Reconquista with a North African crusade, and it subsequently became one of a chain of garrison-fortresses or *presidios* that Spain established along the North African coast. In the late nineteenth and early twentieth centuries both Melilla and Ceuta became the springboard for Spain's bloody North African colonial campaigns—an enterprise that was spearheaded by the Spanish Foreign Legion and the troglodyte militarism of its first commander, General José Millán-Astray. These colonial campaigns also provided the young Francisco Franco with his military and political education, as well as the soldiers and Moroccan mercenaries that enabled him to launch the coup attempt that began the Spanish Civil War in 1936.

Melilla was also the temporary home of Abd el-Krim, the remarkable Moroccan nationalist leader, who received his political education while working on the Arabic-language supplement of the local newspaper. In 1920, inspired by a combination of Rif nationalism and Salafi Islamic reformism, Abd el-Krim united the feuding Rif tribes in a revolt against the Spanish Protectorate in Morocco, subjecting Spain to a series of stinging and humiliating military defeats. By the time the rebellion was snuffed out six years later by half a million French and Spanish troops, Abd el-Krim's Republic of the Confederated Tribes of the Rif had acquired all the trappings of an independent state, with its own army, tax system, and government.

Today Melilla remains a contested frontier. I arrived in the city in the midst of a minor diplomatic incident, when Moroccan customs officers placed a placard in a window describing Melilla as an "occupied city." Both the Melilla administration and the Spanish government were demanding a retraction from Morocco, which was not forthcoming. Relations between Melilla and its Moroccan neighbor are punctuated with such episodes. Every day thirty thousand Moroccans cross the border to work for wages that are well below the Spanish average, and the relationship between the Spanish police and Moroccans often replicates the colonial hierarchies of the past. One evening I watched a bulldog-like Spanish policeman snarling and waving his truncheon at a group of Moroccan women, who moved quickly away as if they were used to being on the receiving end of such treatment.

Perhaps because of its greater distance from Spain, the Melilla border feels tenser and more abrasive than Ceuta. One afternoon I was standing near the border checkpoint when a Spanish plainclothes cop thrust his badge into my face and, with a slightly hysterical urgency that had no obvious cause, shouted at me to take my sunglasses off and produce my ID. Even the border fence is higher than Ceuta's. Since the 2005 "crisis of the fences" the fence has been doubled in height and Moroccan army units and sentry posts are dotted all along the frontier, in addition to the Civil Guard patrols on the Spanish side. A series of watchtowers and a hundred cameras look out over the narrow strip of no-man's-land that has been stripped of trees or cover, and fiber-optic sound and movement sensors automatically direct the attention of the rotating cameras toward any human or animal approaching the fence.

The razor wire that wrought so much havoc in 2005 has been replaced by an automated wire hinge, which folds outward at the impact of a human body and draws the attention of the cameras, enabling the Civil Guard to deploy a patrol in less than a minute to any point along the fence. Anyone who succeeds in getting over the first layer in this time still has to cross the thirteen-foot gap that separates the outer fence from the inner one and circumvent an additional "tri-dimensional fence" of interlocking cables that rise diagonally from the concrete walkway, ensnaring the legs of intruders and slowing their progress, and trigger a pipe running at eye level along the length of the fence to spray pepper-infused water into the gap.

All this has been designed with a single objective in mind: to stop migrants crossing the border to seek work or asylum. Before its construction began in the early 1990s, the border consisted of a few rolls of wire fence that were easily penetrated. The Melilla Civil Guard is proud of the effectiveness of the *valla no agresiva* or "nonaggressive fence" in preventing unauthorized entries, and insists that it is not intended to cause injury. "Some people describe us as if we were heartless," says a Civil Guard officer, Lieutenant Juan Antonio Martin Rivera, "but we're often the first people that migrants see. When we see mothers coming with children, we don't treat them like enemies. We give them bread and milk."

Some officers may well behave like this, but the Civil Guard's behavior has not always been exemplary. A video of the 2005 crisis made by the Melillan human rights activist José Palazón shows African migrants in a Moroccan hospital with broken arms and bandaged legs and ankles, injuries that they received at the hands of the Civil Guard and the Moroccan Auxiliary Forces (known as "Alis"). In one sequence, dated August 29, 2005, more than a dozen African migrants stand around the corpse of a Cameroonian migrant named Akabang Abuna in the Marihuari Forest near the border fence and describe how he was hit in the stomach by a Civil Guard officer with a rifle butt and began vomiting blood before he died.

Médecins Sans Frontières and the Rif Human Rights Association in Morocco have also documented incidents in which the Spanish and Moroccan security have used excessive force. A report to the Spanish Parliament by Spain's human rights ombudsman noted the "great violence" with which both the Civil Guard and Spanish Foreign Legion responded to the 2005 incursions.[2] The Civil Guard in Melilla and Ceuta has also been accused of pushing migrants back through the access points along the border fences into Morocco in order to deny them the opportunity to apply for asylum.

The commander of the Melilla Civil Guard emphatically denies these allegations and insists that his men have never used live ammunition against migrants. "My officers can't even take their guns from their holsters without having to explain why they did it," he says. I had no reason to doubt his sincerity, but he was not in Melilla in 2005, and his insistence that only nonlethal weaponry had been used ignores the fact that rubber bullets too can kill—especially when fired from close range against men perched on a high wire fence. "I'm not saying the Civil Guard shot people, but people were shot," says the director of the Melilla Human Rights Association, José Alonso Sanchez, who witnessed some of these clashes. "Doctors have seen the cadavers—with bullet wounds from below and above. People were shot in the back on the wire. One man was shot with a rubber bullet in the trachea and the government said he died of 'displacement of the trachea.'"

No one has ever been held responsible for the deaths that took place that year, though both Spain and Morocco claim to have carried out their own internal investigations, each of which blamed their counterparts on the other side of the border. This absence of accountability may well indicate the value placed on the lives that were lost in 2005, but it is also facilitated by the ambiguous status of the Melilla frontier. In theory, migrants should come under Spanish legal jurisdiction even before they reach the border, because the fence was constructed a few meters inside Spanish territory. But according to the 2005 Spanish ombudsman's report, there is a "neutral zone of variable length" adjoining the border fence for which neither Spain nor Morocco accepts legal responsibility.[3]

To complicate matters further, the Melilla regional government regards the fence as a "complex barrier" and insists that Spanish and international law do not apply until migrants have actually entered the space between the two tiers.[4] These ambiguities have in effect transformed the border into a legal no-man's-land in which anything can happen to those who enter it and no one is ever responsible, and no government appears to have any interest in changing this situation.

The Penal Colony

Despite the fence, men, women, and unaccompanied minors still find their way into Melilla in boats and homemade rafts, in the false bottoms of cars and other vehicles, by swimming round the edge of the fences, or even by crawling through a water pipe leading into the port, in the expectation that they will be able to apply for asylum and continue their journey to the Spanish mainland while their applications are processed. These aspirations are generally disappointed. In the past Melilla was used as a penal settlement for Spanish convicts. Today the exclave has become an offshore outpost of Schengenland, where migrants may be technically in Europe but unable to proceed any farther.

Most migrants who reach Melilla stay at the Temporary Immigrant Reception Center (CETI) near the Barrio Chino checkpoint and the local golf course, where they live in dormitory accommodations while their asylum applications are considered. Originally built with a capacity of 480 people, the center once housed 1,135 at the height of the 2005 crisis. The CETI is not a detention center, and its occupants are free to come and go during the day, but they cannot leave Melilla until their asylum claims have been resolved— a process that can take months or even years. Rejected appeals are often followed by a protracted waiting period, which can end abruptly with a police raid in the early hours of the morning, when residents are taken to the Spanish mainland for deportation.

In November 2009 these raids were so frequent that more than a hundred residents abandoned the center, preferring to sleep rough or under plastic sheets on a hillside in the Melilla suburbs. I was not permitted by the Melilla authorities to visit the center a few months later, on the grounds that my presence would violate the privacy of its residents, but the administration may have other reasons for such reticence. The CETI's population included Kashmiris, Punjabis, and some fifty-odd Bangladeshi migrants who had been living in the city for nearly five years. "Los Banglas" had become a seemingly permanent presence in Melilla, where they cleaned cars and carried shopping bags at the supermarkets to earn a few euros. Once a week they staged a quiet demonstration in the city center to demand a resolution of their legal status.

Alcoholism, drug addiction, and depression were rife in the CETI, and there have also been a number of suicides over the years. "There are people there who are totally destroyed. They're never going to work again in their lives," said José Palazón. "How can it be that when someone from Bangladesh arrives here after leaving his country in search of work, just as the Spanish, Italians, and English once did, they can detain you for five years?" Palazón introduced me to three Kashmiri men from the CETI, all of whom were clearly under severe strain. One was seeing a psychiatrist for depression and sat frowning at the floor without speaking a word; another was so withdrawn that he barely made eye contact. Gulsahan, a gaunt and haunted-looking young man in his early twenties, told me how his family had sold half their flock of goats to send him to Europe, and of his desire to escape the violence in Kashmir and find a country where it was possible to "live normally."

These aspirations had plunged him into the harsh abnormality of twenty-first-century irregular migration. Like many Asian migrants heading for Spain, Gulsahan originally flew to Conakry, Guinea, where he was forced to spend six months with a group of migrants in a windowless room. Eventually "the boss" in charge of the next phase of his journey took him and his companions to Mauritania, where he found himself on a wooden fishing boat with 335 other passengers heading for the Canary Islands. Shortly after the boat left port, its engine cut out and the passengers drifted for more than a week before they were spotted by a Spanish helicopter. Gulsahan was brought to Melilla and three years later he was still trapped there, unable to work, out of touch with his family, and desperate to go to any country that would take him. The three Kashmiris were nevertheless in better shape than one of their companions, who no longer left his dormitory room at the CETI but spent his days staring into the mirror, laughing and crying and talking to his own reflection.

Later that day I met Harmit, the son of an Indian Punjabi farmer, and his Moroccan girlfriend, Fatima, who were also staying at the CETI. Harmit had persuaded his father to sell half his land to pay smugglers to take him to Europe in 2006 at the age of nineteen—a journey that he said was inspired by the Western travelers he had observed in his own country. After flying to Mali he had crossed the Sahara and entered Melilla in the false bottom of a car hoping to get to Barcelona, only to be issued with an expulsion order. Four years later he had yet to leave Melilla, and Fatima had a three-month-old baby, even though she also had no papers and was at risk of deportation to Morocco despite fears about her safety should she return to her family because she was in an unmarried relationship. "In the CETI they give us food, clothes and shoes," Harmit said, "but you can't live like this. When someone leaves their home they have one dream, to have a house, children, money—here there's nothing to do but clean Spanish people's cars."

In September 2010 the couple was allowed to go to the Spanish mainland, but this concession was unusual. In the early hours of September 7, Melilla police raided the CETI and rounded up "los Banglas." Some of the Bangladeshis tried to escape and jump over the fence, but forty-seven were taken to the Spanish mainland as a prelude to deportation, and two months later seven were flown on a military plane to Dhaka. The remaining forty were released from a detention center in Barcelona, because the sixty-day maximum limit for detention allowed by Spanish law had expired.

It is difficult to detect the logic behind these seemingly random and arbitrary procedures. In January 2011 an Algerian asylum seeker in Melilla was given the much sought-after yellow card by the Melilla police, which should have granted him permission to travel to the Spanish mainland while his asylum appeal was being processed. On boarding the ferry for Málaga, however, he was turned back by Spanish immigration officers. Other asylum seekers with the yellow card have met with similar rejections when they tried to leave Melilla. Amnesty International and UNHCR both criticized these refusals as a breach of Spain's Schengen accession agreement, but the Spanish Ministry of the Interior argued that they were justified under Article 5 of the Schengen Borders Code, which specifies that "Spain shall maintain checks . . . on sea and air connections departing from Ceuta and Melilla and having as their sole destination any other place on Spanish territory."

The asylum seekers who were not allowed to go to the mainland had already been checked by Spanish officials in Melilla and given permission to leave, but it was nevertheless in keeping with Melilla's role as a *tapon* or cork on irregular migration that the Ministry of the Interior should overrule its own officials and introduce what was effectively a new border inside Spanish territory in an attempt to avoid what the Spanish authorities call the *efecto llamada*, or "call effect," which they fear might attract other migrants to Spain's Moroccan exclaves.

The "Zone of Violence"

Morocco has been an essential component of Spain's migratory controls. Spanish officials I spoke to often praised Moroccan cooperation and gave the Moroccans credit for the fall in irregular migration. This cooperation, which includes the presence of Moroccan security forces at the Ceuta and Melilla fences and stepped-up naval patrols by the Moroccan Royal Gendarmerie along the Mediterranean coast, dates back to the Euro-Mediterranean Partnership, launched in Barcelona in 1995, and was subsequently intensified following Morocco's inclusion in the 2004 European Neighbourhood Policy.[5] In 2003, the Moroccan government introduced harsh criminal penalties for Moroccan citizens attempting to enter Spain without documentation, and it has also played a key role in preventing migrants from transiting Morocco en route to Europe.

This role has generally been restricted to repression and deterrence. Morocco is a signatory to the 1951 Geneva Convention on Refugees and cooperates with UNHCR. It also has an Office of Refugees and Stateless Persons

(Bureau des Réfugiés et Apatrides) to assist refugees. But few people get refugee protection in Morocco, and such protection often means little more than the right to remain in Moroccan territory. In any case, the majority of sub-Saharan African migrants in Morocco are economic migrants, not asylum seekers. Thousands of them have found themselves stranded in the country as a result of Morocco's increased control over its coastline, and eke out a living through begging, scavenging, occasional temporary work in construction or agriculture, street vending, petty drug dealing, and prostitution.

Some sleep rough in the countryside and streets; others share overcrowded flats in the slums of Rabat, Tangier, and Casablanca. In Tangier, African migrants are a ubiquitous presence at the port area and the beach, where they come to beg or look for a way to get across to Spain—a passage that has become even more difficult since the opening of the new port an hour's drive outside the city.

Morocco is a poor country with high levels of unemployment, but the harsh treatment of African migrants by the Moroccan state is not merely a question of resources. The city of Oujda is located some two hours from Melilla. Formerly a center of anticolonial unrest during the last years of the French Protectorate in Morocco, the city once provided a safe haven to anti-French rebels during the Algerian War of Independence. In his autobiography Nelson Mandela describes how he was inspired by the sight of the Algerian Army of National Liberation parading in Oujda in 1962 to seek a similar outcome in his own country.

The proximity of Algeria was once a major source of income for Oujda, but since 1994 the border has been closed as a result of political disputes between the two countries. Today this bustling, traffic-bound modern city of 500,000 has come to play a little-known role in Europe's border wars. This role is partly due to Oujda's strategic location at the end of the Saharan migratory route and its proximity both to the Algerian city of Maghnia (a center for organized people-smuggling networks) just across the border and to the area where migrants deported by the Moroccan security forces are routinely deposited.

In 2005 hundreds of the migrants rounded up outside Ceuta and Melilla were herded across the Oujda border before the Moroccan government succumbed to international pressure and brought them back. Nowadays these expulsions are carried out more discreetly and usually take place at night, when migrants rounded up in other parts of the country are brought to the border and forced to walk across it, after being stripped of their mobile phones and in some cases their shoes. These deportees are frequently pushed back by the Algerian security forces in what Hicham Baraka, co-founder of the Oujda-based Association Beni Znassen for Culture, Development, and Solidarity (ABCDS), calls a morbid game of "human ping-pong," or else they slip back across the border themselves.

An estimated seven hundred migrants live in and around the city, though no one knows for sure. Some can be found in the faculty grounds of Oujda's Mohammed I University, where the university authorities have allowed them to build shacks and lean-tos in a dirt compound a few hundred yards from the main administrative offices. The presence of students and staff at *la fac* provides some protection from police raids, but not much. At nights and at weekends when the campus is empty, police routinely enter the university to harass and arrest them and destroy their shelters, and so most migrants prefer to live in the so-called *tranquilo* camps in the forests just outside the city.

I visited one of these Nigerian semi-permanent *tranquilo* camps with Hicham Baraka and his ABCDS colleague Noureddine, after telephone negotiations with the camp's representative or "chairman." We took a taxi to the edge of a plantation forest of low pine trees. After about ten minutes, a tall, powerfully built Nigerian named Anthony came ambling out of the forest in plastic sandals, jeans, and T-shirt, and led us through the neat rows of planted pine trees. A former truck driver and jack-of-all-trades, Anthony had been living in Oujda on and off for three years, and had previously worked in Madrid and Valencia before he was arrested and deported. Now he was the official water carrier for his camp. Each day he walked back and forth to the nearest tap, more than a mile away, laden down with plastic water bottles, and his shoulders were bruised with rope marks from the effort. Anthony displayed a gift for pithy and expressive phrasemaking as he talked about the snakes that sometimes crawled into the tents and the risks of arrest and police harassment that made him wary of buying food in Oujda. "In my country we were kings and queens," he said. "Now we live like rabbits here. We hide by day and come out at night."

Anthony had clearly not been living that well in Nigeria. He had no parents, he said, and only one sister, whom he had not seen in years, and he had no desire to go back despite the primitive conditions in the forest. After about fifteen minutes, we reached the plastic bivouac of Chris, the chairman of the Nigerian *tranquilos*, which was set apart from the other tents as a mark of his authority. Chris was a charismatic and handsome young man, and it was impossible to know whether his leadership position was due to his personal qualities or his connections to the transnational networks that organized the trans-Saharan migrant trail. The *tranquilo* camps are divided by nationality, language, and ethnicity, and most of the Nigerians were members of the Yoruba ethnic group. Their camps consisted of the same identical tents and homemade bivouacs built with plastic and found materials on a frame of sticks or branches, with clothes hanging from lines between trees, and cooking pots and bottles of plastic water piled outside them.

Some were larger and better constructed than others and a few had strips of carpet or thin mattresses, but most had only blankets and scattered clothes on the hard dirt floor. All of their occupants had come to Morocco via the Sahara with the same dream: to get to Spain or elsewhere in Europe and find work and a better life for themselves and in some cases for the children they had brought with them. Some, like Anthony, had made it to Spain only to be sent back to Morocco. Others had been deported a number of times across the Algerian border, but there were also more recent arrivals from Algeria and Libya, whose occupations included beautician, hairdresser, and mechanic; there was also a surprising number of welders.

Most of the Nigerians were Christians. One man came walking through the forest dreamily carrying a battered Bible, like some itinerant preacher from the Mississippi Delta. In one camp a group of women were singing hymns, chanting prayers, and dancing with their children and babies on their arms to the accompaniment of a drum. "We all believe in God and we are calling upon him to help us," one of the Nigerians told me while we waited respectfully for the service to end.

Afterward I spoke to the women. All of them were stressed and anxious. Some had brought their children with them across the Sahara, while others had had babies in the forests, and they wanted to know if I had brought "gifts" for the children. Missy, a pretty, well-groomed twenty-three-year-old Nigerian in a fashionable black coat, had only recently arrived in the forest a few weeks ago after making the journey across the Sahara, and she was so shocked at finding herself in this situation that she wanted to go back to Nigeria. "I didn't expect this," she said, "but now I have to live here like these people."

Single women such as Missy are in an especially precarious situation. In 2010 Médecins Sans Frontières published a grim report on the sexual violence inflicted on female migrants in Morocco, based on interviews with sixty-three sub-Saharan women in Rabat and Casablanca. The report found that one in three interviewees had been raped during their migratory journeys, and that many of these incidents had taken place between Oujda and Maghnia, where female migrants routinely experienced serious sexual assaults at the hands of Moroccan police, bandits, and fellow migrants. One woman told her interviewers how she and two of her companions were raped by bandits after being forced across the Algerian border by Oujda police. A fourteen-year-old girl described how she had been arrested in Casablanca and taken to the Oujda police station, where she was escorted to the border and gang-raped by the police who deported her.[6]

The prospect of deportation constantly hovers over migrants in Oujda, where migrants are likely to be arrested at any time during police raids or when they go into the city to beg or buy food at the market. Near one of the Francophone camps a Congolese woman named Dolita was living in a bivouac with her three children, whose ages ranged from eight years to two months. She had come to the forest in 2009 from Rabat, where her partner died while she was pregnant, leaving her unable to pay the rent or electricity for their flat. She had given birth to her youngest child, Sabrina, and a twin brother at the Al Farah hospital in Oujda, but her other baby died shortly afterward, while she was still in the hospital.

The day after her release she was arrested by Moroccan police and taken to the border at night with her children for a deportation that was only prevented by Hicham Baraka of ABCDS, who went out to the border in the middle of the night and managed to persuade the Moroccan soldiers to let her go. Dolita had the numb, resigned expression of a woman who knew that she was trapped in a kind of hell. She was twenty-three years old and had fled one of the most war-torn and violent countries in the world, and now she was stranded in the forest with her three children, dependent for her next meal on her new partner, who was not present.

No government has shown the slightest interest in doing anything to assist the inhabitants of the forest camps. The only authorities who ever came here were the police, whose sole concern was to carry out arrests and deportations. The only international organization providing the migrants in Oujda with any regular assistance is Médecins Sans Frontières, which maintains a mobile clinic in the region. I met the MSF team at *la fac* and accompanied them on a tour of the migrant camps closer to the border. Driving along the "dead road" that connects Oujda to Algeria, we passed meadows bursting with spring flowers and empty children's playgrounds, hotels and restaurants that had once catered mostly to Algerian visitors from across the border. Now the road was mostly deserted and the only activity consisted of smugglers flitting back and forth on mopeds across the supposedly closed border, half buried under impossible loads of plastic bottles filled with Algerian gasoline.

For migrants, this surreal frontier zone is one of the most dangerous areas of Morocco, as a result of the bandits and criminal gangs operating on both sides of the border. Despite these risks, some migrants prefer to live here to avoid the police. Driving off the main road, the MSF jeep followed dirt roads and tracks that led to numerous migrant camps, some of which had been established in abandoned stables and farm buildings. The relative isolation of the camps does not make them immune to police attention. Only a few months before, a camp next to a nearly dried-up creek known (not without good reason) as Smelly Water was razed by a police bulldozer.

Since then the camp had been rebuilt, and it even had a television powered by an electric generator, so the residents could watch the World Cup. Some of the camps were equipped with long-range cordless phones with antennae that suggested a degree of organization behind them, but they were otherwise as basic as their counterparts elsewhere. At one abandoned farm, migrants slept in rows of plastic cubicles in what appeared to have been a concrete-floored stable, and cane struts were being built to create more cubicles in expectation of new arrivals.

Once again these camps echoed to the sound of hymns and hallelujahs. At another abandoned farm a furious argument was in progress for reasons that were not clear, but this harsh, insecure, and inhospitable environment was clearly not conducive to good community relations. The MSF mobile team provides a weekly clinic for these camps, and responds to emergency calls when possible. MSF also deals with what it calls "psychosocial problems," which are more difficult to treat. Some migrants were suffering from depression, trauma, and even psychosis as a result of their journeys, said Jorge Martín, the Argentine coordinator of MSF's Moroccan mission. Others have witnessed the deaths of friends and relatives on boats heading for Europe. MSF has no facilities to treat the more serious cases, and its treatment for psychological problems is limited to five consultations, without any medication.

Though MSF works alongside the Moroccan Ministry of Health, much of its work is intended to address the needs of a migrant population for whom there is no formal provision for health care. That day a regular clinic was not scheduled, but a constant stream of migrants came to the jeep to report cuts and pains or ask for contraception. As we watched one of these impromptu clinics unfold, Jorge Martín described Oujda as a migratory hot spot marked by a "clear dynamic of violence" in which the EU and Morocco were complicit. Martín believed that this situation was intended to have a "dissuasive effect" and he was waiting to see how Europe and Morocco would respond to the MSF report on sexual violence, which had only just been published.

In August and September that year came the response: Moroccan police carried out a mass roundup of between six hundred and seven hundred migrants from Oujda and other cities across the country and dumped them at night in the no-man's-land between Morocco and Algeria, without food or water. What happened to them is not known, but most will undoubtedly return and stay until this dismal cycle is repeated. The Moroccan government, for its own reasons, has agreed to carry out what is effectively Europe's dirty work, but the Oujda chokepoint is only one of a series of barriers that Spain and the EU have established across the Sahara migrant trail and which extend deep into sub-Saharan Africa itself. Since the 2005 crisis, Spain and the EU have unrolled a series of initiatives in the Maghreb and West Africa in an attempt to pressure African states into closing the trans-Saharan migratory route.

The Spanish Civil Guard now has liaison officers in a number of countries including Mauritania and Gambia, where they participate in joint operations with local police and coast guard officers. In 2006 Spain restored a former school in the Mauritanian city of Nouadhibou, which has become a migrant detention center known to locals as "Guantanamito." Thousands of migrants have been detained in a center that, according to the United Nations Office on Drugs and Crime, is "not known to have any official name or to be governed by any formal regulations."[7]

In 2009–10 the EU funded two new migrant "transit centers" around the city of Agadez in northern Niger, where migrants are provided with food and lodging and given "counseling on the dangers of irregular migration" and "voluntary return and reintegration assistance" by the International Organization for Migration, which works in the centers. A number of African countries have participated in readmission programs with Spain and the EU that make it easier to deport migrants. This cooperation contravenes the spirit, if not the letter, of the "borderless" Economic Community of West Africa (ECOWAS), established in the 1979 Protocol on the Free Movement of Persons, which abolished visa requirements between member states.

Between 2006 and 2008 Spain conducted a program known as Plan Africa, which attempted to make developmental assistance conditional on the ability of various African states to close their borders and tighten their immigration controls—an initiative that the Spanish NGO Intermón Oxfam described as "a perversion of cooperation for development." But such criticisms have done nothing to slow down a policy of Africanization, which effectively demands that African governments override their own immigration and border requirements and traditions in order to accommodate the demands of Spain and the European Union.

4

Mare Schengen

Reinforcing the management of the southern external maritime borders is essential to further develop a European model for integrated border management, based on the principles of burden-sharing, mutual trust and co-responsibility among Member States, which is founded on full respect for human rights.

—EUROPEAN COMMISSION PRESS RELEASE, NOVEMBER 30, 2006

In the course of history the Mediterranean has been variously imagined as a dividing line between civilizations and as a distinct region in its own right—the cradle of a unique Mediterranean civilization that embraces many different influences and components, Christian, Islamic, European, Arab, and African. For the last two decades the ocean that the Romans called Mare Nostrum, "Our Sea," has become the most porous of Europe's maritime migratory borders, and a persistent zone of confrontation between Europe's border enforcement regime and the unwanted intruders who have defied its restrictions.

This confrontation has shifted back and forth in accordance with changing geopolitical developments and levels of surveillance and control. In the first years of the twenty-first century, it was primarily concentrated in the western Mediterranean along the migratory routes between Morocco and Spain. With the construction of SIVE and the intensified prevention and detection measures undertaken by Spain and Morocco, these routes moved eastward into the central Mediterranean, as migrants set out from Tunisia and Libya in overcrowded boats in an attempt to reach Italy and Malta. In peak years migrant "boat people" were arriving weekly and sometimes daily on Italian and Maltese tourist beaches and ports, and navy and coast guard ships routinely returned from patrol with their decks crammed with migrants rescued at sea.

Not all migrants were rescued. In March 2009, a flotilla of four fishing boats carrying African migrants from various nationalities set out from the Libyan coast for Italy. Such flotillas are part of a common strategy used by smugglers in the Mediterranean, based on the calculation that if one boat is intercepted, the others will get through. In this case the strategy went badly wrong. One of the boats, the *Nazar*, was carrying more than 250 people on board even though its legal capacity was fifty. About twenty-five miles off the Libyan coast the *Nazar* got into difficulties in rough seas. Some of its passengers fell into the sea and drowned; others were thrown overboard by the boat's captain in a futile attempt to prevent the vessel from sinking.

By the time a Libyan coast guard patrol boat reached it two days later, ten survivors were clinging to the *Nazar's* overturned hull and the bodies of dozens of men, women, and children were floating in the water all around them. A second boat in the flotilla was subsequently rescued, but the other two were never found. There have been many similar episodes over the last twenty years in what has become the most lethal migrant graveyard in the world. At certain periods during the spring and summer "migration season" corpses and body parts were routinely snagged in fishing nets or washed up on Mediterranean coasts and beaches. In some cases the dead were identified and repatriated to their families, while others were buried in the anonymous migrant cemeteries and ordinary graveyards that litter the Mediterranean coast, identified only by nationality, number, or the date on which they were found.

Most of these tragedies occurred because migrants were traveling in dangerously overcrowded boats without life jackets or navigation equipment. On the night of September 14, 2002, more than a hundred Liberian refugees were found clinging to rocks off the beach at Realmonte, on Sicily's southern coast, where their boat had sunk after striking those same rocks. Thousands of men, women, and children have been saved from certain death during the last twenty years in the course of similar interventions by naval and coast guard services and fishermen from many different countries, both European and North African. But there have also been a disturbing number of incidents in which migrants have been spotted on the high seas and ignored or abandoned, in contravention of the 1979 International Convention on Search and Rescue, which obliges all ships to rescue any person in distress "regardless of the nationality or status of such a person or the circumstances in which that person is found." On July 28, 2009, a large rubber dinghy left Libya headed for Lampedusa with a cargo of eighty-two Eritrean migrants, including three pregnant women. Three weeks later the Italian coast guard found only five survivors, who claimed that numerous ships had failed to rescue them, including a Maltese naval patrol boat that stopped to give them fuel and life jackets and before departing even turned on the dinghy's motor because they were too weak to do it themselves.

In May 2011, at the height of the NATO bombing campaign in Libya, a boat carrying seventy-two passengers left Tripoli for Italy. Sixteen days later, eleven survivors were rescued, who said that their fellow passengers had died of hunger and thirst. The survivors claimed that they had been observed by a military helicopter and a NATO warship, and that they had even made direct contact with the Italian coast guard, none of whom had attempted to rescue them. Despite calls from UNHCR for an investigation into this incident, no government has tried to establish the veracity of these claims. Such incidents cannot be considered the norm. But their frequency—and the general unwillingness of governments to fully investigate them—was such that the UNHCR representative Laura Boldrini declared, "The Mediterranean cannot become the wild west. Those who do not rescue people at sea cannot remain unpunished."[1]

This culture of indifference and impunity is another consequence of the Mediterranean's transformation from a region that most Europeans associate with summer holidays and recreation into the most visible challenge to the European Union's compensatory borders. This visibility was often deceptive. Even in the busiest periods of irregular migration in the Mediterranean, most illegal immigrants who entered Europe continued to arrive legally at airports rather than on Mediterranean beaches and only became illegal after outstaying their visas.

But the media prominence of these incursions, and their frequently horrific human consequences, constituted a litmus test of the EU's ability to "manage" migration and enforce Europe's immigration controls. In addition the central Mediterranean is also the main route for asylum seekers from the Horn of Africa, all of whom were—at least in theory—able to apply for refugee protection from the moment they entered European territorial waters. Detecting and preventing these journeys has therefore been a crucial objective of the EU's border enforcement regime.

These priorities have transformed the Mediterranean into one of the most militarized oceans in the world. In addition to coast guard and naval surveillance by more than a dozen countries and the European border agency Frontex, the Mediterranean is subject to aerial and satellite surveillance, and the European Commission has recently announced plans to integrate the Mediterranean and south Atlantic into the European Border Surveillance System (EUROSUR) using satellite imagery and unmanned aerial vehicles (UAVs) to prevent "unauthorized border crossings." These efforts have also had a transformative impact on the territories that actually make up Europe's Mediterranean borders, nowhere more so than in Europe's smallest island state.

The "Bulwark of Europe"

From a distance, the Maltese capital, Valetta, is a perfect miniature of a European city, with its creamy yellow limestone buildings and stair-stepped streets enclosed by fortified defensive walls, topped by the splendid blue cupola of St. Paul's Pro-Cathedral and its stone cross. According to legend, Malta was the location for the episode described in the biblical book of Luke in which St. Paul was shipwrecked in AD 57 en route to Rome to defend his beliefs before the Roman emperor. Miraculously unscathed by a bite from a venomous snake, Paul went on to convert the locals—an episode that has remained central to Malta's self-image as a nation of devout and hospitable pawlini, or followers of St. Paul.

Catholicism has also defined Malta's historic role as a strategic outpost of European Christendom. In the sixteenth century, Malta was propelled into the front lines of the searing confrontation between the Ottoman Turks and Christian Europe for control of the Mediterranean, when the Holy Roman Emperor gave the islands to a crusading military order, the Knights Hospitaller of St. John, to compensation for their expulsion by the Ottomans from Rhodes, thus beginning what is in effect a form of colonial rule by what one historian has called the "first embryonic council of Europe," which lasted until the expulsion of the knights from the island by Napoleon in the late eighteenth century.

In 1565, the Ottoman sultan Suleiman the Magnificent invaded Malta in an attempt to annihilate the troublesome knights, who had been using the island as a base for raids on Muslim ships. Under the leadership of their

French grandmaster Jean Parisot de La Valette, nine thousand knights and Maltese held off forty thousand Ottoman troops for four months. This epic of heroism and endurance earned Malta the sobriquet *Propugnaculum Europae* (Bulwark of Europe) and was followed by the construction of a new fortress-capital, Valetta, to resist future incursions. Today this brutal history of warfare with the infidel is still firmly engraved on the Maltese national psyche. Every year, on September 8, the Great Siege is commemorated on Victory Day, and Maltese children in some villages still use the word "Turk" as a pejorative term to describe even Maltese outsiders.

During World War II, Malta suffered an even more destructive siege when German and Italian bombers subjected what was then a British crown colony to a ferocious bombardment that leveled much of the city. These historical antecedents have engendered a strong sense of vulnerability that also shaped Malta's response to irregular migration following the republic's entry into the European Union in 2004. For much of the twentieth century Malta, like the rest of southern Europe, produced more emigrants than immigrants. In the bleak decade that followed World War II more than half the population left the island. In 2002 the first migrant boats began arriving on the island from Libya and North Africa, and these numbers reached a peak in 2008, the year after Malta's accession to Schengen, when 2,775 migrants arrived on the island or were rescued in Maltese waters.

In total some eleven thousand migrants arrived on the island between 2002 and 2009. In comparison with other European countries, these numbers were not particularly high, but they nevertheless came as a shock to a small archipelago of islands with only 400,000 inhabitants. "Before 2002 we didn't in any way think that we would have this phenomenon, either as a result of EU membership or not as a result of EU membership," says Joseph St. John, director of policy development at the Ministry for Justice and Home Affairs. Did he feel that Malta was expected to play the role of a migrant trap and buffer zone as a consequence of EU membership? "I don't think it was actually asked to play it," he said. "The rules were there before we joined. I think, if anything, we—and the migrants themselves—ended up being victims of circumstances, really. Of course, if the numbers had not been so great it would not have been such a problem."

Not everyone agrees that the numbers were so high. "There was talk of a tsunami of immigration," says Matthew Vella, a journalist with the newspaper *Malta Today*, which has campaigned strongly against the treatment of Malta's migrants by the Maltese government and society. "I mean, this is an island that caters for 2 million tourists every year, and a maximum of two thousand migrants is not a big logistical problem."

Logistical problems, whether real or imagined, do not account for the xenophobic and sometimes openly racist hostility directed toward Malta's *klandestini* from some quarters of Maltese society. Immigration—in Malta, the term invariably refers to nonwhite migrants—was a direct contributing factor to the formation of two extreme-right parties, Imperium Europa and the now defunct Alleanza Nazionale, and was expressed in racial abuse and physical attacks on African migrants in the street and on public transport, in threats and arson attacks on Maltese NGOs and journalists who were regarded as excessively pro-immigrant, and in apocryphal claims that the bodies of dead migrants were even poisoning the *lampuki* fish, a Maltese specialty.

Such animosity was not confined to the extreme right. "Have we joined Europe to be invaded by Africa?" asked the *Sunday Times of Malta* in an article in August 2005 that described Malta's migrants as "The Third Great Siege."[2] That same year the president of the General Workers Union, the largest trade union in Malta, accused illegal immigrants of taking jobs away from Maltese workers, spreading sexually transmitted diseases, and "jumping the line" in local hospitals.

This image of an island inundated by African migrants tended to ignore the fact that most migrants who came to Malta did not want to stay there. Most were trying to get to Italy, and some had never heard of Malta or believed that it was part of Italy but found themselves obliged to seek asylum on the island because of the Dublin Convention requirements. When migrants first arrived, Malta had a barely functioning asylum screening system, and its government was reluctant to do anything that it believed might attract more migrants to follow their example. Under Maltese law, all undocumented migrants are categorized as "prohibited immigrants" and subject to mandatory detention regardless of their motives. As a result, both asylum seekers and economic migrants were sometimes incarcerated for as long as five years in overcrowded cells and tents in makeshift camps and military barracks, without exercise or ventilation.

"I know people that have spent eighteen months in prison, tried to leave, been imprisoned for six months, tried to leave again, been in prison for six months," says Maria Pisani, a former researcher with the International Organization for Migration in Malta. These conditions were denounced by Maltese and international NGOs, and the Maltese government has since tried to ameliorate some of them. Today the maximum period of detention has been shortened to eighteen months (in line with EU directives), asylum assessment procedures have been improved, and many of those whose claims have been accepted have been resettled in other countries, particularly the United States. Approximately three thousand migrants have been granted refugee status or some form of "subsidiary protection" in Malta itself. Most live in the eight "open centers" run under the auspices of the Organisation for the Integration and Welfare of Asylum Seekers (OIWAS), where they are allowed to come and go during the day and can even receive temporary "Geneva Convention passports" that enable them to leave the island for limited periods to visit relatives elsewhere in Europe.

These freedoms do not amount to a great deal on an island that often functions as a de facto detention center in itself. Situated in a dilapidated former school adjoining a shipyard in the red-light district of Valetta, the Marsa open center is home to some five hundred Sudanese, Eritrean, and Somali migrants, who include refugees, asylum seekers, and migrants whose claims have been rejected. Some have jobs, but most subsist on a monthly allowance of €130, while "Dublin cases" who have been returned to Malta after leaving it without authorization have this allowance automatically reduced to €80. Conditions in the center are primitive; up to thirty-six people are crammed into former classrooms on bunk beds, as many as sixty migrants share showers and toilets that are filthy and stink of urine, and the residents must cook on blackened camping gas stoves.

A group of Somalis showed me a grimy two-burner gas stove on a metal cabinet, whose gas cylinder had recently exploded and set fire to one of the rooms, forcing its inhabitants to save themselves by jumping out of the window. The open center also contains a number of cafés and shops run by migrants and former residents, as well as an Internet café that during our visit had been closed on the orders of the center's unpopular Ghanaian manager, Ahmed Bugri.

Before Bugri's arrival Marsa was run by Terry Gosden, a blunt and outspoken London social worker and Maltese trade union official with dual British and Maltese nationality. Gosden was Marsa's first manager and held the post for four and a half years. Running an open center with a variety of different ethnic and national groups, most of whom did not want to be in Malta, was no easy task. When Gosden took the job, many of his service users had only recently come out of detention and were so confused about the requirements of an open center that he had to get them to walk back and forth through the main gate various times to prove to them that they were free to leave it. Tensions between different groups sometimes broke out in fights. But with the help of his multilingual translator, Warsame Ali Garare, a Somali anthropology student and a migrant himself, Gosden and the residents managed to establish a modus vivendi that was conspicuously absent with his successor.

In the two hours that I spent in the center, the police came twice to deal with acrimonious arguments down in the yard, and the relationship between the residents and Bugri was clearly close to breakdown. Various residents accused him of running the center like a dictator, and a number of them spoke warmly of his predecessor. But Marsa is positively utopian in comparison with the bleak desolation of the Hal Far open center in southern Malta. To get there you take a forty-minute bus ride from Valetta and walk the remaining ten minutes to the Maltese army's Lyster barracks, which also doubles as an immigrant detention center, across a sparsely populated coastal plain that was once filled with British military and air force installations. Situated in the middle of a mostly featureless plain, the open center bears more than a passing resemblance to a POW camp, with its rows of army tents and temporary buildings, enclosed by a wire fence and floodlights.

Between fifteen and twenty people share these tents, where some of them have hung blankets and towels around their beds in an attempt to preserve some privacy. One tent functions as a common room, where a few men and women were listlessly watching a soap opera on daytime TV. Approximately a thousand people live in this dismal compound, and some have been here for years. Adam, a Somali student from Mogadishu, described what he called a "very difficult journey" that had begun in 2007, when he left Somalia after two of his brothers were killed in the ongoing civil war. Adam set out across the Sahara hoping to find work in Libya, and after bribing his way across several borders he eventually made it to the southern Libyan desert and the border with Niger, where the pickup truck in which he and his companions were traveling slipped off a mountain road.

Some of his fellow passengers were killed, but he was taken unconscious to a hospital, where he remained in a coma for twenty-one days. After recovering, he spent the next two years doing occasional jobs before he and his friends decided to try their luck in Europe. On August 27, 2009, they set out for Italy in the usual overloaded boat. As was often the case, none of the passengers had life jackets. On approaching what they thought was Italy, their boat ran out of fuel, and they used empty fuel cans as oars to bring them to what turned out to be Malta.

"Unfortunately, as we were approaching the shore two of my colleagues fell in the water and drowned," Adam said in the matter-of-fact tone in which so many migrants often related even the most grueling and traumatic ordeals. After more than a year in Hal Far, he was considering going back to Somalia, and it was difficult to avoid the conclusion that this was precisely the objective of Malta's open centers. Though OIWAS provides language classes and "lessons in Maltese and European culture" in the open centers, it was difficult to see how a thousand mostly unemployed Africans stranded in an isolated fenced-in compound were going to be integrated into Maltese society or any other in Europe.

Everyone I spoke to at Hal Far complained of the same things: isolation, freezing temperatures in winter and excessive heat in summer, no exercise facilities, no books or Internet, boredom, frustration, and continual uncertainty about their future and the fate of their relatives back home.

"Some people come here and they think, 'Oh, this is all right for us—we're Africans,'" complained Abdi, a twenty-year-old biology student who had been in Hal Far since 2006. "But everybody here is thinking about their future all the time. Nobody knows what it will be like. You just live from day to day."

These conditions cannot be attributed to the limited resources of a small island economy. Just around the corner, the Franciscan monk Dionysius Mintoff provides prefab accommodations for migrants in the grounds of the pacifist educational foundation he calls the Peace Laboratory. Forty-two African migrants, including families, live in small rooms with an average of three or four beds. In one room four young African men were sitting on the carpeted floor eating grapes.

It was not luxurious, but the carpets, wall hangings, and stereo provided some of the trappings of a home rather than a holding center, and Father Mintoff's guests displayed an optimism and a sense of purpose that were entirely absent on the other side of the road. Moussa, a teenager from the Ivory Coast, told me how he had left his country four years ago, when his parents were killed by a bomb when he and his brother were coming home from school. He had worked his way up to Libya, doing various jobs, before he decided to try his luck in Europe. He told me he was glad to be in Malta and liked it there.

Hussein, a young Somali, had got a job with the German electronics company Seifert. Like many Somalis, he had family scattered all over the world. His father was in Canada and his uncle was in Florida, and he had no idea when he would see any of his relatives again, but he clearly regarded his situation as better than the one he had left. "I'm happy now," he said, and he looked as though he meant it. With limited funds but considerable goodwill, Father Mintoff and a former Maltese Labour MP named Joe Abela had treated these young men as human beings rather than migrants and had given them an opportunity to rebuild their lives, one that both of the young people I spoke to were clearly willing to take. And for all the worthy talk of integration from the Maltese authorities, I could not help feeling that open centers such as Hal Far were intended not to extend the same treatment to their residents but to wear down their will to remain on the island, and to transmit a message to their countrymen that Malta was not the place to pursue their European dreams.

Colonel Gaddafi's Guests

In the autumn of 2010 there were certainly fewer people coming. That year only fifty migrants arrived in Malta, compared with 1,475 the previous year, and Malta's detention centers were almost empty. But this steep reduction had more to do with events taking place outside the island than it did with the harsh reception that awaited migrants who arrived there. Most migrants in Malta came from Tunisia and Libya, and the decline in the number of these journeys from 2008 onward was mainly due to the participation of the Zine el-Abidine Ben Ali and Muammar Gaddafi dictatorships in enforcing Europe's offshore border controls.

Libya's contribution was particularly decisive. As early as 2002, the EU began to seek Libyan assistance in stemming irregular migration across the central Mediterranean, and Gaddafi's willingness to perform this role was a significant factor in his short-lived transformation from pariah to international statesman. In July 2004 the European Union lifted its embargo against Libya, and in the years that followed the Gaddafi regime intensified its surveillance over Libya's extensive and often isolated coastline, using equipment and technology provided by Italy and the EU. Libya also participated in joint naval patrols with its European partners, and detained and deported migrants inside Libya who were trying to reach Europe.

The Berlusconi government in Italy was a fervent advocate of this new strategic partnership, whether loaning vessels to the Libyan coast guard, funding immigrant detention centers inside Libya, or deporting rejected asylum seekers en masse to Libyan territory. This relationship culminated in the bilateral "friendship agreement" signed in the summer of 2008 and its subsequent implementation protocol, whereby Italy agreed to a range of measures that would assist Libya in preventing irregular migration. These included the practice known as "pushback" or "towback," in which migrants intercepted in Italian or international waters were towed back into Libyan territorial waters.

On May 6, 2009, the treaty came into effect, and its impact was rapid and dramatic. In 2008, 36,000 migrants arrived in Italy. The following year the number had fallen to 17,000, and in 2010 it was only 10,000. In 2009 Renzo Bossi, son of the Northern League leader, celebrated the pushback policy by creating a Facebook video game called Rimbalza il Clandestino, or Bounce the Undocumented Migrant, in which participants were invited to "defend Italy" and scored points by clicking on migrant boats and sending their country's "enemies" back to Libya. "Abbiamo femato l'invasione," "We've stopped the invasion," boasted the Northern League's regional electoral posters the following year.

The price of this victory received little public recognition from the Italian government or the EU. Libya has never signed the 1951 Geneva Refugee Convention, and tens of thousands of migrants were routinely arrested and detained every year in more than twenty detention facilities dotted across the country. In some cases, migrants were held for years in cells with as many as sixty to seventy occupants, where they were subjected to a regime of beatings, rape, abuse, and torture that many were able to escape only by bribing their guards. In 2007, a Frontex report claimed that 53,842 migrants had been deported from Libya the previous year and that another 60,000 remained in detention.[3] Some of these deportations were carried out on charter flights, but thousands of sub-Saharan migrants were simply abandoned in the Sahara Desert near Libya's southern borders with Mali and Chad, and not all of them survived.[4]

This was the regime that migrants were "pushed back" to. In June 2009 migrants told Human Rights Watch that Italian naval personnel had used electric shock batons and clubs to force them onto a Libyan boat on the high seas. In March 2010 an officer from the Italian Guardia di Finanza (customs and excise police) told La Repubblica how his crew had intercepted and returned a boat filled with African migrants to Tripoli in what he described as "the most despicable order I have ever carried out."[5]

Berlusconi and his Northern League partners were indifferent to criticisms that such procedures breached the Geneva Convention principle of *non-refoulement*: that refugees should not be deported to a country where they may face persecution. In 2009 Berlusconi argued that Italy was obliged to offer protection only to asylum seekers who "put their feet down in our soil, in the sense also of entering into our territorial waters." But UNHCR insists that "the principle of *non-refoulement* does not imply any geographical limitation" and that migrants should be able to apply for asylum from the moment they are rescued on the high seas, in the country of the vessel that rescues them.

Not all of Libya's estimated 1.5 million irregular migrants were trying to reach Europe. By the late 1990s Libya had became a migratory destination in its own right as a result of its booming oil economy and Gaddafi's attempts to court African political support through a more open immigration policy, but Gaddafi shrewdly played on Europe's fears of an immigrant invasion for his own purposes. During a visit to Italy in August 2010, the Libyan dictator asked for €5 billion to help Libya combat irregular immigration and warned that "tomorrow Europe might no longer be European, and even black" if it failed to receive them.

The Maltese prime minister, Lawrence Gonzi, told a radio interviewer that Malta was "ready to do anything to get the EU and the Libya government on the same table and discuss an agreement" provided that the "human dignity" of migrants in Libya could be ensured. But there was no meaningful attempt by the Maltese or any other European government to ensure such "dignity" or change an arrangement that from Europe's point of view was working very well. For this reason there was barely a murmur of protest in June 2010 when Gaddafi expelled UNHCR, which had been lobbying for some years to gain greater access to Libya's migrants in order to assess whether they were in need of refugee protection.

Gaddafi did not get his €5 billion, but in October 2010 he received a promise of €50 million over the next three years as part of a "co-operation agenda" signed by the European Commission. And had it not been for the unexpected events that took place in the spring of 2011, he undoubtedly would have received them.

The Beautiful Island

The cozy relationship between Europe and North Africa was radically altered by the collapse of the Ben Ali regime in Tunisia in January 2011 and by Gaddafi's bloody attempt to suppress a similar uprising in his own country the following month. Almost overnight, the same countries that had courted Libya for years turned against Gaddafi and participated in the NATO bombing campaign in support of pro-democracy rebels. The advent of the Arab Spring also unraveled the migratory barriers and controls that had been so painstakingly constructed over the better part of a decade. Before his overthrow, the Tunisian dictator had received political support and economic assistance from Italy and other European governments in return for cracking down on migration, and the importance of this contribution was dramatically revealed in February and March, when thousands of Tunisian migrants began arriving on the Italian island of Lampedusa.

Situated only seventy-nine miles from the Tunisian coast, Lampedusa is the largest of the Pelagie Islands, near Sicily, and the southernmost border of the European Union. Lampedusa is a flat and mostly barren volcanic outcrop home to more than five thousand inhabitants, but the pristine beaches and transparent aquamarine seas of *l'isola bella* (the beautiful island) attract thousands of mostly Italian tourists every summer. In 1997 Lampedusa became a destination for undocumented migrants from North Africa for the first time. In 2006 19,000 migrants arrived in Lampedusa; two years later the figure had risen to 31,700.

In the nineteenth century Lampedusa was a penal colony for anarchists and socialists detained under the repressive Crispi laws, and the island now began to play a new role as an offshore detention and screening center for Italy's unwanted migrants. Most migrants were detained either in a temporary holding center in the center of the island, which had a capacity of eight hundred people, or in a smaller center in a former NATO base, before being taken to Sicily and the Italian mainland. Others were deported directly from Lampedusa in expulsions of dubious legality.

Conditions in these centers were basic and often were made worse by overcrowding and the prolonged periods that migrants had to spend in them. In February 2009, 1,800 migrants staged an insurrection inside the main holding center, burning part of it down, and hundreds of detainees marched on city hall, demanding to be allowed to leave the island.

That year the Italian government closed the center, as the pushback policy began to take effect and the numbers of migrants coming to Lampedusa once again dropped to the levels of the late 1990s. As a result, the Italian government was completely wrong-footed by the almost daily arrivals of Tunisians that followed the collapse of Ben Ali's regime in February 2011.

By February 25, five thousand Tunisians had arrived in Lampedusa, and Berlusconi's foreign minister, Franco Frattini, warned Europe of an imminent "biblical exodus" of 200,000 to 300,000 migrants from Tunisia and Libya. Frattini was undoubtedly right to appeal for European assistance in dealing with these arrivals, but his melodramatic depiction of a "catastrophic humanitarian emergency" was partly a result of the Berlusconi government's refusal to allow the Tunisians to leave Lampedusa or provide them with any shelter or assistance.

By early March, there were twelve thousand Tunisians on the island and the government was still refusing to open the holding centers. As a result, the Tunisians were obliged to sleep on the streets or on the rocky hillside overlooking the commercial port. This chaotic situation propelled Lampedusa into the heart of Europe's anti-immigration politics. In March, sub-Saharan migrants began arriving on Lampedusa from war-torn Libya, and the Berlusconi government finally began to ease the pressure on the island by reopening the immigrant reception centers on Lampedusa and giving Tunisians temporary permits that allowed them to go to France. The French president, Nicolas Sarkozy, then refused to let them in and ordered the police to stop the trains bringing the Tunisians into France. That same month, the French National Front leader Marine Le Pen visited the island with Mario Borghese, a member of the European Parliament who was affiliated with the Northern League, and called for the Tunisians to be sent back. In May Roberto Fiore, leader of the neo-fascist Forza Nuova political party, visited the island, accompanied by Nick Griffin of the British National Party, who offered to send "volunteers" to defend the island from an "African invasion."

By this time Berlusconi and Sarkozy had come to a mutual agreement and the two leaders issued a joint declaration, which called for a revisiting of the Schengen Agreement to allow the restoration of national border controls in similar situations. To its immense discredit, the EU capitulated to these demands. On May 4, Cecilia Malmstrom, the EU commissioner for home affairs, agreed that limited internal border controls could be reintroduced in "very exceptional circumstances." Incredibly, on the twenty-sixth anniversary of the signing of the Schengen Agreement, a tiny Mediterranean island with a population of five thousand had become a catalyst that had led the EU to call into question one of the great achievements of European integration.

Not for the first time, characterizations of the "invasion" of Lampedusa tended to misrepresent its scale and causes. Most of the Tunisians were looking for work, not refugee protection. Many came from the coastal areas of Tunisia, where the tourist industry had virtually collapsed during the interregnum that followed the fall of Ben Ali. They were mostly young and often highly educated, and arrived in Lampedusa hoping to get to France, Belgium, or Germany, where many of them had friends and relatives. Some had come with the encouragement and assistance of their families, who negotiated directly with Tunisian smugglers in the hope that they would be able to find work and send money back home.

In June that year I spoke to Laura Boldrini, UNHCR's combative and outspoken spokesperson, in Rome. Boldrini was unimpressed by the hyperbole emanating from her own government. "With numbers like these Italy has the resources to deal with them," she said. "There are other countries with bigger numbers." She also condemned the "defensive attitude" of European governments toward the migrants who were arriving on Lampedusa, not only from Tunisia but from the ongoing Libyan civil war, and compared this response to the more positive reception of the refugees she once worked with in Kosovo.

"They were presented as people in need of protection," she said, "and now these people from Libya are presented as a human tsunami, a biblical exodus, and this causes anxiety and also animosity because people don't put themselves into the dimension of offering help and solidarity."

When I arrived on the island it was clear that help was being provided, and the situation was very different from the neglect and chaos seen in February and March. Whenever the sea was calm and the wind dropped, boatloads of migrants were likely to arrive at the island's two ports, where they received medical assessment and treatment from the Italian Red Cross and Médecins Sans Frontières in addition to advice from a phalanx of NGOs including UNHCR, Save the Children, and the IOM.

At four-thirty in the morning I watched a Guardia di Finanza patrol boat escort a fishing boat containing nineteen Tunisian migrants into the closed military port. They included six women, one child, and—to the amusement of the Médecins Sans Frontières team—one sheep. The Tunisians were driven away in a bus to one of the two holding centers, some of them wrapped in silver emergency blankets, but the sheep remained in the port.

Tunisians were now a rarity among the migrants who were continuing to arrive on the island on an almost daily basis, most of whom were African migrants from Libya. The day before my arrival, 1,500 Africans arrived at the commercial harbor in seven boats from Libya. Four days later another 280 people arrived at six in the morning. The frequency of these journeys had led to suggestions that Gaddafi was deliberately using refugees as political counters, as Slobodan Milošević had once done in the Kosovo war. "From the main ports they're leaving in broad daylight in huge ships, nine hundred people at a time," said Barbara Molinario, UNHCR field officer in Lampedusa, "which also means that they take hours to leave . . . and nobody is stopping them even though there are military at the ports."

Migrants were a mostly invisible presence on Lampedusa itself, where they were immediately whisked off from the ports to the two holding centers. Asylum seekers from Libya were screened and transported by cruise ships to reception centers on the Italian mainland, while Tunisians were repatriated via Sicily, following a new agreement between Italy and the Tunisian transitional government. That same week eight hundred migrants were transferred to the mainland, but so many people were arriving that there were still close to eight hundred people in the largest of the two holding centers, and another three hundred in the smaller center. There were also some three hundred unaccompanied minors on the island, including Pakistani and Bangladeshi teenagers as young as fifteen, who were waiting to be transferred to foster homes in Sicily. According to the NGO workers I spoke to, some people had been in the holding centers for more than a month, and there had recently been an attempt to set fire to the main center.

As always, journalists were not allowed to speak to detainees, and it was impossible to confirm these reports. When I tried to bicycle to the main holding center, I found the road blocked by a carabinieri officer, who told me in no uncertain terms that I could go no farther. For all the secretiveness, however, the Italian government had clearly been shamed into showing what it could do. Every day helicopters buzzed overhead, and the orange-trimmed coast guard vessels and armed patrol boats of the Guardia di Finanza skimmed across the water on routine patrol or in response to distress calls. Next to the tourist port, with its rows of bobbing speedboats and mostly empty pleasure boats offering tours of the island, fifty-odd destroyed or damaged fishing vessels were piled haphazardly together in a poignant monument to maritime journeys with a more urgent purpose. In the local cemetery at the edge of town, among the ornate stone tombs with embedded photographs of Italian fishermen and stolid island women dating back to the nineteenth century, a wooden cross designates the humbler graves of *extracomunitaria*—a word used to describe poor non-European migrants. Elsewhere twelve wooden crosses with artificial flowers carry the date "03"—the year in which they drowned—followed by a number.

There were no recent graves, but the migrant exodus from the Libyan civil war was punctuated with maritime tragedies of this kind. On May 10 a boat carrying 650 migrants broke up on leaving Tripoli harbor, drowning hundreds. On June 2, 150 people drowned when a boat with 850 passengers capsized only forty miles south of the island. According to UNHCR, 1,500 migrants who left North Africa between March and June have never been accounted for. Though UNHCR had called upon NATO to provide assistance to any migrant boat spotted at sea, rescuing migrants was clearly not a priority for countries that were more concerned with toppling their former ally.

Drownings were not only due to the poor quality of the boats used by smugglers. Often their passengers were packed so closely together that any sudden movement could overturn the vessel, and such incidents often occurred during rescue operations, when the approach of a coast guard or navy boat would provoke a destabilizing rush toward the would-be rescuers. The commander of the Lampedusa coast guard, Captain Antonio Morana, described one nocturnal rescue attempt in April in which his officers rescued fifty-three people from a capsized boat in rough seas. By the time they got there between one hundred and two hundred passengers had already died, Morana said, and when they returned the next day the seas were still so rough that they were unable to retrieve the twenty-odd bodies still floating in the water.

Morana is proud of the dedication and professionalism of his officers, many of whom have witnessed some truly horrific scenes in the last few years. At one point he showed me a video of the Lampedusa coast guard rescuing a boat packed with African migrants. The tense faces of the coast guard officers and the clearly terrified men and women stuffed together on the deck told a story that has often been repeated in these waters. But there was another, less noble dimension to the search-and-rescue operations in the central Mediterranean since 2009. Had his officers ever participated in pushback operations? I asked. "No, not the coast guard," Morana declared. "Never. We help and rescue people."

Whether or not the Lampedusa coast guard had participated in the pushback policy, such operations had taken place and the Italian government had admitted to them. And despite Italy's improved performance in Lampedusa, its priorities—and those of the EU—remained essentially unchanged. In May the British foreign secretary, William Hague, insisted that European governments would continue to be "tough" toward migrants leaving Libya, on the grounds that "we can't just accept a flow of hundreds of thousands or millions of people into southern Europe and then coming beyond that."

"They Saw Numbers, We Saw People"

These fears were conspicuously absent on the island itself. Lampedusa is a contradictory place. Its long-standing mayor, Bernardino "Dino" de Rubeis, belongs to a local center-right party, and his deputy mayor—somewhat bizarrely—is a Northern League senator. Yet visitors to the airport are immediately greeted by photographs of Tunisian migrants on the island, and even the local tourist magazine celebrates *solidarietà lampedusana*—Lampedusan solidarity.

The Lampedusans I spoke to were more concerned with the drop in hotel reservations than they were with migrants. "Many tourists are scared of this problem," said Giacomo, a receptionist at the Baia Turchese hotel overlooking the port, in a tone that suggested that they had no reason to be. Wasn't he scared? He shook his head. "Lampedusans and Africans get on fine together," he said. "Many of the people who come here are young like us. We have no problem with them."

The presence of soldiers, police, and carabinieri had compensated to some extent for the loss of trade. Military jeeps and vanloads of police with riot shields were a constant presence in the island, but most of the personnel were there on temporary contracts that could be canceled at short notice, and they paid less than tourist rates. No one I spoke to blamed migrants for this situation, and most attributed the fall in bookings to sensationalist and exaggerated media reporting.

On Lampedusa's main drag, a flag of the European Union with a question mark painted on it still hung from the wall of the Café Mediterraneo, where the café's owner, Silvana Luca, had placed it at the height of the Tunisian crisis. I asked her why she had done this. "Because it's the question we asked ourselves," she said. "Where is Europe in this?" Silvana had good memories of the Tunisians who transformed Lampedusa into what she called a "Tunisian city" for nearly two weeks. "They were good to us, and Lampedusans were good to them," she said proudly.

To some Europeans, the media images of Tunisians thronging the streets and squares of Lampedusa were as alarming as the footage of African migrants charging the fences at Ceuta and Melilla in 2005. But in the absence of any intervention from their own government, Lampedusans and Tunisians were largely left to their own devices, and they got along surprisingly well. For nearly twenty-one days Tunisians camped out in plastic tents among the disused concrete pillboxes behind the airport or slept in the streets, with little assistance except the blankets and survival kits provided by the Red Cross and the ubiquitous Médecins Sans Frontières.

At a time when the Italian government was refusing to open the two reception centers, the church and other local institutions gave the Tunisians food, clothing, and blankets. Some restaurants provided free food and allowed the migrants to charge their phones. One schoolteacher took his pupils to meet the migrants for cultural exchanges. "It was the first time you saw so many migrants, and it was really quite weird," remembered Angelo Campiciano, MSF project coordinator on the island. "It was good that they welcomed these people."

The Associazione Askavusa (Barefoot Association), a cultural and social activist organization, cooked a hundred meals a day with money from its members' own pockets or local donations. The association has staged an annual film and video festival dedicated to migration on the island for the last few years, and it is also trying to create Europe's first museum of migration. At its offices, one room is filled with life jackets, shoes and clothes, photographs, letters, and the personalized astrological horoscopes and numerological amulets that Muslim migrants sometimes bring to grant them protection on their journeys, in addition to Bibles, Korans, and other found objects abandoned on the island's beaches. Two of the association's members, Ilaria Vecchi and Giacomo Sferlazzo, explained how they wanted NATO to organize a "humanitarian corridor" from Libya to Lampedusa in order to ensure the safety of the migrants trying to escape the ongoing civil war. When I asked them why the response of the islanders had been so different from that of their own government and Europe in general, Sferlazzo's answer was succinct and unambiguous. "They saw numbers and we saw people," he said.

This response was not unique to Lampedusans. Nearly 700,000 people had fled the fighting in Libya, mostly to Egypt and Tunisia, where they were welcomed by UNHCR and by the local population. In June that year the UN High Commissioner for Refugees, António Guterres, visited Tunisia on Refugee Day and paid tribute to the Tunisians who had played host to some 540,000 refugees, 70,000 of whom were put up by ordinary Tunisians in their own homes. But tens of thousands of African migrants remained trapped in Libya, where they were alternately used as political "weapons" by Gaddafi and victimized by armed rebel fighters and ad hoc militias, who deemed anyone with a black skin a "mercenary" working for the government or simply fair game.

There was a bleak irony in the fact that the same governments who were bombing Libya, supposedly in order to protect its population, were refusing to do anything to protect the migrants displaced by the war. That same week, Berlusconi's Northern League interior minister, Roberto Maroni, urged NATO to prevent migrants from leaving Libya, and the foreign minister, Franco Frattini, signed a new agreement in Naples with the Libyan National Transitional Council in which Gaddafi's successors agreed to play the same role as the embattled Libyan dictator when the war was won, and ensure that migrants would not come to Lampedusa or other parts of Italy and turn Europe black.

5

The Greek Labyrinth

If I send an email from Greece to Germany it will arrive within seconds. How much I would like to be send [*sic*] in an email, wouldn't that be great? Do you think I fit into the computer so that you can send me too?

—Unaccompanied refugee minor in Greece,
December 7, 2009, Birds of Immigrants website

There are few prettier spots in northern Greece than the Ardas River where it flows past the border village of Kastanies. The Ardas is a tributary of the mighty Evros River (known in Turkish as the Maritsa), which begins to separate Greece and Turkey just north of Kastanies before descending southward for 130 miles toward the Aegean, where it breaks up into a swampy delta near the port of Alexandroupolis. This natural boundary is broken by a seven-and-a-half-mile strip near Kastanies where the Evros curves briefly into Turkish territory near the former Ottoman capital of Edirne. In the summertime the water level of the Evros drops and its sandbanks and grassy verges are popular with Greek families, who come here for picnics and leisurely lunches at the Café Artisio overlooking the river.

At night these woods and fields are populated by a different kind of visitor. Almost every day a steady procession of Afghans, Iraqis, Georgians, Pakistanis, Somalis, and Palestinians slips across the narrow land border, carrying their few possessions in plastic bags, a few U.S. dollars, and their European dreams. Only a few weeks ago, according to Stelios, the loquacious owner of the Café Artisio, two hundred people were arrested coming through the woods in a single night.

"I hear that they are very aggressive," he says. "They infect the police with diseases." Stelios does not say what these diseases are, but the numbers at least are not exaggerated. In 2009, 75 percent of 106,200 detected illegal border crossers came into Europe through Greece. In June 2010 Frontex deputy executive director Gil Arias Fernández described Greece as "the hottest area of illegal immigration in Europe."[1]

In the first six months of that year, according to local police, seven thousand migrants had been arrested in Evros prefecture alone—a 30 percent increase over the same period the previous year. Most were caught crossing the border by Greek police and border guards equipped with night vision binoculars, thermic cameras, and other detection technologies. Others were arrested in bus stations or along the main road heading out of Evros toward Thessalonika and Athens, in a sparsely populated rural landscape of gentle hills and cultivated farmland where foreigners tend to stand out.

This bucolic tranquility is deceptive. For decades the Greek and Turkish armies have watched each other warily across the Evros River and still take occasional potshots at each other. Evros prefecture has the highest concentration of soldiers and army bases in Greece, and until recently large sections of the border were littered with antivehicle and antipersonnel mines laid during the 1974 Greek-Turkish war in Cyprus. And in the summer of 2010 this remote militarized frontier had become a new point of confrontation in the most chaotic and dysfunctional of Europe's outlying border countries.

The Armed Frontier

With its proximity to Turkey and the Middle East and a complicated geography that includes three thousand miles of land borders and a seven-thousand-mile maritime border encompassing both the mainland coastline and hundreds of isolated islands scattered across the Mediterranean and the Aegean, Greece has been a porous barrier in the exclusionary architecture of Fortress Europe ever since it joined the Schengen area in 1997. Like so many of the countries that make up the EU's external borders, Greece has traditionally been a country of emigration, with long-established diaspora populations extending to Australia and the United States. Since the early 1990s, the number of Greece's foreign-born inhabitants has grown to just under 1 million out of a total population of 11 million.

This figure does not include up to 800,000 undocumented migrants, most of whom come from neighboring Albania. In recent years, Greece has also become a transit country for migrants from the Middle East, Asia, and also for migrants from Africa seeking to avoid the tighter controls in the Mediterranean and the "Gaddafi camps." Most migrants in the Evros prefecture walk across the land border near Kastanies. Others cross the Evros River in the small inflatable boats used by Turkish smugglers or *kacakci*. These journeys are not without risk, as the militarization of the border presents its own special hazards. Between 1995 and 2009, at least 108 people were killed and another 187 seriously injured straying into minefields. "They had no idea where they were," says George Tentes, the chief surgeon at Didimoticho General Hospital, near the border, which has treated many migrants with mine-related injuries over the years. According to Tentes, these incidents have ceased since Greece became a party to the Mine Ban Treaty in 2004 and began extensive de-mining operations.

Migrants have drowned in the Evros River when their boats capsized or sank, or while attempting to swim or wade across. In May and June 2010, the bodies of nineteen African migrants, including young children, were recovered by the Greek and Turkish border police from the river. In August that year, activists from the NGO Welcome to Europe who were helping a migrant family locate a relative believed to have drowned stumbled upon a mass grave near the border town of Sidero; a bullet-riddled sign described it as an "illegal migrants cemetery." The Greek government initially denied its existence but subsequently admitted that between 150 and 200 bodies were buried there, some of which were exhumed for identification and a proper funeral.

These incursions have added another element of insecurity and paranoia to a border already charged with geopolitical tensions, which I experienced firsthand when I entered a restricted military area near Kastanies with the photographer Steven Greaves in an attempt to photograph one of the few remaining minefields for a magazine assignment. We found no minefields, but as we were leaving the area Greek soldiers riding in a military jeep flagged us down and asked what we were doing there. The soldiers were not mollified by our explanation that we were trying to photograph a minefield for an article about illegal immigration. A series of radio and phone calls ensued before two police cars eventually appeared, followed by the local military commander, who politely divested us of our computer, mobile phones, and cameras and ordered us to accompany the two police cars to the police station at Orestiada, eighteen miles away.

Greece is notoriously sensitive in regard to espionage, whether real or imagined, and we were beginning to wonder where all this might be leading. When we arrived at the station, however, we were greeted amicably by Mr. Charamaloupolos, the acting chief of the Orestiada police, and his intelligence officer, Axis, who told us they had checked with Athens and were satisfied that our reasons for being in Evros were legitimate. We assumed that the affair was closed. But the following morning we realized to our amazement that our car was being followed by a plainclothes policeman. In the course of the day four separate cars tracked us back and forth along the mostly deserted main highway between Orestiada and Alexandroupolis.

The next morning a police escort was waiting outside our hotel, and for the remainder of our stay in Evros he continued to track our movements with a tenacity that was not matched by any attempt to conceal his intentions. This obsessive surveillance was probably not due to our ability to uncover military secrets at the border. Greek and international human rights organizations have accused the Evros police and army of carrying out secret deportations, in which migrants are transported in trucks to the edge of the river, stripped of any evidence that they have been in Greece, from mobile phones to labels on clothing, and ferried across to the Turkish side of the border. These actions are illegal under Greek law, according to a 1999 presidential decree that prohibits the forcible removal of anyone seeking asylum, and Greece has always denied such allegations. But the Turkish military has claimed that nearly twelve thousand people were unlawfully deposited across the border between 2002 and 2007.

For its part, Greece has criticized Turkey for its reluctance to fulfill the terms of a 2001 readmission agreement and accept irregular migrants through more formalized procedures. As a result, migrants have sometimes found themselves shunted back and forth across the border. In July 2001, Amnesty International described how 250 Africans were rounded up in Istanbul by Turkish police and brought to the border, where they were made to walk to the other side, only to be rearrested by Greek police and deported back across the river the following night. After a week in a Turkish prison in the border city of Edirne, they were shunted across the border once again, whereupon the Greek police returned them to Turkey for what appears to have been the last time.[2]

The nervousness of Greek officialdom may also be due to allegations made by Human Rights Watch and other organizations concerning maltreatment and abuse of migrants by the Evros police. Chief Charamaloupolos denied these allegations, insisting, "We are trying to behave in the best possible way toward these people. Every allegation will be investigated and those that have been made have also been investigated. We have nothing to hide."

Our Stasi-like stalkers did not make these claims to transparency entirely convincing. Nor did a carefully controlled tour of Filakio-Kiprinou, the newest of the "special holding facilities" for irregular migrants in the Evros prefecture. Situated in the countryside about fifteen miles from Orestiada, Filakio consists of a large, modern two-story building surrounded by high metal fences topped with barbed wire. A well-drilled lieutenant named George Logathetes showed me around the center's facilities, after the usual stipulation that I could not speak to or even approach any of the 298 detainees. I was taken to the medical room, where a heavy submarine-like metal door led into the detainees' wing and the glass booths where detainees were able to talk to their lawyers and relatives.

The fact that these booths were stacked with rolls of toilet paper and other supplies did not suggest that they had been used recently, and it was difficult to imagine too many lawyers, let alone family members, coming to this remote and inaccessible location, especially since migrant detainees generally have their mobile phones confiscated and lawyers often do not know where they are. Under Greek law, migrants can be held in these conditions for a maximum of six months, though this period can be extended for up to a year, and released migrants are often rearrested.

Under the watchful eye of his superior officer, Logathetes showed me a leaflet that explained Greece's asylum policy in five languages as evidence that "anyone who wants asylum can ask for it." When I asked him how often such appeals were accepted, he replied, "Almost never," and seemed oblivious to the contradiction that this implied. The young lieutenant reminded me that Filakio had been visited by a number of human rights organizations, including the Hellenic League for Human Rights and Médecins Sans Frontières. He did not add that both these organizations had been extremely critical of conditions in the center.[3]

The previous month MSF had published a damning report on Greek detention centers—including Filakio—claiming that detainees were routinely held for much of the day in overcrowded and unhygienic conditions, where they were given almost no exercise and subjected to the "degrading and abusive behavior" of police guards. A 2009 Human Rights Watch report described Filakio as a place where "hitting and slapping by guards appears to be the norm, in part because of the lack of any other means of communication."[4] In Athens I met a Palestinian migrant who had once been detained in Filakio and who told me, "It was incredible. They were slapping everyone—even the women. I've never seen anything like it."

Logathetes emphatically denied these allegations. "It's not happening," he said, and described the relationship between guards and detainees as "friendly and good." It was impossible to find out what the detainees thought, but the somber expressions of the men, women, and children holding up signs in Arabic and Georgian from behind the barred windows suggested that there were other stories that were not being told.

Filakio was nevertheless an improvement on some of the detention centers in western Thrace. Few visitors have reason to pass through the isolated village of Venna in Rodopi prefecture. Situated about half an hour from the nearest city, Komotini, in the midst of cultivated farmland, this whitewashed village is no different from countless others in the region. On the edge of the village, a grain silo next to the local railway station has been converted into a "special holding facility for illegal migrants" with one of the worst reputations of all Greece's immigrant detention facilities. A 2009 report on Venna by the Thessalonika Hellenic League for Human Rights reported that

> the center is extremely filthy, infested with mice and cockroaches and with snakes over summer. . . . We noted an absolute lack of heating. The conditions of detention, the poor light and the ventilation bring to mind medieval dungeons, while sanitary conditions are non-existent to such a degree that the physical and mental health of both detainees and staff are at risk.[5]

Some 130 migrants spent the freezing winter of 2009–10 in Venna, including Iraqis, Pakistanis, and Afghans. On January 3 they set fire to the facilities and began self-harming in protest at their conditions. Forty-three detainees were arrested, thirty-six of whom were sentenced to eight months in prison for rioting and damaging public property. We were not allowed to visit Venna, but one afternoon we managed to shake off our police escort and drove out to try to take photographs.

On an overcast day, with heavy black clouds looming over the Rodopi Mountains in the distance, the center was a dismal and oppressive sight, with its faded yellow walls, barred windows, and high metal fences. We had no idea who was in there, where they came from, or where they were going—the inaccessibility and isolation of such centers and the culture of secrecy that surrounded them was intended to preclude answering such questions. But given what was happening in Evros and elsewhere in Greece, we suspected that the center was probably full and that it would continue to be so for some time.

Securitizing the Aegean

The transformation of Evros into Europe's migrant portal is a relatively recent development. Until 2009 most migrants came to Greece by sea. Between 2006 and 2008, the number of migrants intercepted in the Aegean and the eastern Mediterranean increased from seven thousand a year to just over thirty thousand. Most of them came across the narrow strip of ocean that divides the Turkish coast from the twelve Dodecanese Islands and the islands of Lesvos, Samos, and Chios. Refugees were not an entirely new phenomenon in these islands. In 1922 thousands of Greeks fled to the islands from Smyrna to escape Kemal Ataturk's vengeful reconquest of the city from the retreating Greek army. During World War II some sixty thousand Greek islanders fled in the other direction to Turkey to escape famine and Nazi occupation. Following the 1980 military coup in Turkey nearly thirty thousand Turkish refugees sought political asylum in Europe, many of whom came through Lesvos and other islands.

From 2006 onward these laid-back tourist islands began to receive a new influx of refugees from the battlefields of the Middle East and Afghanistan and the Horn of Africa. It is only a few miles from Lesvos, the third largest of the Greek islands, across the Strait of Mytilini to the Turkish coastal city of Ayvalik. In the summer of 2009 an average of 1,500 people were arriving every month on the island in dinghies, in wooden boats, and even on Jet Skis, hoping to catch a ferry to the Greek mainland.

By the following summer the average number had fallen to fifty. Today the island's beaches are littered with the detritus of these journeys: deflated dinghies, clothes, life jackets, baling jugs used by migrants to keep their boats afloat, a pile of confiscated outboard motors in the coast guard depot at Mitilini. Evidence of these arrivals can also be found at Mitilini's makeshift detention center at Pagani, tucked less than half a mile away from the magnificent blue-domed pink Agios Church and the chic bars that line the town's idyllic harbor. In the summer of 2009, 1,500 men, women, and children were packed into these three disused warehouses with a capacity of 290. In September and October, a series of riots and hunger strikes at Pagani prompted the Greek deputy civil protection minister, Spyros Vougias, to close a center that he compared to Dante's Inferno.

When we visited Pagani the following summer the barbed-wire-topped metal gates were unlocked, but the smell of urine hung in the air from the single toilet as we wandered around the empty buildings, through the rows of mattresses and bunk beds. Parts of the walls and ceilings were still blackened from when detainees had set their mattresses alight the previous year. Some walls bore messages and political slogans in Arabic, Farsi, and English, names such as "Ibrahim from Pakistan," and a particularly poignant anonymous message declaring, "Being away from you is driving me crazy and no matter where I am you are in my heart."

Pagani's closure did not appear to be definitive. A few days later we found an armed policeman in the yard guarding a group of twelve migrants, including a young child who could not have been more than six years old, who were being held overnight before being transported to Athens. Criticisms of Pagani often focused on the fact that unaccompanied minors and very young children were held there, and it was partly in response to such negative publicity that the Greek government established the Villa Azadi ("house of freedom" in Farsi), a reception center for unaccompanied minors, in a former hospital for the disabled about thirty miles from the capital.

As we wound our way up the mountains from Mitilini, the center's Greek-Australian chief social worker, Greg Kavarnos, described in caustic and blackly comic detail the lackadaisical bureaucratic processes that had left him and his staff of social anthropologists, doctors, interpreters, and social workers in a reception center in the middle of the mountains with no clear mandate and precarious funding. Since its establishment in 2008, the center has provided more than 2,300 unaccompanied minors, from very young children to teenagers, with a temporary home.

Many of them have been homeless or living in shared accommodations in Greek cities before coming to the center. Some have become drug addicts and need to be put through detox programs. Others arrive with skin diseases and other health problems. Kavarnos' charges included a discus thrower from the Central African Republic whose father was killed because his son refused to join the national athletic team and a seventeen-year-old Afghan boy who hit his head and fell into a coma when police tried to drag him from a truck in the port of Patras. The hospital had neglected to turn the boy over periodically to keep the blood flowing properly, so he arrived at the center with his back and legs literally rotting and had to be immediately rehospitalized.

The center was obviously a very different place from Pagani. When we arrived there a group of Afghan teenagers were playing volleyball, and a teenage boy who I was told was paranoiac wandered around the grounds with a frown, immersed in his own world. There were no bars or barbed wire, and the residents lived in shared dormitories with pictures on the walls, including their own. Noyan, a thoughtful Afghan Hazara with a constantly perplexed expression, had painted a group of children in a boat half filled with water, rowing their way toward Greece; above them was a speech bubble that read, "Let's go to Europe."

Noyan told me about his strict father, who had been killed four years earlier in Pakistan, either by NATO or by the Taliban. Once, he said, his father had held his hands on a hot stove to punish him for hanging out with a street gang. Now he wanted to save other children from delinquency and he was writing a philosophical book with text and illustrations about "life and terrorism." Noyan was clearly struggling to make sense of some unbelievably harsh experiences, but his immediate prospects were not good. Not a single resident has been given refugee status since Villa Azardi opened. On reaching eighteen they will all have to leave the center and return to illegality in what Toulina Demeli, a refugee lawyer at the center, describes as a "crazy situation. They aren't allowed to come, they're not allowed to stay, and they're not allowed to leave."

Noyan was now eighteen and was no longer entitled to stay in the center. Soon he would be obliged to descend from this mountain sanctuary and return to homelessness and illegality on the Greek mainland. For other migrants, Lesvos marked the point where their journeys ended. At the St. Panteleimon cemetery overlooking Mitilini, more than two dozen drowned Kurdish and Afghan migrants are buried in crude graves, identified only by their nationality, a number, and the date they died. The most recent disaster took place on October 27, 2009, when a boat carrying eighteen Afghans was swept onto rocks off the island's northern coast. Ten passengers were rescued, but three women and five children drowned, most of whom are buried in the cemetery.

The gravedigger did not want us to see these graves and refused to let us photograph them, but we eventually got a permit from the church to do so. In order to avoid a repeat of our Evros debacle, we also asked the commanding officer of the Lesvos coast guard if we could photograph the migrant boats and dinghies in their depot. We were not surprised when the request was refused, and on leaving the office we found ourselves trailed on foot by yet another plainclothes policeman, who was even more hilariously inept at the art of pursuit than his counterparts in Evros.

The decline in the number of migrants coming to Lesvos reflects a general reduction seen in all the Greek islands that has been matched by a concomitant increase in Evros, which the Orestiada police had been at a loss to explain. Some attributed it to the cheaper cost of land smuggling routes compared with sea journeys, others to the increased surveillance in the Aegean, including the joint operations coordinated by Frontex, one of whose ships was permanently moored in Mitilini harbor. Whatever the explanation, there were not many migrants coming to the islands.

Until 2009 the Turkish city of Izmir was a major hub of immigration smuggling. In the summer of that year, migrants from Asia, Africa, and the Middle East were turning up almost daily at the seedy hotels around Izmir's run-down Basmane district, in search of *kacakci* to arrange boat passage to the Greek islands. But when I visited Basmane in June the following year, there were no migrants to be seen anywhere, and the crumbling hotel in Basmane Square that had housed more than ten to fifteen Africans per room the previous year was closed.

Samos

This reduction in migrant traffic was also evident on Samos, the island closest to Izmir. One night we went out on patrol with the Samos coast guard. During the six-hour patrol there were no migrants to be found as the powerful patrol boat sliced back and forth through the moonlit strait between Samos and Turkey. The only people we encountered were an old Greek fisherman alone in his boat and a patrol boat under the command of a Scandinavian army officer, who was presumably part of the ongoing Frontex operations.

Much of the night was spent hovering on the maritime border between Greece and Turkey, fighting off sleep and boredom. In 2008, Lieutenant

Emmaniou "Manny" Schonaraius and his crew once brought back ninety migrants from three separate boats in a single night, but rescue has not always been the Hellenic coast guard's main priority. The Greek coast guard is a paramilitary unit designed to support the navy in wartime, and their Italian Lambro patrol boats are fitted with machine gun mounts. The coast guard's new role in enforcing the EU's maritime border in the Aegean has been accompanied by a disturbing tendency among some coast guard officers to regard migrants as a novel kind of "enemy" to be fought and repelled.

In 2006 *Der Spiegel* reported that the Turkish coast guard rescued thirty-one migrants off the coast of Izmir who had been thrown into the sea by their Greek counterparts. According to the report, six migrants had drowned and three were missing. These allegations have never been fully proven—or disproven. In 2007 the German NGO Pro Asyl accused coast guard officers from various islands of routinely beating up the migrants they rescued, torturing them to extract information about smugglers, casting their boats off in international waters without food, and forcing migrants back into Turkish territorial waters.[6]

Migrants have been known to puncture their own boats in order to pressure the coast guard to rescue them so that they can appeal for asylum, but the Greek coast guard has been accused of puncturing migrants' boats and disabling their engines before dragging them back into Turkish waters and forcing their passengers to row back to shore with just one oar. The coast guard has also been accused of dumping migrants on uninhabited islands and atolls and of generating waves in order to push them back across the maritime frontier.

Zoe Liebetezou, the head of the volunteer emergency rescue organization Hellenika Rescue in Lesvos, has often accompanied the coast guard during migrant rescue operations, and told me that she had personally witnessed coast guard officers jumping into the sea to save people even at the risk of their own lives, but she admitted that she could not speak for every island. Manny Schonaraius and his youthful crew certainly did not look like men capable of drowning migrants at sea, but they were patrolling without a Greek flag, presumably to confuse any migrants they might encounter, and Schonaraius admitted that upon encountering migrant boats his crew sometimes revved their engines in order to generate waves and perpetrated other "jokes to make them afraid."

The lieutenant did not say whether these strategies were carried out on his own initiative or under orders, but he clearly did not have much sympathy for the people he rescued. Most asylum seekers were economic migrants, he said, and some were probably terrorists. When I asked him how he knew this, he told me that he had once rescued a Palestinian from the Gaza Strip who was carrying a photograph of someone holding a Kalashnikov. This did not seem the most compelling evidence of terrorism, but the Greek belief that migrants constitute a potential security threat goes higher up the chain. In 2007 Apostolos Mikromastoras, the chief of the Lesvos coast guard, described migrants as the advance guard of a potential "Islamic invasion" perpetrated by "very well trained" young men who "could strike in Europe, beginning a war here."[7]

Responsibility for defending Europe against this "invasion" is shared between the coast guard and the Samos police, in what has traditionally been one of the softest crime beats in Greece. There has not been a murder on the island in thirty years, and the last bank robbery took place a decade ago. The arrival of migrants on the island meant that police officers were obliged to process asylum claims, using criteria that were difficult to extract from Mr. Condonoris, the chief of the Samos police, who greeted me with the wariness that I was beginning to take for granted from Greek officialdom. When I asked him on what basis his officers accepted or rejected asylum applications, he replied cagily that decisions were made on the basis of "certain information" made available by experts, including linguistic specialists provided by Frontex, who helped determine the nationalities of illegal immigrants in order to eliminate unfounded appeals.

Since 2006 Samos has become the base of operations for Operation Poseidon, an aerial and naval surveillance program that is coordinated by Frontex and involves twenty-four countries. Frontex experts also carry out screening interviews of intercepted migrants at sea or in designated temporary buildings outside the coast guard headquarters in order to distinguish between "returnable" and "nonreturnable" migrants. One of these experts agreed to speak to me on condition of anonymity. As an Arabic-speaker, he was tasked with determining by their accents and dialects whether migrants really were who they said they were. He insisted that translators and lawyers were always present to ensure that asylum claims were correctly and fairly processed.

Dimitrios Vouros, an attorney from the Greek Court of Appeal who has worked with refugees for nearly six years at Samos, had a very different view of these procedures. I met him in his office on a Sunday evening, where he told me how police sometimes pressured detainees to sign forms they could not read in which they renounced their claims to asylum, and described how the absence of trained interpreters meant that he was often obliged to communicate complex legal procedures to detainees in English—a language that he spoke reasonably well but which many of his clients hardly spoke at all.

With his mane of graying hair, lined face, and harassed expression, Vouros was clearly demoralized by the all but insurmountable difficulties in trying to collect evidence in detention centers to support asylum applications—so much so that he was contemplating whether to abandon his contract with the government and work with refugees on a voluntary basis. Vouros was dismissive of the claims by Samos police that all asylum appeals were correctly dealt with. On Samos virtually all asylum appeals were rejected, he said, because police knew nothing about the political situation in the countries where refugees came from and had received no training to prepare them for this role.

UNHCR has made similar criticisms of the Greek asylum system over the years. But Vouros went further, suggesting that the police were under specific orders from within and outside Greece not to grant asylum. Though he praised the professionalism of Frontex officials compared with the local police, he had no doubts about their priorities. "Lawyers must give protection to people that need protection," he said bluntly, "but Frontex wants to stop people coming to Europe."

The Permanent Waiting Room

Until 2009 migrants arrested on Samos were held in a former nineteenth-century tobacco factory not far from the main tourist drag in the town of Vathy, where the Samos police once had its headquarters. From the outside, the yellow and white facade conveys an air of faded bourgeois prosperity that belies its role as a detention center. In peak periods, dozens of migrant detainees were confined for up to twenty-four hours in rooms with a leaking sewage system. In some cases detainees were wedged so tightly on the floor that there was barely enough space to step across them.

In 2009 the center was replaced by the new detention cum screening center built with EU funds. Built on a former police shooting range that overlooks Vathy, its tiered bungalow dormitories represent a considerable improvement on its predecessor, even if the massive two-tiered fences, razor wire, and closed-circuit cameras have more than a touch of Guantanamo Bay, something that the presence of a children's playground failed to dispel. We were allowed to look at the camp from the outside but not to talk to the fifty-odd detainees who had just arrived, who shouted to us that they were Palestinians from Gaza—a claim that was disputed by the Frontex expert, who insisted that they were in fact Algerians.

Like so many of Europe's border countries, Greece is a transit country rather than a destination in its own right. But many migrants are obliged to apply for asylum there under the terms of the Dublin Convention, while fingerprinted asylum seekers who manage to leave Greece and apply in another European country are sent back to Greece, even though applications from deported "Dubliners" were until recently declared invalid by the Greek authorities on the grounds that they had left Greece and abandoned their claims.

Greece is a signatory to the 1951 Refugee Convention and one of the few European countries where the numbers of asylum applications have risen since 2005, but it also has the lowest rate of recognitions in Europe. Few people receive the pink card that gives them limited rights to live and work as registered asylum seekers, and fewer still get refugee status in a country where annual acceptances tends to hover at less than 1 percent. In 2009 exactly eleven people out of nearly thirty thousand applicants were given refugee status in Greece.

The high rate of rejections is due partly to the fact that asylum applications in Greece are processed by police officers with little guidance or expertise in such matters and partly to a poorly administered and underresourced asylum process that makes it difficult for applicants to make their case or appeal against rejections. Rejected asylum seekers are usually issued a "white card" that orders them to leave Greece within thirty days, regardless of whether they have anywhere to go or any documents that allow them to enter other countries legally. Most either remain in Greece illegally or try to continue their journey to Europe. Often they are rearrested and detained again.

The result is that thousands of asylum seekers remain trapped in a country that does not want them and which they do not want to be in. One of them is Sima, a twenty-eight-year-old Afghan woman who came to Samos in 2009 with her husband and two children. Slight and deceptively fragile, with short black hair and an easy smile, she has been an orphan since the age of three, when her parents and eight members of her family were killed by the anti-Soviet mujahideen, and she was brought up an uncle and her grandmother. For some years, she and her husband had been refugees in Iran, but they decided to come to Europe with their children because there was no work there.

The family spent nearly a month trying to cross the Iran-Turkey border, sleeping out in the open or in ruined buildings and living on bread and potatoes, before reaching Izmir, where they crossed the Strait of Samos in a boat with other migrants. At first they lived in an abandoned building. Now they were sharing a small house whose rent was being paid by a local refugee solidarity group and a charity in Athens. Sima's husband was doing occasional work in construction, but they wanted to go to Norway.

When I asked her what she wanted to do there, she looked surprised and said that she had never really thought about it, but she thought she would like to work as a hotel receptionist. Her twelve-year-old son wanted to play soccer for Barcelona, while his pretty young sister wanted to be a singer. There was little likelihood of any of these aspirations being fulfilled: the family had no legal status in Greece and had just been told that the charity that paid their rent might not be able to do so for much longer. This was not the Europe that Sima had imagined. "We had this image of freedom, that people lived better," she said. "But now we see that it isn't better. We're looking for work and we can't find any."

At Sima's house I met Inayat and Younis, two young Afghans in their early twenties from the Hazara ethnic minority, both of whom expressed a similar disenchantment. The two of them had come to Lesvos together by boat from Turkey in 2004, hoping to reach the United Kingdom. After a convoluted trajectory that included three months in Pagani, a failed attempt to reach Italy from Patras, and off-the-books work in Athens, they had decided to apply for asylum in Greece and had received their pink cards. Now they were obliged to present themselves at the Samos police station every six months to get their cards renewed, and they were reluctant to leave the island in case they encountered a less sympathetic police officer elsewhere who might not issue the renewal. In effect they were trapped on Samos, amid the tourist cafés and restaurants, with the beach and the sea as consolations while they waited for the Athens bureaucracy to decide whether they would be given the opportunity to restart their lives.

After thirteen years as a refugee in Pakistan, Iran, and Europe, Inayat no longer felt any affinity to his native land and wanted to study art, while Younis wanted to go to Norway to live with a relative. Both of them emanated the anxiety, uncertainty, and frustration that I encountered so often among migrants caught in similar situations. Why was it, Inayat asked me, with more bewilderment than anger, that governments that were fighting a war in his country were so unwilling to let him go to theirs? It was a good question, and not one that I was able to answer. It is not surprising that, faced with these unpromising possibilities, most migrants try to avoid being fingerprinted and seek to make their way to other European countries. But getting out of Greece is often harder than getting in.

The Bottleneck

Lying 213 miles north of Athens along the Ionian coast in the district of Thesprotia, the port of Igoumenitsa is the gateway to the Ionian Islands and Corfu, with daily ferries to the Italian ports of Brindisi and Bari. Since 2009 this ferry traffic has increased as a result of the completion of the 416-mile Egnatia Odos highway, which connects the town to the Evros border and now brings a steady stream of trucks and vehicles heading for Italy. Few of the foreign visitors who catch the ferries each summer stay long enough to sample the smart bars and cafés that line the main street overlooking the bay.

Together with Athens and the port of Patras, this remote town of fifteen thousand inhabitants has become one of the main staging posts for migrants trying to get out of Greece. In the autumn of 2010 I arrived in Igoumenitsa by bus from Athens in the early hours of the morning, in the middle of one of the dense monsoon-like downpours that take place several times a day in the rainy season. After a tormented few hours trying to evade the assault from a seemingly endless legion of tiger mosquitoes in my hotel room, I woke up to see two African migrants looking for food in the trash bins in the market down below.

Migrants are a frequent presence in the town, where they come to beg for food in the supermarkets or look for scraps in the market. But most of them remain in the hills, close to the barbed-wire-topped fence that surrounds the new port facility, hoping to smuggle themselves onto one of the ferries and reach Italy, more than twenty-four hours away. Getting onto the ferries is difficult and dangerous. Migrants routinely risk injury by clinging to the underside of trucks, and run the chance of beatings by police or coast guard if they are caught. In April 2009 a twenty-nine-year-old Iraqi Kurd named Arivan Osman Abdullah was taken to the local hospital in a coma after being caught by port police underneath a truck; he died four months later. An internal police inquiry later concluded that he had had an epileptic fit, but his companions claimed that police officers had beaten his head against the pavement.

Directly opposite the compound I found a group of Somali, Eritrean, and Iraqi Kurdish migrants staring disconsolately across the metal-gray sea toward the distant islands that Homer once chose as the setting for the *Odyssey*. One Kurd showed me a bruise on his arm where he had been hit with a police truncheon a few days before. "They are very stubborn, these people here," said a haggard-looking Somali who had been in Igoumenitsa for eight months. "They are just treating us like beasts. They are saying, 'Go to the mountains and live there.' It is not good, it is not fair. We are all human beings." Was anyone getting out of Igoumenitsa? "Some of our guys are lucky enough to move," he said. "They go under the trucks and they call us about the life they are living and they say it's better. Some of them are in Italy, some are in France. All Europe is good, only here is not good for us."

Arrival in Bari or Brindisi does not necessarily guarantee entrance to Italy. A bilateral agreement between Greece and Italy allows the Italian port police to send back migrants they catch in the port compound on the same boat they came on. Yet migrants continue to hide in trucks, swim into the port compound, or disguise themselves as ferry workers or tourists. Others are using sophisticated false documents, according to Mr. Varelas, the diminutive second officer of the Igoumenitsa Port Authority.

When I met him Mr. Varelas was a busy man. Greece was in its third week of a national truckers strike, and stationary trucks were lined up all along the bridge leading into the port. His officers had just arrested an Afghan couple and two children traveling with false Spanish passports and a Kosovan family with a baby who let out piercing wails outside his office. Others were being held in the port's temporary holding center. Preventing migrants from getting to Italy seemed to have become the main occupation of the port authorities and the regular police.

Directly opposite the port compound, some four hundred men were camped out in the forested slopes. Dozens of them were milling around at the base of the hill on the other side of the coastal road, washing and hanging their clothes out to dry, cooking over gas stoves and fires, or waiting for the camp's only shower. I drank tea with a group of Iraqis who were sitting on wooden benches beneath a plastic sheet. Hassan, a car mechanic and former interpreter with the U.S. Army in Mosul, told me how he had recently spent five days in a hospital suffering from malnutrition and liver failure; a sympathetic Greek doctor had managed to get him admitted. Salim was one of the fifty-five Kurdish asylum seekers forcibly removed by the U.K. government in a widely criticized deportation in February 2009, and he was trying to return to England, where he had lived for seven years.

Farther up the steep forested slopes a number of Sudanese, Eritreans, Somalis, and Moroccans were camped out in tents, while others had only plastic sheets. Abdel Aziz, a freckled and astonishingly optimistic twenty-two-year-old from Casablanca who had been in Greece for a month, told me how he had been a migrant since the age of fourteen. In Spain he had been a farm worker and a bricklayer, now he was hoping to join his brother, who was working in the construction industry in Milan. In all that time he had seen his parents only once, he said, when he went back to Morocco earlier that year, but he had never ceased to send money back home. Now he was sharing one of the sturdier-looking bivouacs with two other Moroccans from his native city.

"It doesn't let in any rain," he said proudly, smacking the timber door frame to prove it. Like many of the migrants in the hills, Abdel Aziz had no proper shoes, only a pair of plastic sandals that were cutting his feet and were painful to walk in, but he was cheerfully confident he would make it onto one of the ferries in the port below us. When I pointed out that others had been in Igoumenitsa a lot longer and hadn't succeeded, he grinned and said, "They're not trying hard enough." Abdel Aziz was trying very hard indeed. Three times in the last three days he had made it onto a ferry underneath a truck, only to be caught by the port authorities.

But new arrivals were coming almost every day from Athens and Patras, winter was approaching, and the heavy rains had already turned the camps to mud. With four hundred people competing to get into the fortified port compound, frustration sometimes boiled over. Two weeks before my arrival Somali and Kurdish migrants had thrown stones at each other before the police fired their guns in the air to disperse them. Vassilios Miaris, the smooth commissioner of the regional police, expressed sympathy for the migrants and told me he had repeatedly asked the mayor to build a reception center where they could be housed and fed. But there were no plans to build one, and Miaris' humanitarian sentiments were somewhat undermined by his insistence that any such center should be built away from the town to avoid attracting any more migrants. "They should go back to their homes," he said. I pointed out that many of them were unable or unwilling to go back to their countries. "We understand that," he replied, "but Greece can't do anything for them."

According to Miaris, the local population was "terrified" of the migrants, because they robbed cars and broke into people's houses. But these allegations were rejected by Haris Kostinos, a marine biology student and a member of the local migrant solidarity group. Kostinos admitted that migrants sometimes stole food from shops to survive, but he insisted that the police exaggerated the threat they posed. There are certainly not many towns of comparable size that would respond positively to the sudden presence of four hundred homeless strangers on their doorstep, and it was clear that the migrants were not liked. One local stationer told me how puzzled he had been when migrants came continuously to his shop to buy palette knives and masking tape—until he realized that they were being used to slit the canvas on trucks and seal it afterward to avoid detection.

Like many people in the town, he described the migrants as a "big problem" and pointed out that Greece had enough trouble looking after its own population. This was true, but Greeks had not yet been reduced to living in the hills in homemade tents, and Igoumenitsa's unwanted migrants were part of a wider failure on the part of Greece and the European Union, the consequences of which were becoming increasingly difficult to ignore, even in the Greek capital itself.

Meltdown

Every Monday hundreds of asylum seekers and refugees queue up outside the Central Aliens Police Directorate at 24 Petrou Ralli in Athens beginning in the early hours of the morning, hoping to get or renew their pink cards or simply to be able to claim asylum. Some have spent the previous night there, hoping to be among the 20 percent allowed to make their claims each week.

At the offices of the Greek Council for Refugees (GCR), Spyros Koulocheris, the GCR's legal coordinator, described the "humanitarian crisis" that was unfolding in the capital as a result of Greece's chaotic and dysfunctional asylum system. The majority of asylum applications were turned down because the police chiefs knew nothing about asylum, lawyers were increasingly refusing to take on their cases because they no longer knew when or if they were going to get paid, and even asylum seekers with six-month residency permits were not getting their pink cards renewed.

As a result, thousands of migrants were stranded in the city without work, health care, or housing, and there were so many people coming to the GCR offices looking for help that Spyros and his colleagues were obliged to concentrate only on the most vulnerable, including pregnant women and women with children.

At the UNHCR offices in the wealthy Neo Psychiko district, I found thirty Palestinians from the Gaza Strip camped out in tents on the pavement. Most of them had been in the country for at least five years, working illegally. Their spokesman, Hazim, told me that he had recently lost his job as a painter and decorator and that he was homeless. Now he and his companions were asking the Greek government to either give them legal residency or allow them to leave Greece, and they believed that UNHCR would be able to help them. But UNHCR officials told me that there was nothing they could do and that the Palestinians had little chance of achieving their objectives.

Thousands of migrants are trapped in a similar situation. Many are homeless or living in overcrowded rented accommodations, surviving from occasional off-the-books work in construction, on the islands, or in the countryside. Others have no jobs at all. A few blocks north of Omonia Square, I spoke to a group of Somalis in a former office building that they had established as a community center. Maye Abdul, a former social worker in his late twenties, told me how he had left Somalia in 2007 after his parents were killed in the civil war, intending to go to the United Kingdom, where his brother worked for the Southall council. Like many Somalis, he had become trapped in Greece, surviving through occasional work and sporadic donations from his brother, sharing a room with six other people in a house rented by sympathetic British Somalis.

Maye Abdul summed up the consequences of illegality for the 1,500-odd Somalis in Athens with a list of negatives: no rights, no education, no passport, no safety, no security. The absence of the last was evident in the nervous Somalis who kept watch outside the building. Police routinely carry out aggressive raids on the center in search of illegal migrants or simply to harass the *malaka*—"idiotic" or "useless people," as Greek police often refer to migrants. In addition, said Maye Abdul, the Somalis face verbal and physical attacks from "racist people who can't see any color but black"—a category that includes neighbors who spit at them or pour water on them, along with the predatory vigilante groups connected to the ultranationalist political party Popular Orthodox Alarm (LAOS) and the neo-Nazi organization Chrysi Avgi (Golden Dawn).

The activities of these groups have created a siege-like atmosphere among the immigrant communities in the capital, many of whom live in the St. Panteleimon district a few blocks north near Attiki Square. In the last three years they have been attacked by far-right gangs armed with clubs and iron bars, or stabbed in hit-and-run attacks by Golden Dawn militants on scooters and motorbikes. In May 2009, Father Prokopios, a priest at the St. Panteleimon church, was forced to close a soup kitchen for homeless migrants after an arson attack on the church basement. That same year the nearby children's playground was closed by the local council after a group of "concerned citizens" harassed and attacked migrants who brought their children to play there. More than twelve months later the playground remained closed to both Greeks and immigrants—a cowardly decision that was justified by the local council as an attempt to keep the peace.

But peace was increasingly absent in the cramped urban spaces of downtown Athens. In addition to constant clashes between the Greek police and those protesting austerity measures, attacks on immigrants were taking place on an almost daily basis. In September a member of the Médecins Sans Frontières team in Athens was beaten unconscious not far from the church. Naseem, an Afghan who has been living in Greece for seven years and one of the few people to have received full refugee status, told me that he no longer dared to walk back home at night from his job and preferred to take a taxi or stay with friends. "It's a catastrophe for society that you cannot feel safe in a civilized European city," he said. "You feel it, that you cannot go to certain areas, you cannot walk, you cannot go, you cannot feel free. Something is really changing in this society."

One evening I sat in Attiki Square opposite the Hotel New Dream in downtown Athens, one of the main gathering places for Afghan and other Asian migrants in the capital. The atmosphere in the square was relaxed and familial. Women in hijabs were talking animatedly on benches while men stand around smoking and chatting and children darted around the fringes of the square playing catch or chasing each other. Apart from a handful of uniformed police, the only Greeks present were sitting in cafés around the edges of the square.

I was not there around ten o'clock that night, when a group of local vigilantes and far-right activists calling themselves "Citizens of Athens" descended on the square and aggressively drove the migrants away, dispersing leaflets written in English that accused migrants of "insulting all us Greeks, all Greek women, our Christian religion, our civilisation, our pride, our lives" and promised "every possible action" to drive out immigrants and the "traitor-politicians" who had allowed them into the country. The next day the migrants had gone and the square was guarded by a group of sour-looking Greeks, who shooed away a lone Asian man with the temerity to approach them.

The "Hellenization" of Attiki Square was one episode in a concerted campaign to drive migrants from the city center. Riot police were a frequent presence in the area, largely in response to clashes between far-right and anarchist/leftist groups. But migrants and antiracist campaigners have frequently accused the Athens police of tacit collusion in extreme-right violence, and a video apparently showing members of LAOS being transported in a police van was recently raised in a parliamentary debate as evidence of such collusion. In May 2011 the anti-immigrant climate in downtown Athens reached a new level of intensity when the murder of a Greek father-to-be in a criminal attack sparked a racist pogrom. For three days mobs rampaged through the streets around St. Panteleimon beating up any dark-skinned migrant they found, and one Bangladeshi man was killed.

These tensions have been exacerbated by the Greek debt crisis, but they are also a consequence of a dysfunctional system for which both Greece and the European Union bear responsibility. Like Malta, Greece clearly did not anticipate the consequences of its new role as an EU border country when it joined Schengen, but European governments have shown little inclination to change the policies that have transformed Greece into a migratory barrier and a migrant trap. There have been some tentative attempts by both Greece and the EU to improve the quality of its asylum procedures. In the autumn of 2010, the United Kingdom, Norway, and the Netherlands announced that they would stop transferring "Dublin cases" back to Greece, although the U.K. government subsequently continued with Dublin deportations. That same month the Greek government adopted a National Action Plan on Asylum Reform and Migration Management, which pledged a raft of reforms, including the transfer of the asylum process from the police to a civilian authority.

Both the UNHCR and the Greek Council for Refugees cautiously welcomed the new asylum plan, and the European commissioner for home affairs, Cecilia Malmstrom, pledged European assistance to facilitate reforms. But these tentative gestures have been accompanied by an intensification of police repression across the country. On December 27, 2010, the Palestinians outside the UNHCR offices were violently evicted and their tents demolished by police bulldozers. Throughout the winter, Igoumenitsa police escalated their raids on the migrant camps in the hillsides in an attempt to drive migrants from the town, a campaign that resulted in four hundred arrests between April and May 2011. Between November 2010 and March of the following year, some two hundred officers from twenty-six countries took part in Rapid Border Intervention Teams (RABIT), which were deployed for the first time at the Evros border in order to assist Greek police under the coordination of Frontex. And in February 2012 the Greek authorities began the construction of a wire fence along the twelve-mile land border near Kastanies, with EU funding.

Despite this offensive, Greece's migrants have won some victories. On March 9, 2011, three hundred migrants in Thessaloniki were granted six-month residency permits after a forty-four-day hunger strike that had brought some of them to the brink of death, but such concessions are unlikely to become the norm. The EU is currently negotiating a readmissions agreement with the Turkish government that will eventually enable Greece to deport migrants more easily. Though a signatory to the Geneva Refugee Convention, Turkey is one of the few countries to retain the "European clause," which obliges it to provide refugee protection only to European refugees; migrants seeking asylum who returned to Turkish territory will have little chance of getting such protection.

Should this agreement be concluded, then Turkey may well end up playing a similar role to Greece in the EU's migratory controls, and the humanitarian crisis unfolding in the streets of Athens and the hills of Igoumenitsa may finally be solved—or at least shifted to a country where it may be less visible. And if this happens, it will be not only because Greece wants it but also because powerful countries a long way from Europe's new borders are determined to ensure that migrants do not come anywhere near their own.

6

Small Island: British Borders

Surely John Bull will not endanger his birth-right, his liberty, his property, in fact all that men hold dear . . . simply in order that men and women may cross to and fro between England and France without running the risk of sea-sickness.

—Lieutenant-General Sir Garnet Wolseley, 1882

Britain's border security controls are among the toughest in the world, and by using the latest technology we are continuing to improve our ability to ensure only legitimate travellers and goods enter Britain.

—Phil Woolas, MP, December 4, 2009

The United Kingdom occupies an anomalous position within Europe's exclusionary border regime. On one hand, the United Kingdom has been an ardent advocate of tighter restrictions on immigration and asylum across the European Union, and British police and Home Office officials have played a key role in the various European working groups that have formulated European policy on immigration over the last three decades. Britain also participates on a formal or informal basis in most of the key EU conventions and mechanisms pertaining to illegal immigration and asylum.

Together with Ireland, however, the United Kingdom is one of two EU member states that have remained outside the Schengen area and retained their own distinct immigration controls and border checks. These arrangements are partly an expression of lack of confidence in the EU's ability to police its borders, but they also reflect the British belief in a distinct "island destiny" that separates it from the rest of Europe. For centuries this geographical separation was seen as a strategic barrier against invasion and an essential guarantor of the British national character, and this "splendid isolation" was one of the reasons for the long delay in constructing the Channel Tunnel. Between the mid-nineteenth century and World War II, various governments considered and rejected various proposals to build a tunnel, though many of them came close to acceptance. In 1917 the *Daily Chronicle* even contained a special supplement promoting a plan to build a "transcontinental highway from Charing Cross to India" that would isolate a postwar Germany and secure the survival of the British Empire into the indefinite future. This visionary scheme was illustrated with an artist's impression of an intercontinental road stretching from London and under the Channel toward a domed Baghdad silhouetted against the rising sun.[1]

The main opposition to these proposals came from the War Office, which argued—however improbably—that a foreign army might use a tunnel to launch an invasion or a surprise attack. Others feared "invasion" by an array of undesirable foreigners that included Russian Nihilists, Jewish criminals, and French artists with lax sexual mores. In 1919 Colonel Charles Repington, a former intelligence officer and a prominent critic of the tunnel, warned that its construction would lead to the "loss of our insularity and the easy access of shoals of aliens upon our shores" who would breed with British women and "Latinize" the national "stock."[2]

These "intangible psychological factors," as one 1930s parliamentary committee subsequently described them, were as significant as military objections to the tunnel. It was not until 1994 that the opening of the tunnel from Calais to Folkestone finally ended this physical separation from Europe, but the "psychological" factors that had once prevented its construction were if anything intensified by the new proximity of the wider world. By this time the notion of an unbroken highway between London and the Middle East had less positive connotations, and in the last years of the century a sudden influx of "shoals of aliens" aroused old phobias and prejudices that converged on Britain's most famous border town.

The Siege of Dover

Situated on the southeast English coast, only twenty-one miles from France, the port of Dover occupies a special place in British mythology. For centuries the stolid presence of Dover Castle marked the first line of defense against potential invaders, and the town's celebrated chalk cliffs constituted an iconic symbol of Englishness. Dover's emblematic place in the national imagination owes much to the way it has been imagined by artists and writers, from Matthew Arnold's "cliffs of England . . . glimmering and vast in the tranquil bay" to Vera Lynn and the American poet Alice Duer Miller's paean to English wartime resilience in her verse novel *The White Cliffs* (1940).

These associations with war, patriotism, and national purity were crucial to the bleak sequence of events that followed the sudden appearance of asylum seekers from eastern Europe in Dover in 1997. Most of them were Roma from the Czech Republic and Slovakia, who were given temporary accommodations by the Kent County Council in local bed-and-breakfasts and hotels in accordance with the Conservative government's recent directives delegating responsibility for receiving asylum seekers to local councils. Their presence quickly became the focus of bitter local animosity, much of which emanated from the *Dover Express* and its twinned newspaper the *Folkestone Herald*. Edited by the former tabloid journalist Nick Hudson, these papers published a series of inflammatory articles accusing asylum seekers of prostitution, criminality, and spreading an "epidemic of venereal disease."

This campaign reached a peak in October 1998, against the background of the Labour Party Conference in Blackpool, when a *Dover Express* editorial raged against the "illegal immigrants, asylum seekers, bootleggers and the scum of the earth drug smugglers [that] have targeted our beloved coastline" and left Dover "with the backdraft of a nation's human sewage and no cash to wash it down the drain."[3] Hudson's cri de coeur was swiftly picked up by the national tabloid press, which carried a series of articles claiming that Kentish seaside towns were being overrun by "bogus" asylum seekers who were intent on "milking the system" and who were displacing British pensioners from hotels and bed-and-breakfasts.

Much of this was willful exaggeration and distortion. According to Kent Social Services, there were approximately 750 asylum seekers in Dover at the beginning of 1999 out of a population of just over 23,000. These numbers undoubtedly posed a challenge to the local authorities, but they did not bear out the tabloid imagery of Dover and Kent as a "broken" frontier. Such rhetoric was not without repercussions. Between 1997 and 1999, the National Front staged three marches in Dover, and there were a number of physical and arson attacks on asylum seekers in the town.

In the spring and summer of 1999, Kosovan refugees began arriving in Kent from NATO's war with Serbia. They were initially given a more positive reception in the national press—at least until the war was over. In August 1999 eleven people were injured during a fairground brawl between local youths and Kosovan asylum seekers, and Dover became national news again. The veteran *Daily Telegraph* reporter William Deedes reported that asylum seekers had created a "tinder box situation" in the "garden of England," while the Shadow Home Secretary Ann Widdecombe also visited Dover and accused the Labour government of turning Britain into a "soft touch" for asylum seekers.

Against this background, Parliament approved the Immigration and Asylum Act, Labour's first piece of immigration legislation. In addition to a series of measures aimed at preventing asylum seekers from reaching the United Kingdom, the 1999 act announced that financial support payments for asylum seekers were to be paid in the form of supermarket vouchers equivalent to £35 a week, that the immigration "detention estate" was to be increased by four thousand places, and that all asylum seekers entering the United Kingdom were to be given no-choice accommodations in towns and cities far from London or the southeast in a new policy of "burden sharing." In effect the "siege of Dover" had become a catalyst for an essentially punitive model of border enforcement that was to define Labour's thirteen years in government, but it was also symptomatic of the toxic and pernicious attitudes toward immigration that were percolating through British society long beforehand.

Island Under Siege

British politicians have sometimes referred coyly to the "extreme sensitivity" of immigration in British politics as an explanation for Britain's reluctance to join the Schengen area, but these sensitivities are invariably directed at very specific categories of immigrants and tend to rely on very similar imagery and vocabulary. As early as 1900 the *Daily Mail* was describing Jewish refugees from the Boer War in Southampton as "so-called refugees."[4] The 1905 Aliens Act was specifically designed to limit Jewish immigration from tsarist Russia, and it followed anti-Semitic lobbying from the right wing of the Conservative Party and the prefascist British Brothers League, against the "destitute foreigners" and "scum of the earth" who were gaining unfair access to jobs and housing at the expense of the indigenous population. The act was also supported by the *Manchester Evening Chronicle*, which celebrated the fact that "the dirty, destitute, diseased, verminous and criminal foreigner who dumps himself on our soil and rates simultaneously, shall be forbidden to land."

The history of British immigration controls since the 1905 act is punctuated with episodes in which governments have introduced restrictions in response to xenophobic or racist political campaigns, while taking pains to present such legislation as racially neutral. Britain was one of the first European countries to begin recruiting migrant labor from its former colonies after World War II, but it was also one of the first to enact legislation to prevent it in the shape of the 1962 Commonwealth Immigrants Act.[5] This act was intended to limit Commonwealth immigration and followed a prolonged campaign by the Tory right wing for more restrictions and the outbreak of serious racist riots in Nottingham and London. Subsequent immigration controls introduced by Conservative and Labour governments were similarly aimed almost exclusively at nonwhite immigrants, and calls for restrictions were often steeped in coded references to the threat to Britain's national identity and fears that Britain risked being "swamped by an alien culture," as Margaret Thatcher once put it.

By the late 1980s legal routes for unskilled economic migration from the Commonwealth had been drastically curtailed, but right-wing politicians and the media continued to paint a grim picture of a country that was being inundated by "alien" or "unassimilable" foreigners. As was the case elsewhere in Europe, these narratives increasingly focused on the issue of asylum. Coverage of asylum seekers in the U.K. tabloid press was generally unconstrained by any considerations of morality, accuracy, or humanity. Asylum seekers were variously vilified as "health tourists" seeking to access the National Health Service; as carriers of HIV; as criminals, beggars, and sexual predators; and as a parasitical "army of spongers" seeking to access U.K. security benefits, lolling in Jacuzzis at the taxpayers' expense or receiving "free golf lessons" from local councils.[6]

The tabloid image of the United Kingdom as a "soft touch" besieged by "bogus" asylum seekers attracted by its generous asylum policies was not borne out by statistics on the numbers of asylum seekers actually granted refugee protection in the United Kingdom, which were generally smaller than in many European countries, but it was often reinforced by the dramatic attempts to evade the United Kingdom's restrictions. From the late 1990s onward, men, women, and even children attempted to cross the Channel by jumping from bridges onto passing trains or hiding underneath them, concealing themselves in trucks, walking through the Eurotunnel, or even clinging to the outside of a SeaFrance ferry. In December 2001 more than five hundred migrants broke through the wire fence at the Eurotunnel depot near Calais and ran into the tunnel before they were driven back. In 2002 two Lithuanians tried to cross the Channel in a child's inflatable boat, using their hands as paddles.

Throughout this period most irregular immigrants in Britain were visa overstayers who had originally entered the United Kingdom with passports and visas, but these cross-Channel incursions were nevertheless depicted by the *Daily Mail* and other newspapers as the most visible manifestation of a tsunami of immigration that was usurping its jobs and resources and fatally transforming the British national character. Since 2001 these arguments have been made most forcefully by the anti-immigrant lobbying group MigrationWatch. Founded by Sir Andrew Green, a former ambassador to Saudi Arabia, MigrationWatch has become a ubiquitous point of reference in the right-wing media through its often tendentious statistics and demographic scenarios, which depict Britain as a "full" society on the point of saturation and collapse as a result of "mass immigration."

Green's emphasis on numbers and statistics rather than nationality and ethnicity has provided a useful semblance of legitimacy to the mainstream right-wing press, which tends to dismiss any suggestions that its hostility to immigration is racially motivated as part of a conspiracy to silence legitimate public "concerns" about immigration—regardless of the fact that such concerns are often at least partly due to assumptions and prejudices that its own distorted coverage has done so much to create. The fact that such a fig leaf is considered necessary is nevertheless a testament to the evolution of British society as a result of postwar immigration. There is no need to exaggerate either the failures or successes of British race relations to note that as a result of immigration from its former colonies, postimperial Britain has become a more ethnically diverse and cosmopolitan society in which overt expressions of racism are no longer considered legitimate. But some sections of the British public and the political class have never accepted this transformation, and it is these forces that have either directly or indirectly shaped British immigration policy in the new century.

Labour's Hard Borders

Both Conservative and Labour governments have attempted to demonstrate their "toughness" on immigration and asylum, but Labour's three terms in office since 1997 were marked by a striking contradiction. On one hand, both legal and illegal immigration rose to unprecedented levels. At the same time Labour introduced a stream of draconian laws and procedures aimed at restricting and preventing irregular migration, measures that often outdid those proposed by their Tory predecessors.

This paradox is partly due to Labour's attempts to reconcile the demands of a booming economy with its opportunistic desire to please the anti-immigrant lobby, but it also reflects Labour's very specific ideological perspective on borders and immigration. Labour governments have often argued that immigration restrictions are a prerequisite for good race relations, and New Labour often presented the ability to enforce these restrictions at the border as a confidence-building measure to promote "social cohesion." In the 2002 white paper *Secure Borders, Safe Haven*, home secretary David Blunkett argued that "we need to be secure within our sense of belonging and identity" in order "to enable integration to take place and to value the diversity it brings and therefore to be able to reach out and to embrace those who come to the UK."

Published in the aftermath of 9/11 and the violent racial clashes in Bradford the previous summer, the white paper described "secure borders" as the essential foundation of a "safe, just and tolerant society" in which the restoration of public confidence in the asylum system would "defeat those who stir up hate, intolerance and prejudice" and simultaneously provide a safe haven to "genuine" asylum seekers.[7] In the wake of the September 11 attacks and British participation in the "war on terror," the pursuit of "secure borders" increasingly overlapped with broader questions of national security. All these considerations combined to give border enforcement an unprecedented prominence in U.K. domestic politics under the Labour Party, which was symbolized by the fusion in 2008 of customs, border policing, and immigration control into a single bureaucracy, the U.K. Border Agency (UKBA), and which continued to generate a constant series of laws and procedures at U.K. ports and airports throughout the Blair and Brown administrations.

Today Dover is no longer the besieged border town depicted by the British media as the crystallization of Britain's "asylum madness" in the late 1990s. Its port remains the busiest in Europe. Every year some 3 million trucks roll off the ferries and drive straight through the town. The Churchill Hotel, where the Home Office once occupied a suite of rooms in 1999, has closed down, and Folkestone Road's "asylum alley" has fallen on leaner times since the high point of the Kosovo war, when up to a hundred asylum seekers were arriving daily in the town.

Migrants still cross the Channel in trucks carrying everything from diapers to flat-pack furniture and sugar. In the winter of 2009–10 immigration officers in Dover discovered a Vietnamese woman concealed in the dashboard of a car, a Sri Lankan man in an adapted gas tank, and twenty-seven Chinese migrants in the false bottom of a bus. Irregular migration falls under the purview of UKBA, the Kent police's Frontier Crime unit, and the Joint Intelligence Unit, a secretive body based in Folkestone that works closely with its French counterparts on the other side of the Channel in correlating intelligence information on "clandestines" and organized immigration crime.

Migrants detected at Dover and Folkestone automatically have their mobile phones examined so that police can build up a profile of the smuggling or trafficking networks that may have brought them to the United Kingdom, and asylum seekers from "countries of concern" such as Iraq, Somalia, and Afghanistan are also likely to be questioned by specialists in counterterrorism and "domestic extremism."

Technology has played a key role in Britain's attempts to detect unwanted travelers. UKBA officers at Dover are equipped with mobile X-ray and gamma-ray scanners that can see inside vehicles, handheld carbon dioxide detectors, and heartbeat and body heat sensors. Labour has been an avid promoter of the e-Borders system, which uses biometric identification data such as fingerprint, iris, and face recognition to fix the identities of travelers coming to the United Kingdom and screen unwanted visitors at the point of entry. As in the United States, these technophiliac demonstrations of national sovereignty at the border have provided a lucrative industry for the private sector. In 2007 the bid for the latest phase of the British government's £1.2 billion e-Borders program was won by the Trusted Borders consortium, which includes the U.S. weapons manufacturer Raytheon and the Serco Group.

By 2014 this program is expected to be able to monitor and collate information on every traveler leaving or entering the United Kingdom's airports and territorial borders from the e-Borders Operations Centre at Wythenshawe near Manchester, and a 2005 Home Office report predicted that these "pre-entry controls" will eventually make it possible to eliminate anyone not considered to be a "bona fide traveller" from the moment he or she buys an airline ticket.[8] Identifying and preventing the movements of unwanted travelers before they reach Britain is a crucial objective of U.K. border enforcement—with particular ramifications for unwanted visitors who may be seeking refugee protection. In 2007 immigration minister Liam Byrne declared an end to "the days when border controls started at the white cliffs of Dover" and argued that "our immigration control needs to start well before people come anywhere near our shores."[9]

Under the new system of juxtaposed border controls established by Britain and France in 2003, British immigration officials can now check the documents of Eurostar passengers in Paris, Calais, Lisle, Coquelles, and Brussels, while the French Police aux Frontières also maintain their own controls in Kentish ports. British airline liaison officers and immigration liaison officers can be found as far afield as Pakistan, Nigeria, Malaysia, South Africa, and other countries defined as "nexus points for illegal immigrants."

These efforts have not achieved any of the objectives outlined in David Blunkett's 2002 white paper. Refugee organizations initially welcomed Labour's determination to reform a dysfunctional asylum system that had left thousands of cases unresolved. But Labour's commitment to refugee protection was repeatedly called into question by its willingness to impose visa restrictions in countries that were generating refugees, upstream immigration controls that made it more difficult for potential asylum seekers to reach the United Kingdom, and a series of harsh and ruthless postentry measures that were designed to "minimise the attraction of the UK to economic migrants," as the white paper that preceded the 1999 Immigration and Asylum Act described it.[10]

Not only have these measures undermined Britain's commitment to refugee protection, but they have failed to placate the anti-immigrant lobby and reinforced the general climate of suspicion and mistrust of asylum seekers as serial abusers of British generosity. To some sectors of the British right, the increase in immigration that took place under Labour is not just a demonstration of its inability to secure Britain's "broken borders" but a sinister conspiracy to ethnically and culturally reconfigure British society.[11]

The Coalition government initially benefited from such bitter and delirious accusations—but not for long. The Conservatives' election manifesto declared its intention to cut immigration to "tens of thousands a year, not hundreds of thousands"—a promise that was essentially incompatible with Britain's membership in the European Union and was criticized by David Cameron's coalition partners. In November 2011, it emerged that the U.K. Border Agency had waived biometric checks and follow-up questions of incoming travelers during the summer, largely in order to reduce congestion at ports and airports. These revelations provoked a chorus of entirely baseless accusations from the right-wing media that UKBA had allowed criminals, terrorists, and other dangerous migrants into the country.

The furor over "Bordergate" was another product of a mutually reinforcing consensus between governments, the media, and the public that invariably depicts immigration as an endless crisis and often reduces undocumented migrants to the status of dangerous and dehumanized invaders massing outside the nation's borders. And for much of the last ten years these phobias have been directed toward Dover's twinned city on the other side of the Channel.

The Cleansing of Calais

For nearly two centuries Calais was an integral part of Britain, with its own representatives in Parliament. "When I am dead, you will find Calais lying on my heart," declared Mary Tudor following its repossession by France in 1558. Today this port city of just under 75,000 inhabitants is the gateway to Europe for British tourists and truck drivers by virtue of its ferry ports and the nearby presence of the Eurotunnel at Coquelles, and an easily accessible day-trip destination for those in search of French wine. For more than a decade Calais has also been the main staging post for undocumented migrants seeking to cross the Channel in the opposite direction. In the first years of the new century, so many migrants were passing through the city that the Red Cross established a reception center in a former Eurotunnel warehouse at Sangatte to take care of them.

Sangatte quickly became the bête noire of the U.K. press, where it was depicted as a base of operations for an invading "army of migrants." It also became the object of an acrimonious dispute between the French and British governments, each of whom blamed the other for the presence of migrants in the city. In September 2002 the French government ordered the closure of Sangatte, and hundreds of migrants established a shantytown in the woods and fields outside Calais that became known as "the Jungle." In September 2009, following further pressure from the British government, French police demolished these settlements in the presence of the French immigration minister Eric Besson.

The evictions were not the most uplifting example of intergovernmental cooperation, as television footage showed Afghan teenagers crying as their shelters were destroyed. But France and Britain celebrated what they described as a major blow to the Calais smuggling networks—regardless of the fact that the victims they had "saved" were now homeless. At that time the population of the Jungle was about eight hundred, most of whom slept rough in the streets of Calais or in smaller camps elsewhere along the northern French coast while they tried to get to the United Kingdom. By the winter of 2009 these numbers had dwindled to an estimated three hundred to five hundred people.

Approximately 150 migrants were living in Calais itself when I visited the city in March 2010. I arrived in the middle of a regional election campaign, in which the National Front leader Marine Le Pen was predicted to make strong gains. Le Pen had recently described the migrants of Calais as a threat to local security, and the political pressure from the far right on Nicolas Sarkozy's Union for a Popular Movement party, which ran the Calais council, may have contributed to the disturbing events that coincided with my arrival.

On my first morning in the city I found some fifty Afghan and Iranian migrants camped out on the steps of the Bureau Central Main d'Oeuvre (BCMO) gymnasium in the Rue de Moscou that was designated by the authorities as a winter shelter. Two days beforehand they had been evicted from the gymnasium because temperatures had risen above freezing. It was still very cold, and some of them were lying on the steps, wrapped in blankets and sleeping bags to keep off the cutting sea wind that was blowing off the nearby docks. All of them were male, and they looked tired, unshaven, and disheveled. Some were in their teens, but there were also two older men who might have been in their fifties. Some activists from the European anti-immigration control network No Borders were also present, together with two volunteers from the local charity Association Salaam, which organized one of the soup kitchens at the nearby food distribution center.

In January No Borders had tried to convert a rented warehouse into a new social center for the migrants of Calais, but the authorities had closed it down in order to avoid the possibility of a "new Sangatte." Now the police appeared to be acting against the migrants themselves. That morning they had been arresting migrants on their way to the nearby dock where NGOs and charities provided breakfast, and no one had eaten. Some of the older Afghans with connections to the smuggling "mafias" or *passeurs* who controlled access to the Calais truck depots were trying to pressure their younger compatriots into mounting a hunger strike in protest, but most of their compatriots were hungry and more interested in breakfast.

The Iranians also showed little enthusiasm for a hunger strike. Relations between Afghan and Iranian migrants in Calais are not exactly harmonious, and the two groups soon began shouting at each other until a fight seemed like a possibility. The No Borders activists attempted to arbitrate this dispute and supplied banners and spray paint to facilitate the protest. Someone got as far as writing the word "no" on one of the banners, and slogans were painted on the walls of the gym, but the momentum soon evaporated, and two Afghans began kicking a deflated soccer ball, while another group began playing cricket with a piece of wood as a bat.

Most of the migrants sat in silence on the steps of the gymnasium amid the chaos of sleeping bags, clothes, and blankets, drawing occasional stares from people in passing cars. Sami, an Afghan in his early twenties, told me how he had left his home in Jalalabad eight years earlier, at the age of sixteen, shortly after the NATO invasion of Afghanistan, when his family became involved in a feud with a local warlord because of his brother's involvement with the Taliban. He had worked in London and Cardiff before he was arrested and deported back to Afghanistan. For a while he worked as a UN interpreter in Kabul, until his brother resurfaced at the head of a hundred Taliban fighters and told him that he would be killed if he remained in the country.

Sami headed for Europe once again, traveling through Iran and Turkey and across the Aegean into Greece. He showed me his scar on his forehead where he had been clubbed by Greek police. Somehow he had avoided being fingerprinted and continued his journey into Italy, where he was beaten up by police again. Eventually he made it to Calais, only to be arrested by the French police this time and sent back to Italy. Now he was back again. After three months in the BCMO he had given up on the United Kingdom and decided to apply for asylum in France instead. This decision clearly did not fill him with much enthusiasm, but his reason was simple. "I'm tired," he said, showing me the asylum application papers that might eventually make it possible for him to remain in France.

Throughout this conversation, vans from the CRS, the French riot police, sped away from the gym, carrying arrested migrants, and some of the No Borders activists ran after them to take pictures. At eleven o'clock a convoy of police vans pulled up outside the gym and a line of helmeted riot police advanced upon us, bearing gas guns and truncheons. The police began arresting some of the Afghans for spray-painting slogans, while the No Borders women flitted around them taking photographs with their mobile phones.

At one point the police knocked one of the women to the ground and began dragging her toward the waiting vans, but then they let her go and went to arrest some of the migrants instead.

In the midst of this mayhem I spotted a man in a suit calmly observing the proceedings from the other side of the road, and I went over to speak to him. He was Philippe Mignonet, the deputy mayor, and I asked him why the police were carrying out these arrests. "It's England's fault, because you won't join Schengen," he replied nonchalantly. "These people all want to go to the U.K. and the U.K. should take them."

It was an odd experience to hear the deputy mayor go on to talk about the need to ameliorate the conditions that made migrants want to leave their countries even as the police continued to drive away with their vans full of arrestees. At one o'clock the remaining migrants filed off to the designated feeding area, and they were soon joined by Sudanese, Somalis, and Eritreans from squats around the city. Soon there were more than a hundred men in the dock compound, eating their meals on the ground or leaning up against trash bins, washing their hands or kneeling on prayer mats, or charging their mobile phones at the outlets provided for that purpose, an incongruous presence against the industrial backdrop of cranes, warehouses, piers, and water.

The food distribution fulfilled a vital function for both the migrants and the local authorities in Calais. For political reasons, Mayor Natacha Bouchart's administration was reluctant to do anything that might attract migrants to the city, but neither did it want them starving in the streets. So the authorities allowed the dock to be used as a food distribution center, even if they now appeared to be doing their best to stop migrants from going anywhere near it.

The police were also making an increasingly vigorous attempt to drive migrants from their squats around the city. One night I visited the squat known as Africa House with the photographer Steven Greaves, who had been taking pictures of migrants in Calais for the previous six weeks. Africa House was located a few tree-lined blocks from the main railway station, in a former factory building surrounded by a large patch of waste ground. Its entrance was sealed off with a cinder-block wall that police had built in a vain attempt to keep the migrants out, and a French tramp whom the migrants suspected of being a police informer was sitting alone by a fire in a dilapidated wooden annex.

We climbed a wooden palette leaning up against the wall and dropped into a narrow courtyard. Inside the darkened factory building, groups of

African migrants were sitting on makeshift benches, staring into the fires that they called "television" or "CNN." The floor was pockmarked with gaping holes, and a flight of steps led down into a dank and fetid basement piled with blankets and clothes. I was astounded to find what looked like a scene from a Hollywood postapocalyptic film in the heart of an affluent European city, yet these men had spent one of the coldest winters in living memory living in these conditions.

Most of them were Sudanese, many of whom came from Darfur, but there were also some Somalis. Abdi, a car mechanic from Mogadishu, was describing a gun battle in his native city that he had seen on CNN that day. "Two hundred dead—bam, bam, bam," he said, firing an imaginary machine gun. Later he smiled as he spoke of the future that he hoped to find in the United Kingdom, when this "dirty life" would end and he would have a job and a house, but there was a note of mockery in his voice, as if he no longer believed it was going to happen.

That week a Palestinian had walked into the Eurotunnel and had nearly made it to Dover before he mistakenly opened a security door and alerted the police, and some of the men were encouraged at the news that someone had nearly made it to the other side. Few of them spoke much English or seemed to have any idea of what awaited them, yet they had crossed deserts and oceans to get here, blown by the world's political storms to a city that did not want them in an attempt to reach a country that was determined to see them go no farther. It was difficult to believe that the U.K. government was unaware of the ongoing repression in Calais—or that it did not support it.

The following morning the CRS carried out one of their frequent raids on Africa House in the early hours and told the Africans to leave. Shortly after breakfast at the food distribution center, police began confiscating blankets and sleeping bags from the Afghans and Iranians who were sleeping on the steps of the BCMO. The ubiquitous Philippe Mignonet was there to oversee the process, but there was no more talk of global solutions to poverty as the *maire adjoint* coolly described the police action as a "cleaning operation" while council workers wearing protective white suits piled their blankets into vans. I asked Mignonet where they were going to sleep that night. "It's not freezing," he said. Watching police and council workers calmly remove the blankets from homeless men, I thought of other episodes in European history when the removal of unwanted people was described as a form of hygiene, and I wondered if the deputy mayor was aware of them.

That night some migrants returned to the same Jungle they had been evicted from six months before. Others slept in railway sidings or under bridges. Throughout the night the police hunted them down and hauled them off to the detention facility at Coquelles, where they were held without charge before being made to walk back to Calais, a journey that took just over two hours. Some were arrested several times and obliged to repeat the journey. The following afternoon I took a bus out to the mammoth Cité Europe shopping complex near the detention center at Coquelles. A young Afghan named Khalid with a bandaged hand was just preparing to walk back to Calais for the third time in twenty-four hours. He did not speak much English, but he managed to convey that he had sprained his hand playing soccer and that the police had arrested him when he left the hospital.

I paid his bus fare back to town. It was midafternoon and the schools were closing, and the bus soon filled up with French school kids who looked about Khalid's age. I left him at the fashionable Boulevard St. Jacques, and later that evening I met him again at the distribution center with a group of his friends. The food queue had dwindled by almost half, since many migrants were staying away to avoid arrest. One Afghan teenager was hobbling along with his right leg strapped in a splint, which he had injured jumping from a train to escape a police raid. Jamal, an Iranian with a striking resemblance to President Mahmoud Ahmadinejad, told me how he had been arrested sleeping under a railway bridge and spent the night at the police station. He looked shattered and said that he had given up trying to get to the United Kingdom and was going to apply for asylum in France. Atif, a gregarious young Afghan from Kabul with the gleaming smile of a Bollywood star, told me how he had been arrested in a disused train and held for most of the night.

Atif spoke fluent English, and he talked about cricket, his hero the cricketer Sachin Tendulkar, and his pride that Afghanistan had beaten Ireland in the final of the Twenty20 World Cup. In Kabul he had worked as an accounting officer in a bank, he said, and his main reason for wanting to leave Afghanistan was the security situation. Bombs were always going off in the Afghan capital, and there had been two explosions outside his bank. Now after three months in Calais, he was pondering the wisdom of that decision. "Even Afghanistan is better than this," he said.

Like most of his compatriots in Calais, Atif wanted to go to the United Kingdom because there was already a sizable Afghan community living there, and he was genuinely mystified at the unwillingness of the U.K. government to allow him to do so. Atif was also ashamed of the situation he was in. Whenever he called his parents he told them that he was staying in a hotel and that everything was going well. But things were clearly getting worse. That night I went out to the abandoned train cars where he was staying, together with Steven Greaves and an Italian No Borders activist named Chiara. We walked for about a mile past the ferry port, through a landscape of highway overpasses, cranes, and docks, before turning off onto a darkened footpath beside a narrow railway track. To our left the cars whizzed back and forth along the motorway as we walked alongside a dank and evil-smelling stream past a factory. Eventually we saw figures moving about in the darkness and the outline of trains up ahead.

I had expected to find covered cars. Instead we were confronted with a scene that would not have been out of place in the American Depression or the Emir Kusturica epic film *Time of the Gypsies*. About thirty Afghans were sitting or lying in shallow open cars of the kind used to transport coal. Some had strips of plastic to keep off the rain and cold, but most had no belongings at all. The two older men I had seen at the BCMO were lying silently under blankets and leaning up against a bundle of clothes. They looked exhausted, but the younger Afghans were laughing and talking animatedly as though they were on a rollicking adventure.

Just then Atif loomed out of the darkness and asked cheerfully if I thought it was possible to swim to England. I said it was probably not a very good idea, and we sat on the edge of the car as he talked nostalgically about his bank colleagues in Afghanistan and his ambition to become a branch manager or even regional manager someday. This rather surreal conversation was interrupted by the appearance of a CRS van. "Goodbye, Mr. Matt," Atif said, flashing a brilliant smile before vanishing into the darkness with Chiara and the other Afghans. Within minutes only Steve Greaves and I were left on the train as a police searchlight played across the deserted rail cars, and a moment later a CRS officer gruffly demanded to see our passports while his colleagues rounded up some of the Afghans.

As we walked back to town past the docks and ferry port I wondered at the fear and loathing that could lead two of the most powerful countries in Europe to unleash such a petty and vindictive campaign of harassment against men whose sole crime consisted of the absence of a visa and passport. But this "cleaning operation" was only the beginning of a war of attrition that continued throughout the year. In April the CRS raided Africa House a number of times to confiscate blankets, pour off drinking water, and even spray the factory with insecticide. That same month the railway cars where I had last seen Atif and the Afghans were taken away. In June Africa House was finally demolished.

Little of this appeared in the mainstream U.K. media. In April that year hundreds of British vacationers found themselves stranded in Calais after their flights had been disrupted by the Icelandic volcanic ash cloud. British newspapers devoted considerable attention to their frustration, despair, and stoicism in the face of adversity. Some papers evoked the "Dunkirk spirit" as a flotilla of privately owned speedboats attempted to rescue these stranded travelers. There was no mention of the migrants who had been trapped in the city for a lot longer.

7

The Internal Border

We now remove an immigrant offender every eight minutes—but my target is
to remove more, and remove them faster.

—U.K. immigration minister Liam Byrne, May 2008

In 2008 an independent television company produced the first episode of a
new reality series for Sky TV called *UK Border Force*. Initially funded in part
by the Home Office, the series was billed as an unprecedented opportunity
for viewers to "see exactly how our borders are protected and how immigrants
and visitors to Britain are dealt with on the front line." The program was an
essentially hagiographic portrayal of the newly created U.K. Border Agency
fused with entertainment, featuring fly-on-the-wall coverage of officers
detecting "illegals" and "clandestines" in trucks at Calais and Dover and
carrying out deportations and immigration raids, accompanied by an atmo-
spheric thrilleresque soundtrack.

The sight of immigration officers in SWAT team mode chasing down illegal workers in supermarket parking lots and takeout pizza restaurants or
subjecting humiliated and sometimes distraught men and women to inquisi-
torial interrogations with an undisguised air of superiority may not have been
a particularly edifying spectacle, but the series did provide a rare glimpse
into an aspect of border enforcement that is rarely visible to the general public.
In the last two decades, Europe's attempts to prevent migrants from crossing
its borders without authorization have been accompanied by a range of measures aimed at removing those who have succeeded. These include random

identity checks, immigration raids on private homes at dawn, deportation and detention, and a number of exclusionary postentry policies designed to isolate asylum seekers and control their movements.

These policies and procedures are part of an internal enforcement program that extends into neighborhoods, streets, workplaces, railway and bus stations, and private homes, and which has seen a general intensification across the continent in recent years. And it is here, in the ruthless and often pitiless enforcement of these boundaries, that the gulf between Europe's political ideals and the crude realities of its fight against illegal immigration is often most glaring.

The Expulsion Machine

In May 2011, the U.K. Border Agency informed a disabled and wheelchair-bound five-year-old Algerian girl that her appeal to remain in the United Kingdom had been rejected and that she would be returned to Algeria. Rania Abdechakour had been living with her English aunt Jo Taleb and her Algerian uncle Moussa in Bolton for more than three years, and the Home Office had rejected their application to grant her leave to remain so that they could adopt her.

That same month I met Jo Taleb in a Bolton café, accompanied by Rania and Jo's two-year-old daughter Karima. Jo looked tired and under strain. For more than three years she had looked after Rania, a demanding, twenty-four-hour task that involves at least one hour of daily massage plus vision and speech therapy. The previous night she had slept for only three hours. She was eight months pregnant, and now she was trying to organize a Facebook campaign to prevent the deportation of the child she and her husband had come to regard as their own.

The Talebs' attraction to Rania was not difficult to understand. She was a gorgeous child who had made remarkable progress since coming to the United Kingdom, despite formidable disabilities that include quadriplegic cerebral palsy, life-threatening epileptic fits, gastrointestinal problems, and reflex anoxic seizures that cause her heart to stop beating. She attended a mainstream primary school, where her teacher described her as "cherished by pupils, parents, and staff."

Rania originally came to the United Kingdom in 2008 to stay temporarily with the Talebs in order to give her mother a respite from caregiving. At that time her disability was limited to her right arm and leg and strabismus in her left eye, and her mother agreed that her daughter could stay in the United Kingdom for six months and receive conductive education—a form of physiotherapy that her aunt and uncle arranged to pay for privately. As a former health care professional, Jo Taleb was used to dealing with children with disabilities, and when Rania's health problems turned out to be more serious than originally diagnosed, she and her husband applied for her visa to be extended on two separate occasions so that she could receive further medical assessment and treatment. After eighteen months, the Talebs had become so attached to Rania that they wanted to adopt her, and with her mother's agreement they applied to the Home Office to grant Rania indefinite leave to remain.

On May 6, 2011, however, the Talebs had been informed by the Home Office that Rania would have to return to Algeria, and now they were waiting to present their case before an appeals court. The Talebs were convinced that the Algerian health service would not be able to provide Rania with the same level of care that she was receiving in the United Kingdom, and her primary care physician, Dr. Roger Walker, also believed that her removal was potentially life-threatening and told me that Rania's stay in the United Kingdom had had a transformative effect on her health. The Home Office does not comment on individual cases involving minors, and UKBA sent me a formulaic statement insisting that "the UK Border Agency is committed to a fair system which provides emergency health care to those in need, and cares for the vulnerable who—through no fault of their own—cannot return home."

In a letter of rejection addressed—somewhat bizarrely—to Rania herself, the Home Office declared that "in order to protect the wider interests and the rights of the public it is vital to maintain an effective Immigration control" and warned of "the damage to good administration and control if a system is perceived by applicants internationally to be unduly porous, unpredictable or perfunctory."

This was really the heart of the matter. The episode ended happily in August that year, when the Talebs won their appeal and Rania was given leave to remain. But the fact that a quadriplegic five-year-old girl should ever have been categorized as a danger to "the wider interests and the rights of the public" is an indication of the enormous importance that immigration deportation or "removal" has acquired in recent years among European governments and the European Union as a whole.

The ability to expel or remove unwanted people has always been a symbolic test of the state's sovereignty over its national borders. In the last two decades, however, this ability has become an essential component of Europe's border enforcement efforts. According to a 2009 European Commission report, some 500,000 irregular migrants are apprehended inside the continent every year, of whom approximately 40 percent are forcibly or voluntarily repatriated.[1] For many governments, deportation has become a kind of political theater in which crowd-pleasing statistics and deportation quotas are presented as evidence of toughness and implacability in the fight against illegal immigration.

In 2005 the U.K. home secretary, Charles Clarke, boasted, "We have removed many more failed asylum seekers and other immigration offenders from the UK than ever before, but we will substantially increase the number in future."[2] Declaring "swift removal" to be "central to the credibility of our system," Clarke promised "a new drive to secure more effective returns arrangements with the countries from which most of our failed asylum seekers come."

Today the Home Office publishes quarterly "enforcement and compliance" statistics on the removal of foreigners "who do not have any legal right to stay in the UK"—a category that includes migrants engaging in "illegal working," "bogus students," rejected asylum seekers, and foreign-born criminal offenders, some of whom may have spent most of their lives in the United Kingdom. Other governments have also stepped up the pace and scale of deportation in recent years.

In 2009 the Sarkozy government carried out thirty thousand deportations in France—a quota that was sometimes achieved by intensifying police ID checks and searches in order to scoop up migrants of particular nationalities to meet deportation targets. In February that same year, a leaked internal memo from a police station in Madrid's Vallecas district revealed that police were under orders to arrest monthly quotas of illegal immigrants, with a particular emphasis on Moroccans because they were considered cheaper and easier to deport.[3]

At times governments have been so determined to carry out deportations that they have sought to sidestep their international treaty obligations or even their own national legal parameters. Article 4 of the European Convention on Human Rights explicitly prohibits the "collective expulsion of aliens." In September and October 2002, however, Malta deported 220 Eritreans after rejecting their claims for asylum en masse, despite evidence that Eritrea was a dictatorship and police state where political dissidents and military deserters were routinely tortured and imprisoned. On arrival, the deportees were immediately arrested and taken to prison, but thirty of them subsequently escaped to Sudan, where they told Amnesty International how they had been beaten and whipped during their imprisonment.[4]

Between October 2004 and March 2005 the Italian government deported more than 1,500 migrant "boat people" from Lampedusa to Libya on military and civilian planes. As a signatory to the Geneva Convention, Italy was obliged to assess whether any these migrants were in need of international refugee protection. On the basis of evidence from two North African translators, however, the Italian authorities decided that all the migrants in Lampedusa were Egyptians and that there was no need for an asylum assessment process.

Even then, Italian law stipulates that deportations must be assessed on an individual basis by a judge, but the government got around this requirement by recategorizing them as acts of *respingimento* (refusal of entry) rather than *expulsione* (expulsion) and therefore not in need of a judicial assessment. The Italian interior minister, Giuseppe Pisanu, was unapologetic, and celebrated these deportations as a successful response to what he described as an "organized assault on our coasts."

In some cases governments have attempted to carry out deportations below the radar of public or legal scrutiny through summary deportations at their land borders and maritime "pushbacks," or by redefining or "excising" territorial spaces at airports, transit zones, and port facilities as international territories or *zones d'attente* where asylum seekers are deemed to be outside national boundaries and therefore liable to removal without the need for formal deportation or asylum screening procedures.

All these developments are part of a conveyor-belt-like deportation machinery that has no precedent in European history in its scale or intensity. Every week men, women, and children are deported on passenger airlines, charter flights, military planes, or the joint European charter flights organized by Frontex, or shunted across the EU's eastern land borders. Some are taken onto planes in handcuffs and leg irons, blindfolds and straitjackets; in other cases they are bound with rubber straps on stretchers or obliged to wear "expulsion helmets" with muzzles. Sometimes they are driven in vans across Europe's eastern borders to be handed over to Ukrainian or Belarusian border guards and police.

In recent years the urgency that European governments attach to deportation has been reflected in attempts to pressure or cajole other countries to facilitate "readmission" and accept deportees, regardless of the circumstances that await them on returning. In 2007, a number of countries began forcibly repatriating Iraqi asylum seekers to Iraqi Kurdistan and Baghdad, despite the violence and insecurity prevalent in many parts of the country. In December 2008 forty-nine Iraqi Kurdish asylum seekers were deported from London's Stansted Airport, many of them in handcuffs and leg irons. One man who had previously sewed his mouth up in protest was put on the plane after his stitches were forcibly removed. Another slashed his stomach while on the plane, and a third gave himself a concussion by banging his head against the window. On June 16, 2010, forty-two Iraqis were escorted by immigration officers on a charter plane from Heathrow to Baghdad, where they were beaten up by both their British escorts and Iraqi police officers at the airport because they refused to get off the plane.

Coercion is always implicit in the act of deportation, but the removal process has often been characterized by more overt brutality. In a 2004 report on deportation in the United Kingdom, the Medical Foundation for the Care of Victims of Torture described incidents in which deportees were dragged on their backs by their handcuffs up airplane steps, punched in the head and face, sat on, choked, and beaten up inside escort vans, and racially abused by immigration officers.[5] In July 1996, 103 African migrants in Melilla were secretly doped with tranquilizers and transported to Málaga, where they were put on a plane and flown to various African countries.[6]

Allegations of violence and excessive force have often centered on the private security companies that often provide the escorts for deportation flights. In February 2011 whistleblowers from the security company G4S told the *Guardian* newspaper that its immigration officers were routinely using dangerous coercive techniques to control deportees on deportation flights. One of these techniques included a practice known as "carpet karaoke" in which deportees on airplanes were bent almost double with their heads forced to the floor.[7] On March 16 that year, this procedure was used by G4S guards to restrain an Angolan named Jimmy Mubenga, who died of asphyxiation after shouting that he could not breathe.

In other European countries, deportees have died of positional asphyxia, heart failure, or suffocation in the course of deportation. On May 28, 1999, a Sudanese asylum seeker named Aamir Ageeb died during a deportation flight from Frankfurt to Cairo after police forced his helmeted head between his knees to restrain him. In December 2003, four Belgian police officers were found guilty of "involuntarily" suffocating a twenty-year-old Nigerian woman named Semira Adimou during a deportation flight five years previously. In

March 1999 a Palestinian deportee named Khaled Abuzarifa died after being taken to the Zurich airport under sedation with his feet and hands strapped to a wheelchair and his mouth covered with adhesive tape.

Forced deportations are not only brutal and sometimes lethal but also expensive and often complicated to coordinate and arrange. For these reasons a number of European governments have implemented voluntary return programs, in which migrants agree to go back to their countries of origins in exchange for small cash incentives. Some of these programs are organized by individual governments, while others fall within the rubric of the EU's Voluntary Assisted Return and Reintegration Program, established in 1999 in collaboration with the International Organization for Migration.

Originally established in 1951 as a specific response to Europe's postwar population displacements, the IOM has become a multinational intergovernmental organization dedicated to the principle of "humane and orderly migration" and has played an important role in organizing Europe's voluntary and involuntary return programs. At the Bratislava airport leaflets in various languages offer stranded migrants and asylum seekers the possibility of a "dignified, safe and legal return back to your home country . . . without any mental or physical pressure," and the IOM assists these returns by booking flights, buying tickets, and arranging travel documents and financial reintegration packages.

The extent to which these returns are truly voluntary is questionable, since migrants are often subjected to a range of indirect pressures before they make these choices. In 2009 Adam Osman Mohammed, a Sudanese asylum seeker from Darfur whose appeal was rejected by the U.K. Home Office, agreed to accept a voluntary return package to Khartoum. Within months of his return he was shot dead in front of his wife and son by Sudanese security officers who had followed him from the airport to his home in Darfur.

Both voluntary and enforced returns reflect the same determination of governments to ensure that their immigration controls are "credible"—and to demonstrate such credibility to their electorates. But deportation often has grim consequences for the immigrants on the receiving end of these displays. In March 2005 a Russian couple and their son jumped to their deaths from a Glasgow housing estate because they faced deportation. On March 7, 2008, a seventeen-year-old Georgian asylum seeker hanged himself in a Hamburg cell because he was about to be deported to Poland under the Dublin II rules. In 2011 I corresponded with an Algerian woman named Samia, who had been deported from the United Kingdom in 2009. Samia had arrived in the United Kingdom in 2005 with her husband and two children using forged French passports. She settled in Dover, where she worked illegally at various jobs. Only after she was detected by immigration officers did she apply for asylum, on the grounds of maltreatment by her in-laws in Algeria.

While her application was being considered she studied English, took a computer course, and obtained a driver's license. She also worked as a volunteer, visiting detainees at the Dover Immigrant Removal Centre and unaccompanied minors in the Bernardo's children's charity. Her two sons went to a local school, and Samia believed that she had found a permanent home. "I loved England," she wrote. "I loved living there. I thought I would live all my life there." In July 2009, however, her application for asylum was definitively rejected, and she and her family were arrested at the immigration office in Folkestone where she signed in each week, and taken to the Yarls Wood immigrant removal center.

The immigration officers prepared their case well, obtaining passports for the family from the Algerian embassy beforehand and waiting until school term was over before carrying out the deportation in order to avoid the possibility of a local campaign to prevent it. In a long email, Samia told me how she had left Algeria to escape her tyrannical in-laws, who treated her "like a slave," and came to England because she believed it was a country that "respects women." She described her pride at a local newspaper report on one of her sons, who scored a hat trick playing for the Dover Rangers. And she told me about the eight days she had spent at Yarls Wood Immigration Removal Centre before she and her family were deported.

> I thought life stopped for me. It was the worst time of my life. The hardest one was when I had to tell the boys that they are not going to see their friends again. If I had a choice in that moment I rather be dead than to see their sad faces. I will never forgive myself I feel so bad about it now when I remember. I don't know what I did wrong but I feel responsible. I feel so disappointed and let down by the system. I trusted them. I did everything I was asked to do and they put us in prison with criminals. . . . I didn't do anything bad and yet I didn't have any rights. How come is it fair!

Samia had clearly not understood the "rules." Her case for asylum was undoubtedly weak, but she had managed to find a place in a society that she wanted to belong to and contribute to. "She put a lot into it," remembered

Vebi Kosumi, the director of the Dover Detainee Visitor Group. "She would have been more British than 90 percent of British citizens." To the Home Office, however, she and her family were just four of the 67,215 immigrants "with no right to remain" who were removed from the country or who returned voluntarily in 2009.

Lockdown Europe

The detention of unwanted or harmful foreigners is not a new phenomenon in Europe. During World War I various European countries interned "enemy aliens" for the duration of the conflict. At the end of the Spanish Civil War, Republican refugees who fled to France were placed in internment camps that would shortly send some of them to the Nazi death camps. In all these cases internment was seen as an exceptional administrative expedient. Today the incarceration or detention of migrants and asylum seekers has become a crucial instrument in the enforcement of Europe's borders, which has evolved in tandem with its deportation conveyor belt.

In 2011 there were 250 designated detention centers for third-country nationals in twenty-seven EU member states—a figure that does not include detention facilities in Ukraine, Turkey, and North Africa that are outside European territory but which also play a role in Europe's border controls, or the temporary holding facilities of indeterminate status in ports, airports, and border police stations. No one knows how many people are detained each year, but the Jesuit Refugee Service estimates that the number is in the hundreds of thousands.

Immigration detention differs from penal incarceration in that it is not a punishment for an individual criminal act and does not have a fixed sentence or time limit; its legal parameters are often murky and opaque. Various European and national laws stipulate that asylum seekers should not be detained for seeking asylum, yet some countries automatically detain all migrants on arrival, regardless of their reasons for entering the country. European law also forbids the detention of minors except as a last resort and only for the shortest time possible, yet unaccompanied children have sometimes been placed in detention facilities with adults.

Until 2008 nine member states had no fixed limits on detention. In December that year the European Parliament and Council approved the so-called Return Directive, which set a limit for detention of six months, with the possibility of further extensions of up to twelve months. The adoption of an eighteen-month maximum was widely criticized by human rights organizations as excessive, but even this limit has not always been observed. In the United Kingdom, Home Office figures published in February 2010 revealed that 225 asylum seekers had spent more than one year in detention and another 45 had been detained for more than two years.

Detention is often justified as a predeportation measure to prevent migrants from absconding, but the length of time migrants spend in detention—and the fact that they are often automatically detained in some countries regardless of whether deportation has even been decided upon—makes such justifications less than convincing. In 2011 a UNHCR study found that 90 percent of migrants released on bail had observed the terms of their release and did not abscond, and it described detention as "an extremely blunt instrument to counter irregular migration."[8]

Given these limitations and contradictions, it is difficult to avoid the conclusion that this "blunt instrument" is primarily intended to reduce the supposed "pull factors" that attract migrants to Europe—and to transmit a deterrent message to others thinking of following their example. Few governments will admit this, but punishment and deterrence are implicit in the length of time that migrants spend in detention, and in the frequently dire conditions of so many of Europe's immigration facilities. In 2010 the Jesuit Refugee Service produced a comparative report on detention in twenty-three EU member states that painted a common picture of vulnerable and often traumatized people driven to despair, depression, self-harm, suicide attempts, stress, insomnia, and other mental health problems by the unclear terms of their detention and the conditions in which they were held. The report described a common profile of a European detainee "who is trapped and cannot escape" and for whom "the inability to establish a future perspective is crippling."[9]

Not surprisingly, the history of Europe's detention archipelago is punctuated with insurrections, riots, hunger strikes, protests, suicides, and acts of self-harm. Such episodes partly explain the improved detention centers that have sprung up along the Schengen borders in recent years. But the absence of a "future perspective" is not limited to closed detention centers. The Temporary Immigrant Reception Centre (CETI) in Ceuta is very different from the Foreigner Internment Centers (CIEs) on the Spanish mainland, which have often been condemned by human rights organizations and the Spanish Red Cross for their treatment of migrant detainees.

Situated on the outskirts of Ceuta in a forested hillside overlooking the coast, the CETI consists of dormitories, classrooms, office buildings and a basketball court enclosed by a low wire fence and monitored by security guards at the main gate. But its occupants are allowed to come and go during the day and are attended to by a humane and professional team of psychologists, lawyers, doctors, social workers, and teachers who provide weekly classes in Spanish and English.

With his graying shoulder-length hair and open-necked shirt, Valeriano Hoyes, the center's laid-back director, looks like an aging Pink Floyd fan as he describes the facilities and programs that the center provides, including classes in Spanish language and culture to help integrate migrants into Spanish society. But the essential paradox of the CETI is that very few of the people who pass through the center will ever be allowed to go any farther.

When I visited the center there were 360 residents in a building with a total capacity of 512. Most of them were asylum seekers from sub-Saharan Africa, who were waiting for a decision from the Foreigners Office in Ceuta. Some had been there for more than a year, Hoyes said, and few of their applications were likely to receive a positive decision. "The immense majority of people here are appealing for asylum in order to delay their expulsion or in order to continue their migratory journey," he said. On rejection, they would be ordered to present themselves at the police station with their luggage for deportation, or else the police would come to the center to arrest them— usually in the early hours of the morning. I suggested that the CETI's integration programs were somewhat futile and perfunctory, given the fact that so few of its residents would be allowed to go any farther.

"We can't decide the future here," said Hoyes. "What we do is give them a place to stay and provide activities for them, thinking that they are going to remain in Spain, knowing that they might not, and taking care not to generate any false expectations." Javier Espinosa, one of the two psychologists assigned to the center, told me that the main purpose of his work was to help migrants cope with the "disappointed expectations" that followed their arrival and facilitate "a new way of understanding reality," based on the realization that most of them were not going to continue their migratory journeys.

Most of the center's residents were clearly struggling to make this adjustment. A group of Gambian women were braiding each other's hair. "You go crazy in your head here," said one woman who had been at the center for a year. "This is not a good place." Nearby a Somali woman who was sweeping the yard outside her dormitory expressed the same frustration. A former seamstress from Mogadishu, she had been at the CETI for three years. "I'm going crazy here, I can't go anywhere, I want to work," she complained. "I'm a woman, not a man! I'm young and I can't marry!"

As in Melilla, the wheels of Spanish bureaucracy revolve extremely slowly, and few of the CETI's residents could do anything to make them turn any faster. In the evenings and early mornings, they could often be seen near the heavily guarded and fenced-in ferry ports, craning their necks toward the sea and the Spanish mainland beyond. By midnight most of them would be back in the center since, as Alejandro Romero, a refugee lawyer at the center, put it, "Ceuta is a closed territory that you can't leave, and therefore the detention center is the city of Ceuta itself."

The forced immobility of Europe's unwanted migrants is not dependent on the maritime barriers and fences of Ceuta and Melilla. All over the continent migrants may be theoretically at liberty but confined to a particular place by bureaucratic restrictions rather than fences or physical barriers. In Germany asylum seekers are not allowed to travel outside a particular geographical radius—in some cities no more than six square miles—without a special dispensation from the local authorities. In some countries asylum seekers are required to present themselves at police stations every few days or every week. Asylum seekers may also be tied to particular localities by designated no-choice housing and income support conditions that prevent them from working, studying, or moving to other parts of the country. In the United Kingdom income support for a single adult asylum seeker is £36.62 per week, rising to £42.94 for a lone parent with a child.

This drip feed not only is designed to eliminate the United Kingdom's perceived attractions to asylum seekers, who are characterized as parasites and benefit scroungers, but also acts as an instrument of social exclusion and control. Without money, asylum seekers cannot go anywhere or do anything; in some cases they may not even be able to afford the bus to go to the nearest immigration office or immigration court. Such controls enable governments to quarantine asylum seekers from their surrounding society so that they can be more easily tracked and removed if their appeals are rejected, but they are also part of a broader punitive and deterrent agenda aimed at creating as difficult and unattractive an environment as possible for asylum seekers without explicitly rejecting the principle of refugee protection per se.

As a 2007 Home Office report put it, illegal immigrants "not prioritised for removal . . . should be denied the benefits and privileges of life in the UK and experience an increasingly uncomfortable environment so that they elect to leave."[10] But there are those who cannot be removed and cannot—or will not—leave, yet who have found themselves at the receiving end of one of the most brutal and barbaric of Europe's exclusionary instruments.

"Living Ghosts"

It is Thursday morning at the St. Aidan's community center in the run-down Harehills district in Leeds, and the charity Positive Action for Refugees and Asylum Seekers (PAFRAS) is holding one of its twice-weekly drop-ins for homeless asylum seekers. Outside the morning is gray and cold, but the crowded hall exudes physical and human warmth. One counter is piled high with bread and cake, and volunteers are dispensing hot meals to a multinational population that includes Zimbabwean, Iraqi, Iranian, and Congolese asylum seekers, including children. Christine Majid, PAFRAS' founder, flits restlessly around the hall talking to volunteers and service users, and slipping out for periodic cigarette breaks. PAFRAS is not a religious organization, but the church supports its activities, and a monk in a habit and two American nuns from the South Bronx have come to visit.

All of PAFRAS' clients have one thing in common—they are destitute. Most are refused asylum seekers who have lost the Section 95 financial support and accommodations provided by the state because their appeal rights have been exhausted. Some are staying with friends or living in shared housing with the help of refugee charities. Others are sleeping rough and have come for a hot meal and social contact or the free legal advice provided by PAFRAS caseworkers, who include former destitute asylum seekers themselves.

Reza is a thirty-four-year-old Iranian asylum seeker and former economics student who arrived in the United Kingdom in January 2000 in the back of a truck after escaping from a military prison in Tehran, where he had been arrested during a political demonstration. He immediately applied for asylum and was sent to a hostel for asylum seekers in Wakefield. In March 2001 his claim was refused and he appealed against the decision, but in 2004 his appeal was dismissed by an immigration judge and he was told that he would have to return to Iran. By this time he was living with his English partner, with whom he had two children. Under U.K. law, rejected asylum seekers are entitled to Section 4 financial support, a weekly payment of just over £35, which comes in the form of an Azure card, valid in the four main chains of supermarkets. This support is subject to various conditions, including a signed declaration that its recipients will "leave the country at the earliest opportunity."

Unwilling to sign this agreement, estranged from his alcoholic partner, and without any income support or right to work, Reza became homeless. For two and a half years he lived on the streets of Wakefield, sleeping in public toilets or on a strip of cardboard behind Marks and Spencer. It was, he remembers, "a really upsetting time. Nobody's even bothered you're still living. No one helped. People look at you like you're garbage." During this time he survived by begging and occasionally stealing food from shops. On two occasions he was arrested, one time for stealing a cake and the other time for trying to steal a coat. One night he was attacked by a gang of local racists armed with baseball bats, who left him with a scar on his forehead. Throughout this period he made occasional visits—usually at night—to his partner's house to shower and see his children. In 2007 he made a fresh asylum claim with new evidence.

It is three years later, and he is still waiting for a decision, but he is now receiving Section 4 support while his claim is being examined. He has a room in a shared house in Leeds and an Azure card, and he volunteers for PAFRAS, but he is still not allowed to work or study. Reza smiles a lot, but his years as a legal nonperson are etched on his face and in his eyes. His two sons have never found out that he is an asylum seeker, for he has always pretended to them that work keeps him away from home. He talks of his desire to "prove himself" in British society and what he would like to do if he receives legal status:

> I would be a very active person. I would definitely go to college and at least take one course every week. I would definitely start going to the gym, because I could pay for it and find a proper job and try to build a life for my children's future, because they don't have a future with their dad at the moment. I never even took my children to a proper park, because I can't take them. I've got no money.

No one knows how many people are living in a similar situation in the United Kingdom, but many charities and NGOs dealing with destitute migrants report that the number of their service users is rising. In 2009 PAFRAS published a report estimating that between 300,000 and 500,000 migrants were destitute in the United Kingdom, a figure that included both older unresolved "legacy" cases as well as new claimants who had been rejected.[11] PAFRAS regards enforced destitution as a deliberate tool of government policy, and other organizations share the same analysis. In 2006 Amnesty International stated unequivocally that "the very aim of Home Office policy is to make rejected asylum seekers destitute to force them to go home."[12] And a 2007 report by the Joint Parliamentary Committee on Human Rights on the government's treatment of asylum seekers similarly declared, "We have been persuaded by the evidence that the Government has indeed been practicing a deliberate policy of destitution of this highly vulnerable group."[13]

In a parliamentary exchange in 2009, the undersecretary of state, Lord West, rejected these allegations and insisted that "our policies are absolutely such that no person who has sought protection need be destitute." Lord West also insisted that "when a decision has been made that a person does not require international protection and there is no remaining right of appeal or obstacle to their return, we expect unsuccessful asylum seekers to return voluntarily to their country of origin."[14] This choice is not as clear-cut as it appears. Even if asylum seekers agree to leave the United Kingdom voluntarily, their countries of origin may not always facilitate the necessary documentation and may even refuse to accept them. Returning migrants to Somalia, for example, a country with no functioning government and an ongoing civil war, is virtually impossible. In November 2011, the Iranian embassy in London was closed by the U.K. government in retaliation for a mob attack on the British embassy in Tehran. Nor does a negative decision by a Home Office caseworker or immigration judge necessarily mean an asylum seeker is prepared to accept it. Consider the incredible ordeal of Germain Naruhana, a thirty-two-year-old asylum seeker from the Democratic Republic of Congo (DRC) and one of PAFRAS' clients in Leeds.

A secondary school teacher, community organizer, and former choirmaster from the provincial town of Kamayola in the DRC's war-ravaged Kivu province, Naruhana and his father were both members of a local political party campaigning against militia violence against the civilian population. In the summer of 2004 the Congolese army crushed a rebellion in the province led by the Rwandan-backed Colonel Jules Mutebutsi and followed its victory with a spree of rapes and civilian killings. In September that year

Naruhana's father organized a small protest demonstration, and on November 3 he was kidnapped and decapitated.

Naruhana went into hiding with his mother, his brothers and sister, his wife, and their three children. In December, however, he and his fifteen-year-old sister were arrested and taken to a military base, where Naruhana was tortured and subjected to sustained sexual violence while his sister was repeatedly raped. The two of them were released thanks to the intervention of a sympathetic Italian priest, who took them with him on a plane to Italy and left them in a transit lounge at Heathrow Airport during a stopover on January 17, 2005, apparently in the belief that they would have a greater chance of getting refugee protection in the United Kingdom. Naruhana and his sister asked for asylum and were moved to temporary accommodations in Leeds. The next month his case was presented through an interpreter to an immigration judge in Liverpool, who dismissed it as "not credible."

Naruhana appealed the decision and was told to attend another immigration tribunal in Bradford. By this time he was vomiting and urinating blood from the beatings he had received in the DRC, and the judge immediately ordered him to be taken to the local infirmary. After a week in Leeds General Hospital he made his appeal, only to be turned down once again. A subsequent appeal to the Royal Court of Justice produced the same result.

In March 2006 Naruhana reached the end of the appeal process. In a state of severe psychological distress, without financial support or accommodations and fearful of being deported, he began sleeping rough and staying at friends' houses and homeless shelters. In June that year he discovered through the Internet that his mother and two sisters had been raped and killed, and he later learned that his wife and three children were in the hands of a local military commander who had "married" his wife as a sex slave.

Emboldened by this new information, Naruhana filed a fresh claim for asylum and was given temporary housing. But once again his claim was refused and he became destitute, before a local refugee support group managed to find him shared accommodations in a house with other asylum seekers. Throughout these years he continued to carry out voluntary work with his local church and sat in on a postgraduate course on Activism and Social Change at Leeds University. In September 2009 his sister was granted indefinite leave to remain in the United Kingdom—a dispensation that was not extended to him. In November he discovered that the army officer who had kidnapped his wife had been killed, and that she had escaped to a refugee camp in Malawi with his brother and one of his children. Naruhana subsequently heard that they had been granted asylum in Australia, and he asked to be allowed to join them, only to told by the Home Office that he would have to go back to the Congo first and try to get to Australia from there.

When I met him, he was still waiting for the result of an application from his wife to the Australian government to allow him to join her on family reunion grounds. Naruhana told his shocking story calmly, without embellishment, and without bitterness or self-pity, punctuating his account with precise dates, times, and details, as if he were used to not being believed. He spoke of his desire to teach again and the "invisible bars" that had prevented him from being able to work or provide for himself for the last five years.

He still sang in his local church choir and his firm religious convictions had clearly sustained him through an ordeal that would have left many people broken. "The world works according to different sets of rules," he said. "We are ruled by powers and principalities and there is nothing we can do about it. In the Home Office there are good people—I'm not saying that everyone there is bad or wrong. They are good people and they work with the rules that are set before them."

Others may be less charitable and wonder why a country that routinely trumpets its historical generosity toward refugees can allow such things to happen. Such practices are not exclusive to the United Kingdom. Directly opposite the Hungarian embassy in the plush Via dei Vellini in Rome, a faded flag with a white star against a blue background hangs from the peeling orange and gray facade of the former embassy of the Republic of Somalia. For years the embassy was abandoned, and until recently this monument to a nonexistent state served as a squat for hundreds of destitute Somali asylum seekers. When I visited it in the summer of 2011, the gate was locked and the only person there was an elderly Somali, who was sitting on the veranda for reasons that my primitive Italian was not able to discover.

Most of the embassy's former occupants are now living in smaller squats around Rome or in accommodations provided by the Centro Astalli, the Italian branch of the Jesuit Refugee Service, which provides food, accommodations, and legal assistance to some 26,000 people in the city every year. Only a few blocks from the crowds of tourists at the Colosseum and the Via Sacra, stone steps lead into the cavernous crypt beneath St. Paul's Within the Walls Episcopal Church. Here the Joel Nafuma Refugee Center holds its daily drop-in sessions, where up to two hundred homeless refugees and asylum seekers come to eat a free breakfast, play chess, table tennis, and foosball; watch television; and chat.

On the day I visited there were around a hundred people at the center, including a group of young American Christians who had come as volunteers. Most of the clients were Afghans and Somalis and all of them were male, including adolescents who had come to Italy with their fathers and brothers. "They have a very difficult life. Most of them are sleeping in the street and they can't find a job," said Abdullah Akbatar, the center's ebullient multilingual Kurdish coordinator, known to everyone as Tuana. Almost everyone who comes to Italy has to spend at least a month in this situation, he said, because their initial asylum claims are not generally followed by immediate integration into a reception center. But many migrants remain destitute for a lot longer, since asylum seekers in Italy who appeal rejections lose state benefits and accommodations during an appeal process whose average length is four years and can sometimes last as long as seven.

One the center's regular visitors was Victor, a stocky young Sierra Leonean in his late twenties, who had been in Italy on and off for nearly eight years. During most of that time he had been destitute. Twice he had reached the United Kingdom, only to be deported under the Dublin Convention rules. He originally left Sierra Leone at the age of seventeen in the late 1990s with his brother, after their parents were killed during the civil war, and he went to work in Libya. In 2003 he came to Italy by boat and asked for asylum. Two years later his appeal was rejected because he failed to turn up for his asylum tribunal in Rome.

Victor blamed this rejection on the police for not telling him when the tribunal was coming. His unwillingness to tolerate the routine abuse directed at migrants by the Italian police had caused him a lot of problems during his years in Italy. On arriving in the country he was taken to the police station at Foggi with thirteen of his countrymen. When a plainclothes policeman began beating them up for no apparent reason, Victor fought back and took a beating himself before he was arrested for assaulting a police officer. He was subsequently acquitted in court. In 2007 he was arrested again when he got in a fistfight with two policemen who tried to handcuff him while he was sleeping in a park in Rome. This time he landed an eighteen-month prison sentence. After serving three months he was released on appeal and he had been homeless ever since.

Now he had had enough and was planning to go back to Sierra Leone with his brother and see if it was possible to start again. "It's been an education for me, coming to Europe," he said. "I see now how the world works. I see how Westerners think, and it's nothing to do with people, it's only the system."

Victor was a tough and resourceful character, but not everyone is able to cope with the prolonged exclusion and uncertainty of destitution. Osman Rasul Mohammed originally came to the United Kingdom from Iraqi Kurdistan to seek asylum at the age of twenty in 2003. When his appeal was rejected he spent the next seven years slipping in and out of destitution in a vain attempt to gain refugee status. In January 2010 his relationship with his Polish partner broke down, and he left his home and two children in Coventry. He turned up at the offices of the Nottingham and Nottinghamshire Refugee Forum and told them that he was homeless. The Forum referred him to legal advisers Refugee and Migrant Justice (RMJ). For the next six months the Forum provided him with a £10-a-month cash grant, food parcels, and twice-weekly hot meals at its drop-in centers, while he slept at two different houses of people he met at the Forum.

A photograph of a handsome, bearded man smiling shyly at the ground in front of a blackboard gives no indication of the desperation and inner turmoil that reached its tragic culmination in July that year. In June RMJ was forced to close as a result of cash flow problems caused by late payments from the Legal Services Commission. Before its closure, RMJ provided free legal advice and assistance to more than ten thousand asylum seekers across the United Kingdom. Without RMJ's assistance, Rasul, like many others in a similar position, lost any possibility of pursuing his asylum claim. Distraught and demoralized, he made his way to the UKBA headquarters at Lunar House in Croydon and pleaded with officials to help him or send him back to his country.

Not surprisingly, he was told to go away, and he returned to Nottingham in a state of physical and mental exhaustion. An attorney referred him to the Nottingham Arimathea Trust, a local charity that provides temporary housing to particularly vulnerable destitute asylum seekers. The Trust did not have enough bed space, explained its project manager Caron Boulghassoul, who also recalled, "Of all the referrals that we've had from RMJ, his looked the strongest in terms of potential of getting a positive decision."

Rasul had clearly lost faith in this possibility. On Sunday, July 27, his housemates noted that he seemed calmer and more cheerful, and he told them that he was going for a bicycle ride. Early that evening he climbed onto a balcony of the Clifford Court Tower. For nearly two hours he held on to the railings while police and a neighbor tried to coax him down and a small crowd gathered below and started jeering at him to jump. Witnesses later said that he appeared to be praying before he finally placed one hand on his heart, looked up briefly at the sky, and dropped to his death.

Rasul's death was described by UKBA as a "tragedy," which is the usual official response to such events, but it was also an avoidable tragedy. Like tens of thousands of Europe's "living ghosts," he was obliged to choose between an indefinite legal limbo and a return to the country that he had spent seven years of his life trying to escape, because the country that he had appealed to for help refused to believe that he deserved it. No one will ever know whether Rasul saw suicide as the only way of demonstrating his sincerity or whether he simply lost hope that his life would ever get any better. But the society and institutions that cast him into no-man's-land for seven years bear some of the responsibility for the terrible choice that he made, and a country that felt the need to exclude this vulnerable and fragile young man in order to demonstrate the credibility of its immigration controls was a pettier, harsher, and infinitely sadder place than it realized.

PART TWO

Border Crossings

Before I built a wall I'd ask to know
What I was walling in or walling out,
And to whom I was like to give offense.
Something there is that doesn't love a wall,
That wants it down.

—ROBERT FROST, "MENDING WALL"

8

Difficult Journeys

We are all called upon to leave our homes, we all hear the siren call of the open sea, the appeal of the deep, the voices from afar that live within us, and we all feel the need to leave our native land, because our country is often not rich enough, or loving enough, or generous enough to keep us at home.

—Tahar Ben Jelloun, *Leaving Tangier*

Three months that we are crossing the borders we did not smile because we are anxious for crossing the border. Wherever we go somewhere people look at us like we are criminals or have bad manners.

—Anonymous Afghan migrant, Birds of Immigrants website, May 16, 2010

In the pseudonymous B. Traven's novel *Das Totenschiff* (*The Death Ship*, 1926), the American sailor Gerard Gales loses his sailor's card and passport when his ship sails from Europe without him. Unable to obtain a new passport from his own consul because he has no proof of identity, Gales finds that no country is willing to accept him. Jailed, deported, and harassed by one set of European officials after another, he is eventually obliged to make his way back to his home in New Orleans on the *Yorikke*, a hulk or "death ship" that is worth more to its owners for its insurance value when sunk and the only vessel whose captain is willing to take on undocumented seamen.

Traven's bleak satire on the security-obsessed Europe that emerged in the aftermath of World War I was a response to what was then a historical novelty, but the illegal odyssey of Gerald Gales also has some resonance in our own era. Today Europeans on even moderate incomes can expect to travel almost anywhere in the world for work or pleasure. This freedom to change one's country and place of residence at will is one of the privileges of twenty-first-century capitalism in its globalized variant, reflected in travel agencies and low-cost airlines that offer routes to and vacations in every conceivable destination, in television programs that highlight travel and exotic destinations, in travel supplements and magazines offering exotic holidays in the most far-flung places, and in real estate agencies and websites that specialize in foreign properties as first or second homes.

"If you're currently dissatisfied with your life and you want to make changes for the better, one of the ways you can positively affect your life is to start again in a new nation," declares Shelter Offshore in its online guide to "low tax living abroad." Many of Europe's unwanted migrants are motivated by very similar objectives, but the absence of a visa or a passport means that they are often obliged to use very different means to try to achieve them.

In May 2007 twenty-seven Africans from various countries paid £500 each to Libyan smugglers, who equipped them with a boat and compass to make their own way to Italy—a journey they were assured would take only two hours. They soon became hopelessly lost. After seven days at sea without food or water they were spotted by a Maltese tugboat trailing a tuna fishing cage. With their boat shipping water, the migrants pleaded to be taken on board. Incredibly, the captain refused, claiming afterward that he did not want to delay returning to port with his tuna catch. Faced with almost certain death, the migrants jumped onto the circular tuna cage.

For three days and nights they remained there, clinging to the rim, buffeted by seven-foot waves and winds of up to forty miles per hour, singing and praying to keep up their morale, while the Maltese and Libyan authorities bickered over who should take responsibility for them. Eventually they were rescued by the Italian navy and taken back to Italy, where they were given temporary leave to remain for one year. Tens of thousands of men, women, and children have undertaken equally perilous journeys to Europe over the last two decades, using routes and methods that most Europeans would not contemplate in their worst nightmares, but which would not have been entirely unfamiliar to B. Traven's stateless protagonist.

Rites of Passage

For the "legitimate" or "bona fide" traveler in the twenty-first century, foreign travel usually involves the same familiar and predictable preparations and procedures. Prospective travelers book hotel stays and flights beforehand, plan itineraries, and perhaps get the local currency and take out insurance, secure in the knowledge that the burgundy EU passport will enable them "to pass freely without let or hindrance," as its U.K. version requests, and that governments will "afford . . . such assistance and protection as may be necessary" should they get into difficulties.

For travelers without such documentation, travel is an infinitely more hazardous and complicated activity. From the moment they step outside their national borders they become illegal and lose any right to state protection or assistance. If they are sick or injured, there is no guarantee that they will be able to go to a hospital or see a doctor. If they are robbed, they usually cannot go the police, and in some countries they may be robbed by police themselves or obliged to pay a bribe or "migrant tax" to continue their journey.

Illegal travelers may use the same forms of transport as their legal counterparts, but not in the same way. If they go by plane, they might stow away in the wheel carriages of jet planes—a particularly dangerous and frequently lethal mode of transport. They might travel by truck, but only by hiding in the back or hanging upside down underneath the vehicle. If they take the train, they can only travel on the roof or by inserting themselves between or underneath cars. If they come by automobile, they may have to hide in cavities and false bottoms in the trunk or engine, or, in an even more recent innovation, by allowing themselves to be molded into car seats with their heads inside the passenger's headrest in an attempt to physically merge with the vehicle itself.

Other forms of transport are exclusive to illegal travelers, from the creaky fishing boats and dinghies that have so often sunk or capsized on the Mediterranean to the rusty hulks used to bring larger numbers of migrants from Africa to Europe on longer voyages. If their passengers are lucky or have enough money, they may have life jackets, plastic bags of spare clothes, and adequate supplies of food and drinking water. Some may travel on boats with powerful motors and an experienced pilot, but many people have drowned because safety precautions were entirely absent.

To undertake such journeys requires courage and daring, tenacity, foolhardiness, and also physical strength and determination. Not everyone can hang underneath a truck, jump onto a train, or cross snow-covered mountains in the middle of winter, as some migrants have done while trying to get from Bulgaria into Greece or from Ukraine into Slovakia. Not everyone has the nerve to set out in a leaky and overcrowded boat when they can't swim and may never even have seen the sea, or wade across a river at night to evade police and soldiers along a mine-infested border to enter a country where they can't speak the language and have nowhere to stay.

The *"cayuco* route" from Senegal to Spain takes between five and seven days and may take longer in rough seas or if things go wrong. During that time their passengers often have no protection from the sun, increasing the risk of exposure and hyperthermia if they get lost. In southern Spain I met one Malian migrant who had walked across the length of Morocco between Algeria and Ceuta at night in order to avoid police. One Somali at the Hal Far open center in Malta had only one leg and had crossed the Sahara and the Mediterranean on a pair of crutches.

The Sahara Desert is a particularly formidable obstacle in the migratory trail. In some years anywhere between 65,000 and 120,000 people have crossed it in cars, trucks, or convoys of Toyota four-wheel-drives and minibuses. Most sub-Saharan African migrants head north to the migrant hub cities of Gao in Mali or Agadez in Niger, following ancient caravan routes into Algeria, Libya, or Mauritania, while Sudanese and Eritreans move westward through Darfur, Egypt, and Chad into Libya. Pakistani, Iranian, Burmese, and Chinese migrants have also taken the trans-Saharan route, flying to West African cities such as Dakar, Bamako, and Conakry, where visas are easily obtainable, before making their way up through the desert toward Ceuta and Melilla and the coastal cities of Tangier and Larache in Morocco, or Tripoli, Benghazi, and Zuwarrah in Libya, to arrange a sea crossing to Europe.

These desert crossings generally take about ten days, but they may take longer while their drivers wait to collect more passengers or because cars and trucks have broken down or not arrived. Most of the driving takes place at night, usually in convoys. During the day the drivers sleep, while their passengers take turns sheltering from the sun underneath their vehicles because there are usually too many of them to shelter together. For more than 685 miles between Agadez in Niger and the Libyan oasis of Qatrur there are no paved roads, and passengers may be obliged to push and drag their vehicles over towering sand dunes. Supplies of water and food are generally inadequate, and smugglers sometimes mix water with gasoline to stop their passengers from drinking too much of it.

The Sahara is littered with wrecked or abandoned vehicles and skeletons of migrants who fell from their vehicles and were abandoned or succumbed to thirst or hunger. Migrants in the Sahara are also subject to the depredations of bandits, thieves, and corrupt officials. In 2010 the Nigerian journalist Emmanuel Mayah traveled 2,683 miles across the Sahara disguised as a migrant. Traveling in an overcrowded truck from Agadez to Bilma in Niger, Mayah described a hellish landscape that few Europeans have ever experienced:

> The desert has no roads, no trees, no houses, no signpost, no milestone and no friends. We traveled for four days swinging like a pendulum between extremely hot and extremely cold weather as days turned to night.
>
> There was an unbearable stench as adults urinated inside the moving truck. At least once in a day, we came across carcasses of dead animals, human skeletons and personal items like passports and Bible[s].[1]

Mayah's truck was held up by Tuareg bandits who forced the passengers to strip naked, searched their orifices for concealed money, and casually raped a young Nigerian woman who was traveling on the truck.

Bandits are not the only predators along the Saharan trail. At the Libya-Niger border the annual income from bribery and extortion has been estimated at €20 million, while female migrants on the trans-Saharan trail are often obliged to pay a different kind of "tax" as the price of their journeys, in the form of sexual favors "freely" given or taken by force.

These illegal journeys are sometimes more expensive than their legal equivalents. A place on the *cayuco* route between West Africa to the Canary Islands once cost €600 to €700, but migrants have paid upward of $15,000 for "full package solutions" that transport them directly from as far away as China to the United Kingdom. These fees do not guarantee comfort or safety. Without documentation, few migrants are able to stay in hotels, except for shared rooms with ten or more people that can be found in migratory hubs such as Besmane in Izmir. Often they will sleep in the open or spend days or even months confined with other migrants in safe houses or *hawsh*, as they are called in Libya, while smugglers prepare their embarkations or wait for more people to fill their quotas before continuing the next stage of their journey.

For travelers with a passport, crossing borders is generally a formality and a minor inconvenience. For migrants, every border is the place where their journey may end, and crossing borders often requires them to conceal their identities or invent new ones. In 2009 the Swedish Migration Board began using special technologies to identify asylum seekers who had mutilated their fingertips with knives, razors, or acid in an attempt to evade the Eurodac fingerprint database. In Calais migrants sometimes attempt to erase their prints by covering them with polyurethane, burning them in fires or on hot stoves, or rubbing them with sandpaper.[2]

The Promised Land?

Why are so many people prepared to undergo such ordeals? What do they see in Europe before coming? Governments and migration theorists traditionally talk of the "push" and "pull" factors that spur migration. The former may include war and armed conflict, political and cultural oppression, poor governance, environmental degradation, overpopulation, unemployment, corruption, and poverty. All these elements are present to a greater or lesser degree in the countries where Europe's undocumented migrants come from. Today global divisions in income levels, health, education, lifestyle, life expectancy, and security between countries and regions have never been higher, and some of these disparities are visible on either side of Europe's external borders.

In Spain the gross national income per capita in 2009 was $31,870, compared to $2,790 in Morocco. Even among the newer eastern EU member states, the figures for Poland and the Slovak Republic in the same year were $12,260 and $16,130, respectively, compared with $2,800 in neighboring Ukraine and $1,590 in Moldova. Europe is also geographically close to sub-Saharan Africa, where these differences become even steeper. Of the forty-nine least developed countries (LDCs) listed by the United Nations in 2011, thirty were in Africa—a figure that did not include Somalia, for which no economic statistics were available.

The "push" factors that drive people to leave their countries are one thing, but the choice of migratory destination depends on the perceived availability of more positive alternatives. Europe's appeal is not difficult to understand. In 2007 the European Union was the largest economy in the world. Of the twenty wealthiest countries in the world, fifteen are in Europe. Writing of his youth in Enver Hoxha's Albania, the writer and journalist Gazmend Kapllani recalled how Italian and Greek TV shows obtained through illegal aerials provided Albanians with enticing glimpses of "the world-beyond-the-borders" that eventually led him and many of his compatriots to emigrate to Greece and Italy.[3]

Today such information is more available than ever before as a result of all-pervasive global media and the Internet. The cafés of Tangier daily transmit Spanish TV channels that provide a constant reminder of these differences to young jobless Moroccans, and the backstreets of the Kasbah are dotted with Internet cafés and Skype booths that enable prospective migrants to cross virtual borders and stay in contact with friends or relatives on the other side of the Strait. The same information is available in even more distant countries.

Most migrants come to Europe to work or earn higher wages, and some are sent by their families so that they can contribute to the family income. Some migrants raise the money by saving or borrowing money from smuggling networks, which they pay back when they find work in Europe. In other cases relatives and local communities take out loans and invest in their journeys in expectation of remittances. Undocumented migrants may come from poor countries, but they are not necessarily the poorest of the poor. In 2007 the Spanish Red Cross conducted a detailed survey of 5,191 migrants from various West African countries who had passed through migrant reception centers in Mauritania in an attempt to reach the Canary Islands. Nearly three-quarters had gone through primary or secondary education, and more than 85 percent had been working before leaving their countries, mostly in insecure professions such as fishing, agriculture, chauffeuring, and street vending.[4]

These findings are not a universal template. Within Africa, economic and political conditions vary considerably between different countries and within them. Nearly all the migrants interviewed by the Red Cross were unmarried young men, but many of Europe's migrants are children and minors, particularly from Afghanistan. There has been an increase in irregular female migration to Europe—reflecting a global "feminization" of migration that has been estimated at close to 50 percent of the global total.

Most of the migrants I met had come to Europe in search of opportunities for work or study that are not available in their own countries. Some were unskilled or semiskilled and had never been to school. But there were also university graduates, journalists, teachers, social workers, electronics engineers, and businessmen. Some had formed positive impressions of particular countries from films and television or soccer clubs such as Manchester United and Barcelona. The success of African soccer players in European clubs was a particular inspiration for African migrants, some of whom talked of becoming soccer players themselves.

Several Sudanese and Nigerians told me that they were going to the United Kingdom "because you colonized us"—an explanation that was partly an indictment and also a straightforward recognition of the historical and/or linguistic connections that made migrants choose some countries rather than others. Many if not most of the migrants I met were following routes already taken by relatives, friends, and neighbors, and some had clearly come with an excessively rosy notion of the future that awaited them.

In tabloid mythology the stereotypical illegal immigrant is a devious and calculating opportunist with an expert knowledge of the countries he or she is seeking to reach. But many migrants set out on their journeys with remarkably little idea of what awaits them. On my first night in Calais, I was taken by taxi to the wrong hotel, where I met a short black woman in her mid-forties, with bouffant hair and a long quilted coat, scarf, and boots. Her only luggage was a carryall and a plastic bag. She introduced herself as Ann Mungi and said she was from Kenya and that she had just arrived from Sweden. She had no passport and very little money, and it was cold and getting late, so I gave her something to help her pay for a room and left for my hotel. Two days later I saw her at the migrant food distribution center, still carrying her bags, the only woman among the lines of men waiting for the soup kitchens.

She told me that she had spent the previous night walking the street and various drivers had propositioned her. Now she was worried about where she was going to sleep and wash that night. "I'm a Christian woman and I fear God," she said. "I don't want to do bad things." She told me that she had relatives in London, and I offered her my phone so that she could call them, but she said she wanted her visit to be a surprise. Given her predicament, this seemed an odd priority. I introduced her to Jacky Verhaegen, the Calais representative of Secours Catholique, a branch of the charity Caritas, who explained to her that it would be very difficult to find her somewhere to stay because she had no papers and her presence in Calais was a criminal offense. He said that she would not be able to go to the United Kingdom either and asked if she wanted to apply for asylum in France and whether she had been fingerprinted. Ann looked as if she had never heard of these concepts, and said that she would need two or three weeks to consider her options.

I said goodbye and wished her luck, but the next morning I met her yet again—in my hotel. Jacky had managed to find her a place there for two nights. After that, she said with the same calm, unruffled composure with which she seemed to react to all the bad news she had received so far, she did not know what was going to happen. We had breakfast together in the café and I asked why she had left Kenya, and she said that she had had some "trouble with Muslims" in her village near the Somali border. When I said I was amazed that she had managed to get so far by herself, she replied, "Sometimes a woman can do what a man can't do, and a man can do what a woman can't do."

She then asked me if there were any Pentecostal Christians in the United Kingdom. I said there probably were, and she proceeded to tell the story of the four lepers from the Bible, who find themselves excluded from the city of Samaria during a siege by the Syrian army, and decide to go to the Syrian camp to ask for food, regardless of the risk. "That is how it is with us," she concluded solemnly. "We always hope for a better life and we will keep on pushing until we find it."

Ann was an enigmatic and in many ways astonishing character. On one hand, she was so unaware of the rules and requirements that Europe's borders entailed that she might have been beamed into Calais through a magic portal, yet she had traveled more than four thousand miles and crossed several international borders without a passport and with very little money. I was often astonished by the naivete and resourcefulness of Europe's migrants. One night in Alexandroupolis Steve Greaves and I met two Pakistani men who wanted to know where they could catch the train to Athens. Their lack of any possessions beyond a plastic bag or any currency except U.S. dollars made it obvious that they were recent arrivals from the Evros border. Neither spoke Greek or much English, but when we told them the last train to Athens had already left, they said they would take a taxi. They seemed mildly surprised but not remotely fazed by the news that Athens was nearly five hundred miles away.

Not many Europeans would contemplate flying thousands of miles from their homes and walking through a militarized border at night to a country they have never been to before, carrying nothing but a plastic bag and a few hundred dollars. In a security-obsessed continent that often seems paralyzed by its own fears of what lies outside it, Europe's unwanted migrants often lived according to the Vietnamese proverb "Venture all: see what fate brings."

Contrary to some media representations, these journeys were not simply a product of misery and despair. There were also those, such as Al John, a supremely optimistic Liberian I met in Tangier, who described his journey to Europe as part of "the great adventure—fleeing poverty in Africa" and exuded confidence that he would find a way to cross the Strait and get to Europe, even though he had no money. Nor are migrants always unprepared for their journeys. In Senegal passengers on the *cayuco* route across the Atlantic often perform purification rites beforehand with the assistance of their local *marabouts* (religious leaders) in an attempt to ensure a safe crossing, while Muslim migrants will often obtain astrological horoscopes and amulets from their imams and/or from fortune tellers to give themselves confidence or provide protection from the sea *djinns* (spirits), suggesting that they are aware of the risks involved.

Nevertheless, I often encountered men and women trapped in situations that they had clearly not expected to find themselves in. Yet even in the worst circumstances, very few were thinking of giving up and going back. In Calais migrants who had spent a sleepless night in a police station would call their families the next day to tell them that everything in Europe was going well. In Malta, Terry Gosden told me how residents at the Marsa Open Centre used to ask him to photograph them leaning proprietarily against his car, for reasons that he did not understand until he discovered that they were sending these photographs back home.

Some migrants are simply too ashamed to tell their families what happened to them. In some African countries, returning home empty-handed brings the stigma that Malians call *la honte* (shame). But returning also means an abandonment of the hopes and aspirations that led them to risk so much in the first place. When I asked one Sudanese migrant who had been stranded in Igoumenitsa for months how he was able to stand such conditions, he told me, "We always go forward, we always believe that there is something better for us in another country."

These aspirations are not unknown to Europeans. In the late nineteenth and early twentieth centuries millions of Poles emigrated to the United States or across the border into Germany in search of permanent or seasonal work, and Italians from the impoverished south crossed the border into France or made even longer journeys to America. Even in the early 1970s

Spaniards were obliged to look for work in Belgian and German factories and construction sites. Since 2004, millions of eastern Europeans have moved to western Europe in search of work and higher wages.

As a result of the global financial crisis, countries that once appeared to have made the transition from emigrant-producing societies to immigrant-receiving ones have begun to generate emigration once again. In 2009, 102,000 Spaniards emigrated to the United States and Latin America. In 2010, the Irish government predicted that 100,000 Irish citizens would leave the country within the next four years. In the same year, a Greek opinion poll found that seven out of ten university graduates were hoping to work abroad. Thousands of unemployed Portuguese graduates have emigrated to Portugal's former colonies in Africa and Brazil to escape the economic crisis.[5]

The push and pull factors that drive migration are not static, and human beings will always look for something better if they see the possibility. For the time being most of Europe's new migrants may find legal routes to realize these hopes, but if not then they too may one day be obliged to look for other routes and methods.

Refugees

There are also those for whom Europe offers not just the prospect of work but an escape from violence, persecution, and war. Until 2004 Adams Saleh Zaid worked as a charcoal burner at the village of Aran in western Darfur, at a time when the region was ravaged by fighting between the Sudanese army and militias and separatist Darfuri rebels. It was, he remembers, a period in which "life is stopped, Africans are targeted. Danger is everywhere. All that area is burning."

One day he and another man from his village were burning charcoal in the forest when they were arrested by Sudanese soldiers and accused of collusion with the rebels. For more than a year Adams was shunted back and forth between Sudanese army bases. Sometimes he was beaten and tortured and deprived of food and water. At other times he was forced to serve his captors. Eventually he became seriously ill and was sent to an army hospital in Khartoum, where he escaped with the help of a sympathetic nurse, who arranged with people outside to get him to Europe. In March 2004 he was smuggled onto a ship at Port Sudan, which he was told was heading for Turkey or Italy.

On April 7, after seventeen days at sea, he was put in a small boat with two other people at night and told to make his way to a nearby island, which turned out to be Crete.

The following morning he went to the nearest town and met some Sudanese workers who were working on the orange harvest, who told him that he had arrived in Greece. After presenting himself to the local police and applying for asylum, he was taken to the Larissa detention center in Athens, where he received medical attention and psychological counseling from a local NGO dealing with victims of torture. Nine months later he received his pink card, with the help of intense lobbying from a refugee lawyer, a social worker, and various other people who had become involved in his case. Today he is the spokesman for the Sudanese community in Athens and runs a little café cum community center in a backstreet near Omonia Square, where he provides help and assistance to other Sudanese migrants.

In principle all European governments recognize a moral obligation to provide protection to "genuine" refugees such as Adams, but these commitments are often at odds with the common assumption that many if not most refugees are economic migrants seeking to flout Europe's immigration laws. There is no doubt that migrants do appeal for asylum in order to circumvent the restrictions that prevent them from entering Europe by any other means, and that some may choose particular countries where they believe they are more likely to succeed. But it is equally true that both the media and politicians tend to exaggerate the number of asylum seekers who do this in order to dilute or weaken the moral case for refugee protection.

Certainly none of the migrants I met appeared to have planned their journeys on the basis of particular countries' perceived generosity on asylum conditions, and many of them were remarkably uninformed about Europe's asylum criteria. Robar, an Iraqi Kurd, arrived in the United Kingdom in 2003 from Calais as an unaccompanied minor of fourteen to claim asylum. He was told by one his countrymen that he would have a better chance of getting asylum in the Netherlands. This was bad advice. When Robar made it to Holland, he was sent back to the United Kingdom, where his asylum appeal was rejected on the grounds that he had left the country. Over the next seven years he was deported from nine European countries.

When I met him in Igoumenitsa in the autumn of 2010 he was trying to get back to Norway, where he had a girlfriend and a seven-month-old son. Robar had lost track of the reasons for his deportations, if he had ever understood them in the first place, and now he was trapped in Greece and trying to cross another border, and there was little possibility that any country would accept him.

Or consider the case of Atifiyah, a nineteen-year-old Iranian asylum seeker who eloped with her boyfriend despite opposition from their two families. The couple made their way to Izmir, where a heavily pregnant Atifiyah and her husband rowed to Samos in a boat with two other migrants. When I met her she had had another baby and was still seeking asylum on the grounds that if she returned to Iran she might be killed by one of the two families. On the wall outside the house where she was staying she had written the word "love" in English. But this Romeo and Juliet scenario was never likely to pass through the narrow Greek asylum filter, nor were other countries likely to be any more sympathetic. Atifiyah and her husband had little prospect of getting refugee protection unless they were able to prove that they would be at risk of serious physical harm even if they moved to another part of Iran.

For many Europeans, the mere fact that asylum seekers have come to Europe instead of remaining in the nearest safe country or refugee camp is proof that they must be bogus asylum seekers and economic migrants rather than genuine refugees. But such accusations are often based on a misconception of what it means to be a refugee. Most of the world's refugees are in fact located close to their own countries or remain inside their national borders as internally displaced persons. But many refugees seek not just an escape from immediate danger or persecution but an opportunity to rebuild their lives, especially when their own countries are in the midst of intractable and long-term conflicts or where political or cultural oppression is an entrenched feature of their societies. In some countries such as Somalia and Afghanistan, the push factors of poverty, unemployment, and lack of opportunity may be exacerbated by conflict and insecurity, making it difficult if not impossible to establish hard-and-fast categorizations between economic migrants and refugees.

In the last two decades, however, the insistence by many governments that many if not the majority of asylum seekers are not genuine refugees has become a justification for intransigence, skepticism, and a new drive to weaken or evade their moral obligations under the Geneva Convention. Asylum seekers, like economic migrants, often come from countries with historic or cultural ties to Europe. Many of them are attracted to Europe because of the political ideals of democracy, tolerance, freedom of lifestyle and human rights that some European governments have proclaimed as a justification for military interventions abroad. In the United Kingdom there are gay and lesbian asylum seekers who have fled persecution in socially conservative countries such as Iran, Cameroon, or Turkey, only to have their applications turned down on the grounds that they could have avoided such persecution by keeping their sexuality secret.

Tens of thousands of people, it should not be forgotten, have been granted refugee status or other forms of protection in Europe. There are wide variations between countries such as Greece, Slovakia, and Malta, for example, which accept very few asylum claims, and Sweden, France, and Germany, all of which have accepted large numbers of refugees. But such generosity also needs to be placed in perspective. Between 2003 and 2007, 1.4 million Iraqis refugees fled to Syria, a country with a population of just over 21 million, and another 750,000 Iraqis found refuge in Jordan, which already has a large Palestinian refugee population. In the same period 60,000 Iraqis applied for asylum across the whole of Europe. In 2009 only 6 percent of the refugee population designated by UNHCR and other agencies for resettlement were resettled in the European Union, compared with 90 percent in the United States, Canada, and Australia.

European policy toward refugees often appears to be pulling in two contrary directions at the same time. On one hand, the EU proclaims Europe to be "a common space of protection and solidarity." At the same time, European governments and the political institutions of the EU itself are constantly seeking ways to limit access to such protection, through upstream migration controls that make it difficult for asylum seekers to reach Europe or by introducing tighter visa restrictions in response to increased asylum flows from specific countries. As a result, refugees seeking protection in Europe are often obliged to make use of the same routes and channels as economic migrants, and they may find themselves obliged to seek the services of specialists who occupy a particularly malevolent position in Europe's immigration wars.

Networks, Smugglers, and Mafias

On June 18, 2000, fifty-eight Chinese migrants either suffocated to death or were poisoned by carbon dioxide in the back of a refrigerated truck in Dover on the hottest day of the year, leaving two survivors. All of them had been transported from Rotterdam to Dover by a Dutch petty criminal, who closed the single air vent, apparently to reduce the risk of his cargo being discovered. This horrendous tragedy produced an outpouring of indignation against what the U.K. home secretary Jack Straw called the "profoundly evil trade" of people smuggling.

Such outrage is often directed by governments, the media, and law enforcement agencies toward the smugglers, *passeurs*, and facilitators who organize Europe's migratory journeys, and it is not always undeserved. In the last two decades there have been numerous incidents in which migrants have drowned because smugglers loaded them into unseaworthy boats in order to maximize their profits or threw them overboard to escape arrest. Others have been brutalized, raped, and sometimes killed by the people they paid to organize their journeys. But there is more than a touch of bad faith in the official vilification of people smuggling.

Smuggling covers a wide range of protagonists, including fishermen looking to make some extra income, corrupt police and border officials, truck drivers, pilots of private planes, and transnational criminal organizations. Most do it for money, but there are also those who see themselves as performing a humanitarian and even political function, such as the extraordinary Amir Heidari. A former Iranian Kurdish guerrilla who fought against the Khomeini regime, Heidari was granted refugee status in Sweden in 1979. Since then he has spent more than fourteen years in jail on various charges relating to the facilitation of illegal immigration.

Heidari has admitted to helping more than forty thousand Iranian and Iraqi refugees enter Europe illegally since the early 1980s and has always insisted that his motives were a natural development of his political involvement in the Kurdish cause. In 1981 he founded an organization called Solh (meaning "peace"), which smuggled military deserters and draft resisters out of Iran during the Iran-Iraq war, and this initiative evolved into a skilled and prolific smuggling network that forged documents, bribed officials, and arranged routes and accommodations for asylum seekers from various countries during each phase of their journey into Europe.

Heidari's clients have included Iranian Jews, Turkish Kurds, and Iraqis from pre- and post-Saddam Iraq. Though he charges for his services, he also claims to have helped people get into Europe who had no money. In an interview with Shahram Khosravi in prison in 2009, Heidari compared himself to the Swedish diplomat Raoul Wallenberg, who saved more than twenty thousand Jews from Nazi death camps during World War II, declaring, "Humane law does not recognize any border. Borders are constructed by inhumane minds. I see no borders."[6]

Heidari's radical idealism may be unusual, but altruism and profit making are not mutually exclusive activities. The restrictions placed on Jewish immigration by various governments during the 1930s and World War II produced a wide range of amateur and professional smuggling networks and individuals whose motives were not always noble. In June 2009 two Afghan brothers, Ahmed and Abdul Sakhizada, were sentenced to between seven and twelve years for facilitating illegal immigration and laundering the profits. The two brothers managed a string of pizza restaurants and brought at least 230 Afghans into Europe as part of a "full package" that included the overland journey from Afghanistan into Turkey, a boat to Greece, and bribes to truck drivers to take their clients to the United Kingdom and other European destinations.

In court their lawyer argued that Ahmed Sakhizada was driven by a desire "to assist others to overcome the harshness of reality in his own country." Such assistance did not come cheap. Their clients paid up to £5,000, and some of them paid off their debts by working in the Sakhizadas' restaurants. Police audio surveillance of the "pizza connection" made it clear that the brothers were not averse to using violence to maintain discipline.

Sakhizada may have attributed his activities to altruism in an attempt to reduce his sentence, or he may have genuinely believed that he was serving a good cause.[7] But whatever the smugglers' motives, their clients often have a very different attitude toward them than their governments do. In China's Fujian province, even the much-reviled "snakeheads" are regarded as heroic and indispensable figures, and the depiction of smuggling as a product of organized criminality also fails to take into account the more informal migrant networks and associations made up of friends, relatives, or members of the same nationality or ethnic group that have sprung up along the migratory trail to Europe. These networks provide crucial advice, information, contacts, and sometimes food and accommodations at all stages of the journey, and are often essential to survival.

Migrants in the *tranquilo* camps around Oujda in Morocco have even established a regional forum for all the migrants in the area that they call ECOWAS, after the Economic Community of West African States, where many of them come from. The camps' ECOWAS comes with its own rotating chairman who is elected every three months. The distinction between informal networks and organized crime in the Oujda camps is difficult if not impossible for outsiders to determine. Some chairmen owe their dominant position to their experience or personal charisma; others have connections to the nebulous transnational groups that organize the various stages of the trans-Saharan migratory routes.

Some of these groups were based in Maghnia, on the other side of the border, where there were rumors of a "national lord" who controlled all the African migrant communities in Morocco and extracted regular payments from their chairmen. In Calais and Igoumenitsa also, migrant "mafias" wield special influence over the shifting migrant populations that pass through the ports. As in Oujda, NGOs, charities, and solidarity organizations working with migrants are obliged to respect these hierarchies and negotiate access with their leaders, but the connotations of an Italian-style "mafia" are misleading. The power of these "mafias" may reside in their ability to control truck deports and port facilities and reserve access for members of their own national or ethnic groups. In Calais certain depots and ports were known to "belong" to Afghans or Nigerians, but some groups have "sold" rights of access to each other.

Passeurs may guard their territory jealously, and they may exploit their clients. Some migrants may well be tempted to set out for Europe by smugglers who raised their expectations in the hope of profiting from their journeys, but most of the migrants I spoke to had clearly made their own choices. Governments and law enforcement agencies know this perfectly well, yet continue to present their attempts to eliminate "organized" smuggling as a humanitarian enterprise and migrants as exploited victims in need of rescue. But even the most amoral and unscrupulous smugglers are helping migrants overcome barriers that were placed in their path by the same governments that aspire to save them—and the smugglers get them to where they want to go. For all the moralistic rhetoric directed toward this "evil trade," it is impossible to avoid the conclusion that this is the real reason why European governments and law enforcement agencies are so intent on stamping it out.

9

Traffic

Mano negra clandestina
Peruano clandestino
Africano clandestino
Marihuana illegal.

—MANU CHAO,
"CLANDESTINO"

The United Kingdom faces a complex and constantly evolving array of threats from terrorism, organized crime and illegal immigration which, left unchecked, can cause untold harm to our communities, businesses, public services and economy.

—*Protecting Our Border, Protecting the Public*,
U.K. BORDER AGENCY, FEBRUARY 2010

European governments and border guards often talk of their determination to "protect the border" from illicit or illegal people and commodities. But this determination to keep unwanted people and things out is sometimes at odds with the equally essential objective of allowing legitimate people and commodities in. On one hand, most European governments subscribe to the philosophy espoused by Renato Ruggiero, the former director of the World Trade Organization, in 1998 that "no country, developing or under-developed, has an interest in building walls against technology and investment flows from outside"—a philosophy that requires borders to be open, flexible, and permeable to goods and people.[1]

At the same time, European governments and law enforcement agencies share a common belief that greater global economic integration has made the continent more vulnerable to the "dark side of globalization" and the various permutations of "cross-border crime"—a consensus that has been reinforced rather than diminished by the abolition of internal border controls within the European Union. In 1999 the European Council's first summit on justice and home affairs, in the Finnish city of Tampere, declared the fight against "trans-border crime" an essential prerequisite for the creation of an "area of freedom, security and justice" in which both European citizens and "justified" non-EU travelers can "enjoy his or her freedoms, can live and work where he/she wishes in safety." The summit concluded with sixty proposals "to stop drugs, smuggled and stolen goods, and illegal immigrants entering the European Union" and undertook to develop "common policies on asylum and immigration, while taking into account the need for a consistent control of external borders to stop illegal immigration and to combat those who organise it and commit related international crimes."[2]

The 2010 European Council's draft *Internal Security Strategy for the European Union* painted an equally grim and alarming picture of a continent that was more vulnerable than ever to the negative consequences of globalization, declaring that

> The main crime-related risks and threats facing Europe today, such as terrorism, serious and organised crime, drug trafficking, cyber-crime, trafficking in human beings, sexual exploitation of minors and child pornography, economic crime and corruption, trafficking in arms and cross-border crime, adapt extremely quickly to changes in science and technology, in their attempt to exploit illegally and undermine the values and prosperity of our open societies.[3]

The idea that illegal immigrants and asylum seekers constitute potential threats to European security comparable to drugs, terrorism, and child pornography is a common theme in the discourse of European border enforcement. One of the key institutions in the European Union's fight against "cross-border crime" is the European border agency Frontex. Created by the European Commission in 2005, Frontex is devoted almost exclusively to combating irregular migration, and its mission statement sums up the contradictory demands of European border enforcement "to ensure that the

EU's external borders remain permeable and efficient for bona fide travellers while being an effective barrier to cross-border crime."

To some extent Frontex's political symbolism as a European border force outweighs its practical ability to realize these ambitious objectives. Because of its limited budget and resources, the agency is almost entirely dependent on equipment and personnel provided by EU member states for the operations that it takes part in. Much of its activity consist of gathering intelligence and statistical information on migratory hot spots and smuggling routes, which it calls "risk analysis." At its headquarters in the Rondo 1 skyscraper in central Warsaw, some fifty officials are permanently engaged in these activities, and their findings are regularly published in graphs and maps that mimic the quasi-military charts favored by drug enforcement and counterterrorist officials, with clusters of arrows thrusting menacingly toward Europe's borders to illustrate new migratory routes.

On a gray Warsaw morning in 2011, I spoke to the agency's executive director, Ilkka Laitinen, in his office on the twenty-second floor, where he outlined the essential philosophy of border enforcement in which he was schooled during his years as an officer of the Finnish border guard on the Finland-Russia border during the Cold War. "At the border crossing point the objective is to facilitate regular legitimate border crossings, to make it happen as smoothly as possible," Laitinen said, and "at the same time to stop such persons who are not allowed to enter on one hand, or who are deemed to be a threat to security."

Earlier that year I had seen a Frontex promotional video at the European Museum in Schengen, which warned of an uncontrollable "human surge" of immigrants spreading across the continent unless the phenomenon was contained. Was this how Frontex saw the security threat posed by irregular immigration? I asked. Laitinen said that he was not aware of the video and did not want to comment on the expression "human surge." So how did he see immigration as a security threat? "This is a delicate issue," he said. "By definition crossing the border against the rules is not an illegal act for all member states. It's not a crime to do it. What we are very much interested in is the organized crime. That is a real threat."

The Frontex director subsequently elaborated further on what this threat consisted of. "It's partly because of the resources, partly because of the readiness of the societies, and partly because of the structure," he said. "We have seen so many negative examples of what can happen if migration is not controlled, if integration is not managed properly."

When I asked for one of these examples, Laitinen cited the 2005 riots in the Paris *banlieues*. The absence of migration management did not seem to me a particularly relevant explanation for disturbances that were rooted in the long-term marginalization of second- or third-generation immigrants in French society, but the Frontex director's nebulous definition of the security threat posed by irregular immigration is not unusual.

Governments and law enforcement agencies frequently view irregular migration through a security prism, in which vague and elastic categories of "trans-border crime" or "immigration crime" are invoked as a rationalization for tighter monitoring and control over their borders. Such representations tend to reinforce an image of migration as an abnormal and criminal activity, perpetrated by harmful and dangerous people, and they often lead to an emphasis on a militarized and security-oriented approach to migration that precludes other responses. Last but not least, such depictions tend to generate security expectations that are difficult if not impossible to fulfill at the border itself. For these reasons, it is worth looking more closely at some of the commodities and people that are included within the rubric of "cross-border crime."

Contraband

Smuggling is always a response to prohibitions, and borders have often been the place where such prohibitions are enforced. Such prohibitions may be intended to prevent the unauthorized smuggling of legal commodities in order to gain revenue for the state or protect monopolies on particular products, or they may be imposed in order to prevent the entry of goods and activities considered to be antithetical to public morality, safety, or security.

Most experts agree that the massive growth in legitimate global trade in the last two decades has been accompanied by an exponential increase in the flow of illicit and illegal commodities across national borders. This includes untaxed cigarettes and alcohol, fake designer clothes, narcotics, weapons, industrial machinery, nuclear material, human organs, stolen cars and jewelry, antiquities, artworks and historical artifacts, pornography, pirated DVDs, gasoline, toxic waste, endangered animal species, and people trafficked for sexual exploitation or forced labor.

All these manifestations of the global shadow economy routinely cross Europe's borders in the early twenty-first century. For years Italian and

Albanian *contrabandisti* have zipped back and forth across the forty-three miles between Albania and Italy carrying cigarettes, migrants, and drugs in powerful speedboats that are capable of outrunning Italian coast guard patrols. In the Strait of Gibraltar the Civil Guard is often equally powerless to prevent the Moroccan launches that bring shipments of hashish to the European market. Contraband also flows out of Europe. The Civil Guard at Algeciras recently established a scuba-diving unit to prevent the looting of sunken Spanish treasure ships and the illegal sale of historical artifacts. At the Terespol border, commodities confiscated by Polish border guards include Kalashnikovs from the former Soviet Union destined for Austrian and German collectors, heroin aimed at the European market, and also methamphetamine manufactured in Europe for sale in Belarus and Ukraine.

The increase in the flow of contraband that has taken place from the 1990s onward is partly a consequence of the new proliferation of global suppliers to meet internal demand, but smuggling is also a product of socioeconomic conditions and income and price differentials closer to the border. In the 1990s smuggling was often a crucial economic lifeline in the former Soviet territories closest to Europe, such as the Russian oblast of Kaliningrad, which became a center for the smuggling of cigarettes, amber, and alcohol. In the same period the breakaway Republic of Moldova became a virtual mafia state that sold anything from black-market gasoline to drugs and weapons, including surface-to-air missile launchers.

The conditions that drive such cross-border traffic are not necessarily permanent, and neither are its markets and commodities. During the 1990s the Polish Border Guard established a special unit to prevent the smuggling of Orthodox religious icons looted from former Soviet churches and monasteries and destined for private collectors in Europe. Today the icons unit has been disbanded, and border guards have noted an increase in the traffic of smuggled luxury consumer goods in the opposite direction, such as antique furniture, Versace porcelain, and stolen classic cars destined for the Russian nouveau riche in Moscow.

Much of the Polish Border Guard's efforts to "protect the border" are devoted to the cat-and-mouse game contest with cigarette smugglers, who smuggle hundreds and even thousands of cartons of cigarettes in cars and trucks, in trains fitted with cavities in floors and walls, or on pulley lines across the narrower points of the Bug River. This traffic is partly driven by the higher profit margins defined by the border itself. In Ukraine and Belarus a packet of L&M cigarettes that costs €1 can sell for more than double that amount in Poland, and even more in western Europe. But antitobacco campaigners have also accused tobacco companies of diverting shipments to illicit suppliers in order to avoid paying taxes and to penetrate international markets.[4]

Whatever the truth of these accusations, the scale of cigarette smuggling on the eastern border is vast, and efforts at prevention have an air of Canute-like futility. Smuggling is not restricted to gangsters and professionals. During the 1990s unemployed or underpaid Ukrainian teachers also participated in the semilegal "ant-hill trade" across the Polish border, and the Ukrainian and Polish authorities effectively turned a blind eye to the processions of people carrying fridges, cigarettes, TV sets, and computers back and forth across the border to make a profit for themselves or receive a percentage from their employers. Ukrainians, Russians, and Belarusians have all made these journeys to local Polish border towns or farther afield to the vast bazaar in Warsaw known as the "Russian market," which once was Europe's largest flea market before it was cleared to make way for a new national soccer stadium in 2008.

Today this trade has been drastically reduced as a result of Schengen, but Belarusians and Ukrainians can still be seen selling cartons of cigarettes in Polish border towns, while Poles and Slovaks regularly cross the border to Ukraine to buy cigarettes and gasoline. The distinction between smuggling and legal economic activity is not always clear-cut in Europe's "frontier economies." Every day thousands of Moroccans cross the border fences at Spain's exclaves of Ceuta and Melilla to participate in the semi-institutionalized traffic of duty-free goods known euphemistically as *comercio atipico* (atypical trade) across the border.

From the early hours of the morning and throughout the day, a procession of mostly female *porteadores* (carriers) comes to collect their loads from warehouses and open markets that have been specially established for the purpose near the border fences. In a strip of waste ground by the Barrio Chino checkpoint in Melilla, hundreds of women strap huge piles of consumer goods to their bodies and carry them across the border through caged tunnels. Most of these "mules" make these trips several times a day, earning €3 to €5 for each journey from the retail outlets in nearby Moroccan towns such as Nador and Tetouan, and some have been doing this work all their lives. One morning I saw a wizened old Moroccan lady at the Barrio Chino checkpoint walking with a crutch and carrying an enormous pile of heavy plates with her free arm.

The sight of these women in hijabs, kaftans, and sneakers staggering through Europe's African frontier with bundles of Huggies, sneakers, and blankets strapped to their bodies, watched over by Spanish police and Civil Guards, is a grim testament to the brutal inequalities on either side of the border—like a cross between some ancient slave society and Mad Max's barter town. Women have been crushed and even killed trying to pass through these tunnels, and from time to time the Civil Guard and police officers bark orders at them and throw their bundles to the ground because they are too large.

In most circumstances the transport of duty-free goods across national borders would be considered smuggling, but it is not always clear which commodities are legal or illegal at Ceuta and Melilla. These activities constitute a vital source of income for the two exclaves and also for Moroccan retailers on the other side of the frontier, so much so that they have been formally incorporated into Spain's Schengen accession agreement.

The Narco-frontier

This tolerance is not extended to all commodities. Narcotics invariably feature among the threats to European security, public health, and safety emanating from beyond the continent's borders. Morocco is one of the largest producers of cannabis in the world, and the main supplier of hashish for the European market. Most Moroccan hashish is grown in the Rif Mountains between Tangier and Melilla, where cannabis production has been a staple of the local economy for centuries.

For decades hashish has been smuggled into Europe from Morocco via Gibraltar, Ceuta, Melilla, and Tangier in private yachts, fishing boats, or trucks and other vehicles before distribution to the rest of Europe—sometimes in convoys of souped-up cars that whiz along the Spanish motorways to France using the so-called *go fast routier* method. Some smugglers have transported hashish in *pateras* carrying irregular migrants, but the more sophisticated groups use powerful dinghies fitted with three or more engines that can get them from Morocco to Spain and back in less than half an hour.

Neither Moroccan nor Spanish patrol boats are fast enough to get anywhere near these vessels, though in some cases early detection by the SIVE network can allow enough time for the Civil Guard to set up an ambush when the boats reach the shore with their shipment. These efforts have not diminished a trade that is essentially demand-driven. According to the European Monitoring Centre for Drug Addiction, more than 22 million Europeans smoke hashish or marijuana on a regular basis, and to some extent Europe's attempts to prohibit this trade at the Spain-Morocco border parallels the failed drug war in the United States in its futility, if not the same level of violence. As in the United States, prohibition has generated a lucrative criminal enterprise on both sides of the frontier. Some of the sumptuous villas in Ceuta are widely reputed to belong to beneficiaries of *narcotraffico*, and in 2005 Spanish police arrested nineteen people in Ceuta and Melilla on charges of laundering drug-related profits worth €350 million through banks in China and Asia.

Despite these arrests and the annual seizures of smuggled hashish by the Spanish police and Civil Guard, there is no indication that these efforts have reduced the drug trade. Between 2003 and 2006 the Moroccan government carried out a campaign of crop eradication in the Rif, in response to pressure from Spain and the EU. Morocco claimed that production had been reduced by half, but these claims were disputed by Chekib el-Khiari, the head of the Association of Human Rights in the Rif, who accused the Moroccan authorities of targeting small-time dealers while ignoring Moroccan politicians and state officials involved in the trade.

An outspoken critic of the treatment of migrants by both Spain and Morocco, in 2008 el-Khiari appeared in a French documentary that showed narcotraffickers' dinghies leaving the coast near Nador in broad daylight despite the nearby presence of Moroccan army units. In February the following year el-Khiari was arrested and charged with defaming Morocco's state institutions and judicial authorities. And in June, despite protests from Amnesty International and Human Rights Watch, he was sentenced to three years in prison and fined 753,000 dirhams ($90,000)—a punishment that was clearly intended to deter others from following his example.

In April 2010 I met his brother Amine at el-Khiari's hometown of Nador, near Melilla. Amine had been campaigning for his brother's release and had no doubt that his brother's arrest was due to the powerful interests that he had tried to expose. On my way up from Oujda to Nador through the Rif I had seen numerous police roadblocks, which he described contemptuously as a form of theater designed to demonstrate Morocco's conformity with the rules of the European Union. Amine insisted that launches carrying hashish were still regularly leaving the Marchica lagoon just outside the city in full view of the authorities.

In April 2011, his brother received a pardon from the Moroccan king after serving two years of his sentence—a decision that owed more to the new political climate of the Arab Spring than any pressure from Spain or the EU, for which Morocco's role as a migratory barrier appears to be more significant than the imprisonment of a human rights activist or his inconvenient allegations that elements of the Moroccan state might be complicit in narcotics smuggling.[5] Whatever the truth of these allegations, the border has clearly been a very weak and even irrelevant instrument of prevention, which has ignored the internal demand that drives the drug trade in the first place and concentrated instead on a futile attempt to enforce prohibitions that have only made it more profitable and more amenable to corruption.

Human Traffic

The question of demand is also crucial to one of the most iniquitous expressions of the dark side of globalization—the trafficking of women and children for sexual exploitation. Trafficking and human smuggling are two very different activities, even if they are often confused or the terms are used interchangeably by the media and politicians. The United Nations defines trafficking as "the recruitment, transportation, transfer, harbouring or receipt of persons, by means of the threat or use of force or other forms of coercion."[6]

The European Union has played a leading role in trying to combat an industry whose annual profits have been estimated by the UN at $15.5 billion. In 2005 the Council of Europe adopted the first international antitrafficking convention, which urged states to develop "effective policies and programs to prevent trafficking in human beings" based on "the protection of victims' rights and the respect for human rights."[7]

The prevention of trafficking is routinely cited by European governments and law enforcement agencies as one of the most serious and dangerous expressions of cross-border crime and a major justification for tougher border enforcement. As in the case of narcotics, trafficking prevention tends to concentrate on cutting off sources of supply rather than on the demand that drives it. Reliable statistics on trafficking in Europe are not available, but the European Commission estimates that hundreds of thousands of people are trafficked into or within Europe for sexual exploitation or other forms of labor.[8] The people brought in for sexual exploitation include Nigerian women and adolescents psychologically cowed by *juju* or magic rituals to bind them to their traffickers, women from Ukraine, Moldova, or the Russian Federation, and other nationalities.

Many of these women are recruited to satisfy a demand for particular exotic nationalities in European brothels. Out of an estimated eight thousand sex workers in London, 80 percent are foreign women. In Spain, some 85 percent of prostitutes and call girls are foreign. In 2009 the English-language newspaper *Athens News* reported that up to twenty thousand foreign women, including a thousand girls between the ages of thirteen and fifteen, have been sold into the Greek sex industry, mostly from the Balkans and the former Soviet Union, and it claimed that "one million men—about 30 percent of the nation's sexually-active population—call on these women regularly."[9]

According to the UN-affiliated group ECPAT (End Child Prostitution and Trafficking), Malta is a "destination country for women and children trafficked for sexual purposes from Eastern European countries such as Ukraine, Russia and Romania."[10] Most women enter Malta on tourist visas, sometimes after having been purchased by Maltese pimps from Ukrainian gangsters. In some cases these women are resold to other pimps. It is impossible to know how many of the foreign women and girls who come to Europe to work in the sex industry fit the UN definition of trafficking, but there is no evidence that Europe's hardened borders have prevented or reduced such exploitation.

Trafficked women and minors generally cross Europe's borders legally, and often voluntarily, at least at first. Some victims may have no idea what is going to happen to them and may even be accompanied by their traffickers, or their families may have been threatened in order to keep them silent. Trafficking is a complex crime, but the border itself is an extremely ineffective means of detecting or preventing it. The detection of trafficking—and successful prosecution afterward—crucially depends on evidence from victims themselves, and such evidence is rarely elicited at the point of entry. Police officers from the Frontier Crime unit at the port of Dover told me that they rarely detect trafficking offenses, and that even when they do suspect that someone is being trafficked, it is often impossible to obtain sufficient evidence to act on these suspicions.

Even after entering Europe, there is often a discrepancy between the EU's commitment to a victim-centered approach to trafficking and its immigration enforcement agenda, since the fear of deportation can make victims reluctant to report their abuse and exploitation to the authorities. In 2010 the Anti-Trafficking Monitoring Group published a report on the U.K. government's implementation of the Council of Europe's Convention on Trafficking, which listed 130 trafficked individuals over a period of nine months who had not gone to the authorities mainly because of concerns about their immigration status. The authors criticized a new government monitoring scheme designed to identify trafficking victims, accusing it of "putting more emphasis on the immigration status of the presumed trafficked persons, rather than the alleged crime committed against them."[11]

The report also included some extracts from letters of rejection from UKBA and other authorities tasked with identifying trafficking victims, including one letter that informed its recipient, "You have highlighted numerous incidents of non-consensual sex . . . and some incidents of violence. Although this experiences [sic] are extremely unpleasant, it is considered that this treatment . . . does not amount to trafficking in your case." Another recipient was informed, "Even if it was accepted that you had been trafficked from . . . to the UK, and held against your will . . . it is not accepted that you currently qualify as a 'victim' of trafficking for the purposes of the Convention."

Such rejections did not suggest the victim-centered approach to trafficking that the Convention recommended. The hardening of Europe's borders may also have provided traffickers with another instrument of coercion and control over their victims. Within the limited set of choices available, some women may choose to sell themselves as sexual commodities in order to finance their migratory journeys to Europe. But women on the trans-Saharan trail may also become dependent for their survival on "companions of the road" who end up pimping them. Whether they are trafficked or smuggled, female migrants without documentation in Europe are often forced to choose between deportation and exploitation, and even women with passports may have them taken away by pimps, madams, and brothel owners in order to control them. One African woman told Médecins Sans Frontières in Morocco how every woman who arrives at the Algerian border city of Maghnia "becomes the property of whoever wants her; she can't refuse, she can't leave, everything is paid for with sex. Even if she is with her baby or child, every woman must go through the same thing."[12]

All this makes trafficking a complex crime, and dealing with it is a complicated and difficult task, but the evidence suggests that border enforcement does not make it any easier and that, far from protecting its victims, it may even have made their situation worse.

Europe's New Serfs

Border enforcement is an equally weak instrument in preventing exploitation in more mainstream economic activities. An estimated 5 million to 8 million non-European migrants work in Europe's informal or shadow economy, most of whom perform menial "3D" (dirty, dangerous, and difficult) jobs that Europeans have tended to avoid in recent years, such as on construction sites and in factories, food-processing plants, nursing homes, hotels, restaurants, and the agricultural sector.

In 2005 a report titled *Forced Labour and Migration to the UK*, commissioned by the Trades Union Congress, described an economic subworld that would not have been entirely unfamiliar to Dickens or Mayhew, in which agricultural workers were forced to work for starvation wages under threat of violence by armed gangs and overseers, asylum seekers worked "voluntarily" for NHS hospitals in Glasgow because they were not allowed to work legally, and foreign domestic servants and factory workers put in seventeen-hour shifts for well below the minimum wage.[13]

These "slavery-like conditions," the report argued, were facilitated by an unregulated employment chain that connected subcontractors and labor recruiters to mainstream employers, including National Health Service trusts and major florists and supermarkets—and also by the fear of deportation that was used as an instrument of control by employers who recruited these workers. In some cases employers retained the passports of their employees in order to withhold or cut their wages. In one incident, sixteen Chinese migrants worked sixteen-hour shifts for twenty days to fill a factory order. On completion of the contract they were denounced by the factory managers to immigration authorities and immediately deported—without being paid.

British governments have not been oblivious to such practices. On February 5, 2004, twenty-three undocumented Chinese cockle pickers drowned in treacherous tides at Morecambe Bay in the north of England while working at night in dangerous conditions. All of them had come from Fujian province of their own volition, but once in the United Kingdom they were entirely dependent on their Chinese gangmaster, who recruited them for a succession of poorly paid and unregulated jobs that culminated in their horrific deaths. This episode provoked a spasm of moral indignation that helped generate momentum for the Labour government's Gangmasters Licensing Act that year. But the condemnation of the gangmaster who controlled the cockle pickers tended to overshadow the broader amorality of an economic system that prioritizes labor flexibility at the expense of workers' rights.

Flexibility often translates into the state of permanent instability and insecurity that sociologists and economists call "precarity" or "precarization," and irregular migrants in Europe tend to occupy a particularly precarious position at the bottom of the economic pyramid.[14] Policies toward irregular migrant workers are not the same in every European country. Spain and Italy have both introduced periodic amnesties to allow limited numbers of migrants to get legal status. No U.K. government has dared propose a similar amnesty for the 618,000 irregular migrants believed to be in the country, for fear of being accused of "rewarding illegal behavior."

Spain is unique in Europe in that it provides access to health care and education to officially registered irregular migrants—albeit according to certain conditions that migrants are not always able to meet. Nor do all employers regard illegality as a competitive advantage. In some northern Italian cities local business associations have actively promoted the social and legal integration of migrant workers in order to ensure a more stable and reliable labor force. In Italy, as in Spain and France, some employers have supported regularization programs.[15]

But the availability of a cheap and flexible labor force will always be attractive to some employers, and there will always be workers willing to fill this demand and routes and channels to direct them to it. The result is that undocumented migrants find themselves in a lose-lose situation. Reviled by governments and the media for working illegally and regarded as a source of unfair economic competition because they sell their labor more cheaply than Europeans—even if the jobs they do are anathema to many Europeans— they are also likely to be resented by the local workforce for bringing wages down.

No European state has signed the UN International Convention for the Protection of the Rights of All Migrant Workers and Members of Their Families, which states that "migrant workers shall enjoy treatment not less favorable than that which applies to nationals of the State of employment in respect of remuneration" and also calls for the same equality in terms of other factors such as "overtime, hours of work, weekly rest, holidays with pay, safety, health, termination of the employment relationship."[16] As a result, Europe's undocumented workers often constitute a permanently marginalized and easily disposable source of labor whose illegality may transform them into economically desirable and even essential commodities, but who can never access the rights and privileges that are associated with national citizenship.

The Almerian Miracle

Sandwiched between the Alpujarra mountain range in southern Spain and the Mediterranean coast, the province of Almeria was once one of the poorest regions in the country. Much of it consists of desert and dry, rocky scrubland that resembles Arizona and which once made the region a favored low-budget location for spaghetti westerns. Until recently this arid landscape generated more emigrants proportionally than any other part of Spain. All this began to change from the early 1990s onward, when local farmers began importing the Dutch technique of intensive greenhouse production of fruit and vegetables that enabled the cultivation of multiple export crops even in winter.

The high yields generated by the "new Andalusian agriculture" transformed Almeria's economic fortunes. Almost overnight peasant farmers became rich by covering their holdings with plastic. Today some 115 square miles of the province are covered in greenhouses producing tomatoes, melons, peppers, and squash for the northern European market, and Almerian agricultural products constitute 50 percent of Andalusia's exports and 18 percent of the national total. In a labor-intensive agricultural season that requires some 45,000 workers at peak periods in the early spring, migrant workers from inside and outside the EU have increasingly taken on the role once occupied by Spanish *temporeros* or day laborers.

Moroccans, sub-Saharan Africans, Latin Americans, Romanians, and Asians all toil in the greenhouses, planting, pruning, harvesting, applying fertilizers and insecticides, and clearing the land at the end of each season in temperatures that reach subtropical levels in June. Though some Moroccan migrants have become legalized and have even become greenhouse farmers themselves, most of Almeria's migrants constitute a rural subproletariat that is physically present but legally invisible.

Many of them work in and around San Isidro, a featureless modern town of 35,000 on the coastal plain below Nijar. In the 1950s the Spanish novelist Juan Goytisolo wrote a celebrated account of the preindustrial poverty that he encountered in the Nijar region.[17] Today the plain around San Isidro is swathed in plastic greenhouses stretching from the sea to the foothills like a

Christo installation. When I visited the town in July 2010 the agricultural season was over, but migrant workers were a ubiquitous presence in the area, traveling back and forth on the bicycles that constitute an essential form of transport between the greenhouses.

All around the town African *sin papeles* sheltered from the searing heat or sat out in the street in the cooler evenings. Most had no work and there was little possibility of finding any until September. Spanish agricultural workers can claim unemployment benefits to tide them over these dead periods, but none of this was available to the migrants of San Isidro, who relied on support from their families, their meager savings, or charity.

All around the dirt roads and nameless avenues that divide the greenhouse cities of Almeria's *plasticultura*, migrant workers live in shared flats or abandoned cars, in abandoned barns and pigsties, in crude plastic shacks or *chabolas* hidden among the miles of dirt roads. On the main road leading into San Isidro six young Malians were living in an abandoned bungalow without toilets, water, or electricity, sharing three rooms filled with single beds and bicycles. All of them had come to Spain via the Sahara and the Mediterranean to work in the greenhouses, and now they were surviving on food packages a local nun brought them twice a month, and occasional work that paid about €20 a day—less than half the sum negotiated between employers and unions for the province.

The previous month two of them had made a verbal agreement with a local Spanish farmer to clear a 100-foot-long greenhouse in preparation for the planting season. The price agreed was €400 and the job took them a week, but when it was over the farmer gave them €200 on a take-it-or-leave-it basis. Not all farmers behave like this. There were those "with good hearts," the Malians said, who "treat you like a human being," but there was little recourse against employers who behaved differently.

On the other side of the town, some fifteen plastic shacks were scattered across a ravine behind a row of greenhouses, some which had generators and satellite discs. This semipermanent *chabola* settlement was inhabited by Moroccans, most of whom had papers and had gone back home for the summer holidays. I spoke to three young workers who had been unable to make the same journey because they had no papers. Like most of San Isidro's migrants, they were waiting out the dead season in these baking shacks.

All of them had come to Almeria for the same reason: higher wages and a chance to send money back home. "You go where the work is," one of them said. None of them wanted to live permanently in Spain, and they all expressed the same desire for a less restrictive system of work permits that would enable them to work in Spain for part of the year and then return to Morocco without losing the chance to come back when the agricultural season started again.

Some migrant workers have brought their families with them, but most are single men like these, without residence papers or work permits. Almeria also has a large population of female migrants from inside and outside the EU, some of whom work in the greenhouses. On the edge of a main road just outside San Isidro a former farmhouse has been transformed into a brothel where African women service a clientele that includes migrant workers, Spaniards, and—according to rumor—members of the police and Civil Guard.

The brothel's facilities were basic. A dirt compound led to a shabby fly-filled room with a television in the corner, where clients buy soft drinks before going into the back rooms. At its peak this rustic *puti-club* (whorehouse) employed up to thirty women of various nationalities, who could sometimes earn more money in a day than most migrant workers in the greenhouses made in a week. Now there were only five Nigerian women, one of whom looked to be in her late teens, and business was clearly not going well.

Beauty, an emaciated-looking twenty-two-year-old whose youth and looks were already falling short of her parents' expectations, told me that she and her three-year-old child had not eaten that day, and there was no reason to disbelieve her. It was impossible to know if she had been trafficked or whether she had "chosen" her profession. But whatever the circumstances that had brought Beauty to Spain, her defeated and demoralized expression suggested that her European dreams had turned very sour indeed.

Other women were doing better. In San Isidro I met Harima, a Moroccan woman in her twenties, who was living with her uncle and some other relatives in a rented bungalow just outside the town. She had come to Spain by *patera* less than three months before, leaving behind her eight-year-old son in her home village near Marrakesh. In Morocco, she said, she was lucky if she made €5 a day. In Spain she had already earned €35 a day picking strawberries near Huelva during the short season from May to June, and her fixed address was the first step toward getting a residence permit one day.

This was not an entirely unrealistic aspiration—at least not then. Tens of thousands of migrants have obtained legal status as a result of Spain's periodic amnesties, but many of Almeria's *sin papeles* have yet to benefit from such largesse. The coastal city of El Ejido lies half an hour south of the

Almerian capital. In 1996 its population was 47,227. Today the figure is almost double, and El Ejido has become the second-largest city in Almeria, an island of concrete, glass, and marble floating in an ocean of plastic. The city's newfound wealth is reflected in a proliferation of disproportionately large shopping malls, hypermarkets, and public squares, and the rows of giant fruit and vegetable warehouses and car dealers that constitute its outer perimeter.

Approximately 35 percent of the population of this soulless boomtown consists of foreigners from inside and outside the EU. Twenty-three thousand mostly Moroccan and sub-Saharan African migrants work in the greenhouses, including an estimated four thousand undocumented migrants living in shacks among the dense rows of greenhouses between the city and the sea. In February 2000 El Ejido became national news when the murder of a Spanish woman by a mentally disturbed Moroccan worker ignited a vicious anti-immigrant pogrom. For three days mobs of local Spaniards roamed the city armed with iron bars and baseball bats, burning Moroccan and African cars, shops, and cafés and beating up any *moros* (Moors) they encountered, in an explosion of racist violence that shocked the Spanish public.

More than a decade later, race relations in the city are still polarized. This situation has not been helped by El Ejido's right-wing former mayor Juan Enciso. A corrupt municipal despot who ran the city from 1991 to 2011 as his personal fiefdom, Enciso was imprisoned on charges of blackmail and money laundering in 2009, and remained in office after being released on bail until his defeat in municipal elections two years later. His attitude toward the city's immigrant population was once summed up by his assertion that "at eight in the morning there are never enough immigrants. At eight in the evening there are always too many of them."

To some extent El Ejido is an unusual, even unique place. Begoña Arroyo, a local social worker, calls it a "town without a memory" whose population consists almost entirely of recent arrivals without a coherent sense of community. But the marginalization of its migrant population is part of a wider pattern that has been repeated in other parts of Spain and Europe. In theory, employers who hire undocumented migrant workers in Spain are liable to fines, but more often than not the attentions of Spanish officialdom have been directed at their employees.

In August 2006 the Nijar authorities demolished an abandoned greenhouse outside San Isidro and evicted the five hundred Africans who were living there. In the spring of 2010, Spanish farmers from the province of

Huelva in western Andalusia were actively recruiting strawberry pickers from Senegal because they did not have enough workers for the harvest. No sooner had the picking season ended in June than dozens of these workers were evicted by police from their shacks, because the local farmers association claimed that their presence was damaging the industry's image.

Italy's Zones of Precarity

These conditions are not unique to Spain. In southern Italy sub-Saharan African workers are recruited each year to work in the Mafia-dominated fruit-picking industry, where they are often housed in abandoned shacks and houses without water or electricity. In January 2010 African migrant workers in the Calabrian town of Rosarno rioted in protest at these conditions. In response, local youths, some of whom were connected to Calabrian Mafia bosses, shot at them and attacked them with iron bars. When the Italian police intervened to quell the disturbances, all 1,300 migrants were arrested and deported, but the following year many of them came back to work in the same conditions.

The exploitation and marginalization of Italy's migrant workers are not limited to the Chinese sweatshop labor depicted in *Gomorrah*, Roberto Saviano's coruscating indictment of the Naples Camorra, or the Mafia badlands of the Mezzogiorno. With its elegant Renaissance porticos and creamy stone palazzos, its statues, museums, and sculptures, the city of Brescia in Lombardy embodies all the historical and cultural riches that attract so many tourists to the Italian north. The province of Brescia is also home to an estimated 200,000 non-EU immigrants, who constitute some 16 percent of the city's population—the highest percentage of any Italian city. Most live in the modern periphery of the city, where they work in the small and medium-sized factories that once laid the basis for the Italian economic miracle or *sorpasso,* in construction and agriculture, or as domestic servants and caregivers for the elderly.

Many of Brescia's migrants have residence permits as a result of the Italian government's periodic amnesties, but thousands have no legal papers. Since residence permits are dependent on the possession of a work contract, even legalized migrants can slip into irregularity if they become unemployed for more than six months. Nadeem Hussain arrived in Italy from Pakistan on a boat from Greece as a seventeen-year-old in 1996. Today he has a residence permit and runs a kebab and pizza takeout shop in the town of Gavardo, near Lake Garda, where he also works as an official for the CGIL trade union. Nadeem is married and his two children were born in Italy, but after fifteen years he cannot vote, and he could lose his right to remain in Italy if his businesses went under. "I feel part of Italian society, but Italian society doesn't feel the same way about me," he says, "but if I had to go back to Pakistan, I wouldn't know what to do with myself."

Both legal and illegal immigrants in Brescia have also been exposed to the segregationist and anti-immigration politics of the Northern League. In 2009 the Northern League council of Coccaglio in Brescia province launched a campaign that it called "White Christmas," which called for the identification and expulsion of all illegal immigrants from the town. In March 2010 the Northern League wrested control of the Brescia city council from its bookish mayor, Paolo Corsini. A Catholic intellectual with communist convictions and a fervent integrationist, Corsini saw his administration brought down by a typically xenophobic Northern League campaign that blamed the city's immigrants for crime and unemployment.

Flushed with their victory, Northern League councils enacted a series of discriminatory anti-immigrant *ordinanzas* across the province. In some towns immigrants were banned from speaking their own languages in public places, and local councils began compiling lists of houses where immigrants were living in order to conduct regular "sanitary inspections" that were essentially a justification for police harassment. In September that year the mayor of the town of Adro ordered the League's Alpine-sun logo plastered all over a local school, and stipulated that pork should be a compulsory ingredient of school lunches—a measure that was specifically aimed at the school's Muslim children. In the town of Gavardo, near Lake Como, the Northern League–dominated town council ordered the removal of all of the town's public benches, where many Pakistani and Moroccan immigrants often congregated.

The Northern League's attempts to enact a de facto apartheid in Brescia reflect wider tensions in an Italian society that has increasingly come to rely on migrant workers from inside and outside the EU but which remains reluctant to accept or acknowledge its new ethnic diversity. On one hand, Italy has gone further than many European countries in granting six amnesties that have enabled undocumented workers to get legal status. But these amnesties generally fail to acknowledge the number of irregular workers in the country.

In 2007, Italy announced an annual quota of work permits for *non comunitari* that would be limited in the first year to 170,000. But in 2008 there were approximately 800,000 applications for such permits from employers—most of which were made for the estimated 670,000 irregular migrants or *irregolari* already in the country. Not only did these new quotas mean that the majority of irregular migrants in Italy would not get legal status, but those who did were replaced by new ones coming in.

In effect, Italy's amnesties have become a kind of lottery, which are conditional on the permanent presence of a large undocumented population. In September 2009, the Italian government introduced the sixth of its periodic amnesties for undocumented workers. Though thousands of domestic workers and caregivers gained legal status as a result, many others paid up to €3,500 to unscrupulous middlemen who promised to get them the work contracts and papers required for residence permits, then took their money and vanished. These partial and often clumsy and unregulated amnesties have been accompanied by the persistent vilification of Italy's *irregolari* from the Berlusconi/Northern League government. Following the 2008 elections, Berlusconi announced a crackdown on Italy's "army of evil" and took the unprecedented step of deploying four thousand soldiers on the streets of major cities in order "to fight crime, stem illegal immigration and defend terrorist targets." In July 2009 the Italian parliament approved a new "security law" that made illegal immigration a crime, punishable with fines of up to €10,000 and six months in detention before expulsion. The law also made it a criminal offense to "aid and abet clandestinity" by providing health care or employment to undocumented workers, and introduced a three-year prison sentence for anyone housing illegal immigrants.

All this has pushed Italy's 600,000 irregular migrants further to the margins. In December 2010, five migrants climbed a crane above Brescia's new light railway line in protest at their continued illegality. All of them had paid €500 to the state during the 2009 *sanatoria truffa* or "fraud amnesty" in the hope that they would able to get legal status. For seventeen days they lived and slept on the arm of the crane in an audacious protest that divided Brescia and transfixed Italian society.

In March the following year I met Haroun, a young Pakistani and one of the organizers of the Brescia protest. Haroun had lived illegally in Italy for years, and he and his fellow protesters had all paid the €500 fee to the state and even larger sums to middlemen during the 2009 amnesty, in the hope of obtaining the coveted *permesso di soggiorno*, but none of them had received it.

Before going up the crane he and his comrades had spent weeks camped outside the Brescia city hall in protest, but the authorities ignored them.

In the end they agreed to come down from the crane after the government promised to consider their demands. But nearly four months later, their situation remained unchanged and Haroun and his friends were considering further action to make their voices heard. "We don't have an army or anything to protest with," he said. "But if they don't give us our rights, then we'll go up the crane again."

Elsewhere in Europe migrants have been forced to undertake equally dramatic protests in an attempt to win their political and civil rights. The Brescia protest was modeled on a similar demonstration in 2008, when more than forty migrants climbed cranes across Brussels to demand ninety-day residence permits from the Belgian government. In May 2010 hundreds of mostly North African *travailleurs sans papiers* (workers without papers) occupied the steps of the Bastille Opera House in Paris and called upon the French government to create a clear path toward legal status for the estimated 400,000 undocumented migrants in France. Bearing a large banner proclaiming "We live here, we work here, we're staying here," the strikers remained camped out until October 10, when the Sarkozy government agreed to some of their demands.

In November 2010 five migrants in Milan climbed a disused smokestack and remained there for two weeks with a banner calling for a general amnesty for Italy's migrants. Increasingly, it seemed, the only way for Europe's illegal immigrants to escape their invisibility was to climb to a place where they could not be ignored or dismissed as criminals, security threats, or "victims of trafficking," and demand that the societies that had recruited and employed them accept their right not just to work in Europe but also to live in it.

10

Hands Across the Border

Let us dream of Europe . . . a space clearly defined by the way in which it successfully distils the dynamism of creation, the need for solidarity and protection of the poorest and weakest.

—Valéry Giscard d'Estaing, 2002

On a muggy evening in June 2010 more than a hundred Turkish and foreign demonstrators converged on a four-story brownstone building in the working-class backstreets of Istanbul's touristic Sultan Ahmet district. The Kumkapi detention center is one of Turkey's designated "foreigner guest houses," and it is occupied almost exclusively by undocumented migrants intercepted en route to Europe or deported back from Greece. For more than an hour, the demonstrators chanted slogans in Turkish, English, and French: "Libere" (the Turkish word for freedom), "Open the door—free migrants," "No borders—stop deportations," and "Solidarité avec les sans-papiers!"

A contingent of armed Turkish police watched over the scene but did not intervene, perhaps because of the presence of foreigners from the European Social Forum (a migrant rights network) and the presence of TV cameras. The detainees pressed their faces against the barred windows, shouting and dropping burning pieces of paper to indicate their appreciation. In a few weeks or even days many of them would be deported to the countries they had come from, to be replaced by others, but for two hours the bond between the anonymous detainees and the crowd gathered outside was palpable.

This powerful demonstration took place in what was a very bad year for Europe's unwanted migrants. The tone was set in January by the pogrom in

Rosarno and the beginning of the police offensive against the migrants of Calais. In April the Catalan city of Vic voted to deny undocumented migrants access to health care and education. In August random identity checks on migrants and police harassment of African *manteros* (street vendors) had become so frequent that the U.S. State Department took the unusual step of warning African American travelers to Spain to expect police attention—a warning that caused some embarrassment in a month in which Michelle Obama and her children visited Andalusia for their vacation.

In the autumn rising anti-immigrant violence in the streets of Athens was matched by a new police offensive against the migrant camps in Igoumenitsa. Even in traditionally tolerant Sweden the extreme-right Sweden Democrats entered the Swedish parliament for the first time in September. In November Swedish police arrested a thirty-eight-year-old man for a series of random shootings of immigrants in the city of Malmö. In October the Birmingham City Council withdrew from a five-year contract with the U.K. Border Agency to provide housing to asylum seekers because its properties were needed for "our own people."

Throughout that year there was another response to Europe's migrants that was generally less visible. In February 2010, the recently formed migrant solidarity group in Igoumenitsa delivered food, clothes, and blankets to the migrants living in the hills. Many of the migrants had spent that winter in subzero temperatures in summer clothes, without receiving any help or support from anyone, and when the distribution was over, they spontaneously applauded the Greeks who had come to help them, in what one member of the group later described to me as "one of the most beautiful moments in my life."

On March 1, more than 300,000 migrants and Italians in more than sixty Italian cities took part in a one-day national strike to protest the marginalization of Italy's immigrant population, under the slogan "One day without us." The protest was organized by a group of Italian women through Facebook and modeled on similar protests in France and the United States. For twenty-four hours migrants and their supporters withdrew their children from school and stopped working, shopping, and using telephones or public services in order to show their contribution to Italian society.[1]

In Brescia in November, hundreds of migrants and Italians, including trade unionists and representatives of more than forty Catholic associations, turned out to support the migrant crane protest. For seventeen days these supporters maintained a constant presence, providing food and water to the migrants camped out on the arm. The broad-based movement was united by the catchphrase "Siamo tutti sulla gru"—we are all on the crane.

"Solidarity" is a word that often appears in official EU documents and policy declarations, usually in the context of collaboration between member states in dealing with crises and emergencies or as a defining principle in Europe's relationships with the developing world. European governments also describe pan-European border enforcement operations as acts of solidarity and "burden sharing."

Across the continent and beyond it, however, a heterogeneous constellation of individuals and organizations has demonstrated a different kind of solidarity with migrants themselves. The scope of these activities is too broad to be encompassed in a single chapter, but at a time when so many European governments are intent on pulling up the drawbridge and reasserting the divisions between foreigners and "our people," and when immigrants are increasingly scapegoated for a crisis they did not cause, it is useful—and perhaps essential—to consider the actions and motivations of some of those who have responded differently.

Affirming the Human

As a political and moral issue, migration has a remarkable ability to attract people from a very wide spectrum of political persuasions and backgrounds, and solidarity with migrants encompasses many activities. For some people it means volunteer work in soup kitchens or collecting food parcels for destitute asylum seekers. There are organizations that work alongside governments and provide support and assistance to migrants in detention, and others that are radically opposed to the principle of detention and the whole concept of immigration controls. Some organizations work exclusively with asylum seekers and refugees. Others campaign for the rights of all migrants, regardless of their motivation. In France the national parents' network Education Sans Frontières (Education Without Borders) campaigns for the children of *sans-papiers* to attend school.

All these individuals and organizations share the same underlying determination to "affirm the human" that Bea Tobolewska, the manager of the Nottingham and Nottinghamshire Refugee Forum, defined to me as the guiding principle behind her work with refugees. Jacky Verhaegen is the legal adviser and jack-of-all trades in Calais for Secours Catholique, the French branch of the Catholic development organization Caritas. With his ponytail, pointy-toed boots, and cigarette constantly in hand, Verhaegen is not the most obvious representative of a Catholic charity. A former social worker, he first began working with migrants at the Sangatte center for another local NGO, La Belle Etoile.

Whenever I saw him at the food distribution center, he was surrounded by migrants, whose problems he did his best to solve. Every day he and his assistants drive an average of sixty migrants back and forth across the city to shower, providing them with soap and towels. Though not a Christian himself, he shares with Caritas a common commitment to "humanism" and a desire "to make the world better and do as much as we can to help people who are in need."

Most people who have become involved with solidarity work with Europe's migrants share this aspiration. On October 27, 2003, Rafael Quiroz and his wife, Violeta Cuesta, two teachers from the town of Rota near Cádiz, Spain, discovered the corpses of thirty-seven migrants on a beach not far from their home. None of the bodies carried any documentation, but with the help of an *El País* journalist, Quiroz and Cuesta found out that twelve of the migrants came from Hansala, a small Berber village in the impoverished Beni Mellal region of Morocco.

In December Quiroz and Cuesta traveled with three companions to the village, where they were offered tea by a group of local residents, some of whose sons had died at Rota. They later recalled:

> One of the fathers of the deceased told us how one day, two months before, he had come home from work at night, and noticed that his son had left his books in his cupboard. He asked his wife what was happening and why his son's study materials were there but he wasn't and she explained that he had gone to Tangier to get a *patera*. Since then, the father explained, he had not opened the cupboard, he didn't dare. The other father explained to us that life is like these cups of tea, that it can fall through a slip of the hand and it's over. That was what had happened to their children, who Allah had taken away in an instant. In that moment we were so overwhelmed that we began to cry. No one laughed at us, they just watched us with sadness and respect. They knew why we were crying.[2]

On returning to Spain, Quiroz, Cuesta, and their colleagues raised money to send the bodies back to Hansala and attended their funerals. They then established an NGO called Solidaridad Directa (Direct Solidarity) to help improve conditions in the village. Since then more than one hundred people from Rota have made more than fourteen visits to Hansala during the school holidays and raised money to finance a dispensary in the village, a new irrigation system, and an upgrade to the local school building. All this has been done without any official assistance, by ordinary people acting entirely on their own initiative.

Quiroz and Cuesta are Gandhian pacifist activists who were already engaged in peace education work before this shipwreck on their own doorstep galvanized them to trace its origins on the other side of the border. But people with no political or activist history have also been drawn into Europe's migratory drama. Michael Moore, an American engineering student I met in Calais, became a volunteer worker with a local soup kitchen after witnessing the conditions in which migrants were living in the city. Others have campaigned against the deportation of people they have known as friends, classmates, workmates, pupils, or neighbors.

In 2005 seven Glasgow schoolchildren launched a successful local campaign to prevent the deportation of one of their friends, who had been arrested with her family during an immigration dawn raid. The "Glasgow girls" became seasoned national campaigners and visited the Scottish Parliament, where they challenged the Scottish first minister on the Labour government's policy on immigration dawn raids.

In 2000, José Nanclares Mendía, a retiree in the town of San Isidro in Almería, learned that one of his daughter's friends and schoolmates, a fifteen-year-old Moroccan girl named Rachida el Fallaki, had been thrown out of her house by her Moroccan stepmother after her father left Spain and returned to Morocco. Rachida had lived in Spain for twelve years, and even though she had no residence permit she was legally entitled to state support as an abandoned minor, but the Spanish authorities announced that she was to be repatriated to Morocco as an illegal immigrant.

Before his retirement, Nanclares worked as a furniture salesman and had a mobile cinema; he had no history of political activism or engagement. But, shocked by his government's ruthless treatment of a girl he regarded as an adopted daughter, the sixty-nine-year-old began a one-man campaign to prevent the deportation.

Despite his efforts, Rachida was taken to Melilla that summer, escorted in handcuffs to the border, and abandoned on the other side of the fence. Nanclares traveled to Melilla and with the help of José Palazón from the children's rights association Prodein managed to get Rachida back into Melilla, where Palazón found her a temporary place to stay. Nanclares also wrote an impassioned plea to King Juan Carlos asking him to intercede in the affair. Astonishingly, the king acceded to this petition from an unknown retiree, and in 2002 Rachida was allowed to return to the mainland.

Today she lives in Málaga with her partner and baby, and Nanclares continues to live in his humble *cortijo* (farmhouse), with his run-down car, his collection of dusty film reels, his constantly expanding population of cats and dogs, and his letter from the king. As the president of Prodein in Almeria, he still helps the destitute migrants who occasionally turn up on his doorstep, and he campaigns for the rights of children, the disabled, and undocumented workers in the greenhouses, continuing to wage a lone crusade against injustice that began with his refusal to accept the exclusion of a girl who the local authorities regarded as just one more deportable immigrant.

Solidarity at the Border

Firsthand experience of the harsh realities of immigration enforcement is often a decisive factor in motivating people to take action against the exclusionary policies of their governments, and these consequences are often particularly visible at Europe's hardened borders. In 1998 José Palazón was the director of three private academies in Melilla that prepared the city's public sector workers for their civil service exams. That year he and his wife, Maite, were walking their dog on the beach when they discovered an eleven-year-old Moroccan boy living under a trash bin. The boy had crossed the border fence as an unaccompanied minor three years before and had been sleeping rough in the city ever since.

Palazón and his wife befriended the boy and eventually became his legal guardians. Galvanized by this chance encounter, Palazón established the children's rights association Prodein to campaign on behalf of other street children in Melilla. Prodein subsequently widened its activities to include adult migrants passing through the city, and Palazón went on to become an uncompromising and outspoken critic of Spanish and Moroccan government policy. Palazón is gaunt and middle-aged, with a passing resemblance to the French actor Jean Reno, and his soft, mumbling voice and sardonic wit belie a fierce indignation at his government's treatment of migrants, an anger that is not moderated by tact or diplomatic niceties.

His criticisms have not made him popular in his home city. The Melilla local administration has issued various lawsuits against him for defaming the city and its officials, without success. One former mayor of the city declared Palazón an "enemy of Melilla" and accused him of smuggling unaccompanied minors across the frontier. His contract with the Melilla authorities to prepare candidates for the civil service exam has been terminated and his schools have been whittled down to a few dilapidated classrooms in the city center, none of which has prompted him to moderate his criticisms.

Solidarity with Europe's migrants also extends beyond the continent's borders. In Uzhgorod, the Border Monitoring Project Ukraine (BMPU) is staffed by five women, most of whom are volunteers, and came into existence as a specific response to the unexpected emergence of the city as a migrant bottleneck on Europe's eastern border. The Association Beni Znassen for Culture, Development, and Solidarity (ABCDS) in Oujda was founded in 2005 by a group of students from the university there who wanted to do something to improve their neighborhood, which was known as "Vietnam" because of its poverty and drug-related crime.

The ABCDS began to focus on migration following Morocco's mass deportations from the migrant camps at Ceuta and Melilla that year. Today it has more than three hundred members. In addition to social and cultural activism in Oujda itself, it collects food and clothing for the migrants and campaigns internationally to draw attention to their situation. The driving force behind the ABCDS is its president, Hicham Baraka, a thirty-year-old former drama student and Samuel Beckett fan with a pale complexion and a babyish, slightly Asian face, known as the "white chairman" to the migrants in the forest camps.

Whether heading to the border in the middle of the night to try to prevent deportations, transporting migrants to and from the hospital in emergencies, taking food to the forest camps, or arbitrating disputes between different ethnic groups, Baraka has been a tireless and relentless advocate of migrant rights in Oujda.

At their sparsely furnished offices near the headquarters of the local gendarmerie, Baraka and his colleagues showed me photographs of migrants playing soccer in an "Africa Cup" tournament that they had organized recently at the university campus to help raise their morale. Another room was piled high with clothes and blankets collected mostly from poor neighborhoods. The ABCDS has also become a prominent international critic of Europe's border controls. Its ultimate aim, according to Mohammed Talbi, a local businessman and one of the association's co-founders, is "to put human rights at the heart of migration," taking its inspiration from Article 13 in the UN Declaration of Human Rights, which declares that everyone has the right to leave his or her country.

Many solidarity organizations share the same human rights perspective on migration. In 2008 Turkish human rights lawyers and activists in Izmir formed Multecilerle Dayanism Demegi (Multeci Der, or Association for Solidarity with Refugees) in response to the transformation of their city into a staging point for migrants heading for Greece. In its mission statement, Multeci Der proudly proclaims that providing assistance to refugees is "not 'burden sharing' but 'honor sharing' on behalf of humanity." In a country that has not generally been well disposed toward refugees, its activists have often swum against the tide in their attempts to lobby state institutions and officials on behalf of Turkey's migrants.

Multeci Der has also tried to change attitudes among the Turkish public through awareness-raising activities, such as the innovative *kayiki* (kayak) campaign conducted in collaboration with Greek NGOs in 2008, which highlighted the issue of migrant deaths at sea with posters and videos under the slogan "Migration and asylum are not a crime—we're all in the same boat."

Like the ABCDS, Multeci Der does not distinguish between political refugees and economic migrants. "The border between them is very weak," says its director, Piril Ercoban, at Multeci Der's offices above the mammoth Salepcioglu shopping mall in Izmir, "so we cannot really say, 'Okay, this is an asylum seeker and refugee and this one is not,' because it is sort of inter-twined." Ercoban listed various universal rights that she considered to be applicable to all migrants, regardless of their motivations. These include the right to freedom of movement (contained in the UN Declaration of Human Rights), rights to education, health, privacy, and liberty, and the right to work. Many of these rights are not guaranteed for migrants in Turkey—or Europe—and without any legal mechanisms for enforcing them, NGOs such as Multeci Der have a limited ability to influence governments that are often more concerned with removing or deterring migrants and which often regard human rights as an impediment to this agenda.

NGOs and solidarity organizations are often obliged to play an ambiguous and difficult role in Europe's immigration wars. In some cases they work alongside governments and are only allowed to operate with government approval. NGOs may also find themselves providing humanitarian assistance that would normally be the prerogative of the state, but which governments prefer not to acknowledge or take credit for. As a result, some organizations may be able to do little more than mitigate the worst consequences of repression and exclusion, which in turn helps to conceal these consequences from the general public.

Médecins Sans Frontières has been a ubiquitous protagonist in Europe's immigration wars for more than a decade, whether providing migrants with medical attention and psychological counseling in detention centers or setting up mobile field clinics in migrant camps and settlements in more remote places. "Some people have a political agenda," says the former head of MSF's mission in Morocco, Jorge Martín. "We're not pro-migrant or anti-migrant; we simply believe that people's basic rights should be respected."

The question of the basic rights of migrants is rarely a politically neutral issue, since it raises wider issues regarding the definition of such rights and the question of who is responsible for ensuring and protecting them. MSF has published some stinging reports on the treatment of migrants in Morocco and also in Italy, Greece, and Malta. But the notion of universal human rights that transcend or override national prerogatives and the rights of states is a relatively recent development, which has always been at odds with the priorities of immigration enforcement.

In principle, all European governments share a common commitment to such rights and are obliged by various treaties to uphold them. No government would reject these rights outright, but many governments have been determined to ensure that these rights do not limit their ability to enforce their immigration restrictions. This enforcement agenda has consistently created situations in which such rights are weakened or conspicuously absent, either as a result of deliberate policy or through the creation of vague areas of jurisdiction.

The Office of the United Nations High Commissioner for Refugees is the highest-profile international organization involved in European migration. Its work consists primarily of capacity-building efforts to help governments, police, and border officials improve their asylum screening procedures, and monitoring activities at migratory hot spots such as Greece and Calais in an attempt to separate "genuine" refugees from economic migrants and ensure that the former get state protection. "Our position is not that Europe should suddenly open the borders to anyone who wants to come here," explains William Spindler, UNHCR's spokesman in Calais. "Governments do have the right to control their borders and decide on their own immigration policies. But we insist that the case of refugees is something special."

Spindler is not oblivious to the difficulties in establishing such hard-and-fast distinctions. Nevertheless, he insists, "We don't believe that immigration is a right. We don't believe that people have the right to go and live wherever they want. But asylum is a right, a basic universal human right." There is no doubt that UNHCR's authority and expertise can be helpful and even essential to refugees seeking protection in Europe, and its recommendations and its criticisms are imbued with a special moral authority that governments cannot easily ignore. But its exclusive emphasis on "genuine" refugees can sometimes place UNHCR in an uncomfortable position when dealing with the mixed flows that characterize irregular migration in Europe.

Since 2009 UNHCR has had a permanent office in Calais that provides assistance and advice to the French government on how to improve its asylum screening procedures, and it also advises migrants seeking asylum on how to access such protection. But these efforts have taken place against the background of a campaign of police repression aimed at removing all migrants from the city, regardless of their motivations. One morning I watched Spindler and the UNHCR Calais officer, Maureen McBrien, remonstrating with the deputy mayor, while police and council employees in white overalls took blankets from migrants who had just been evicted from the winter shelter.

Given its remit, there is not much that UNHCR could have done to persuade the authorities to behave any differently. But it was a reminder that when states place their own priorities first, then moral pressure will not be enough to stop them, and even the world's most prestigious humanitarian organization may be able to do little more than stand back and watch.

"The Border Is the Problem"

UNHCR's close relationship with governments has not made the organization popular with the more radical opponents of European immigration policy, such as the anticapitalist network No Borders. A loose formation of activists rather than a structured hierarchical organization, No Borders is a militant protagonist in Europe's border wars, whether setting up annual international "No Borders camps" near detention centers, monitoring police repression or Frontex operations, or staging concerts and political film shows for migrants in various countries.

No Borders has been especially active in Calais since the demolition of the Sangatte "Jungle" in September 2009. A constant stream of mostly young international volunteers has passed through the city to document the ongoing police repression, and they take the concept of solidarity very seriously indeed. When I was in the city they were a constant presence around the winter shelter in the Rue Moscou and the other migrant camps and squats. They ate with migrants and sometimes slept in their squats in order to monitor police raids and try to reduce their severity. They provided tarpaulins and plastic sheets for migrants to sleep under. They photographed police arrests and pursued police vans to the police station and the detention center at Coquelles. They also played music and staged impromptu parties to cheer the migrants up, and provided language and art classes in their squats. Often they would turn up outside squats first thing in the morning, linking arms outside the entrance to prevent the CRS from entering, and sometimes taking beatings in the process.

Not surprisingly, the police detested them and regarded them as violent anarchist agitators. No Borders activists were not always popular with local NGOs or migrants themselves, some of whom thought that their activities antagonized the police. As far as I could see, the police needed no prompting for an offensive that had already been decided upon, but it was also obvious that No Borders had a broader political agenda that was not limited to helping migrants cross the Channel.

In the spring of 2010 I spoke to Mara and Katerina, two members of the German No Borders contingent, in a café in the city center. A social worker in Frankfurt, Mara become involved with No Borders when she discovered how difficult it was for her South American boyfriend to come to Europe. This was her second visit to a city that she described as a "crystallization of things that are happening on the global scene."

Katerina was a biology student who had only just become involved in the network. She had borrowed her mom's car to drive her friends to Calais, and she was about to return home. In the last few days she had tried to organize a hunger strike and driven back and forth to the Coquelles detention center, and her voice was hoarse from the flu she had contracted while sleeping in the basement at Africa House, but she was exhilarated and inspired by her first encounter with the migrants of Calais.

Both women saw Europe's antimigrant traps as an expression of global inequality and injustice. "It depends on where you were born whether you can move and where you can't, and that's just not fair," Katerina said. "And also we know that rich countries are using the resources of poor countries that can't really organize themselves because they aren't powerful enough."

They also rejected UNHCR's qualitative distinction between refugees and economic migrants. "We think that everyone should have the right to go where he or she wants to," Mara said. "If someone wants to go to England, it doesn't matter if it's because of war or because they fall in love with someone."

For her, the kind of solidarity offered by No Borders was different from what the other organizations in Calais provided, since "the NGOs are interested in helping and that's not our main focus. We want to show solidarity and help the people to help themselves." Did they really believe a world without borders was a possibility? "It will be a mess," Katerina said, "but I think it's better than what we have now." Both women agreed that the abolition of national borders would have to be accompanied by efforts to improve conditions in the countries that migrants come from—an objective that many governments and border guards I had spoken to also agreed on—and both seemed to see the notion of "no borders" as a guiding principle and a metaphor rather than a concrete project. "I personally think it's a utopia and I don't think it will happen in the next few years," Mara said. "I think it's a good idea to work on, but I can't imagine how it will be practically."

No Borders is one of a number of often overlapping networks that have sprung up across Europe that have a broadly anticapitalist and/or antiracist orientation and a similar belief that "the border is the problem," as the Greek network Welcome to Europe puts it. Caminando Fronteras, or Walking Borders, is a group of activists, filmmakers, journalists, and scholars based in Spain, whose membership extends from Europe to Morocco, Libya, and Mali. "We aren't a typical NGO," explains Helena Malena Garzón, one of its founders, in a Tangier café. "We like to imitate the networks created by migrants themselves, forming and dissolving them, depending on the situation."

This modus operandi was already evident in the autumn of 2005, when she became personally involved in the "crisis of the fences" in Ceuta and Melilla. She was woken up in the early hours of the morning in her flat in Madrid by a phone call from an African migrant friend at the fence in Ceuta, who told her that he and his companions were being shot at. Hearing the shots and the insults of the Civil Guard in the background, Garzón immediately alerted the UNHCR representative in Madrid, and the next day she traveled to Morocco with two companions to monitor the situation.

When the Moroccan government began its mass deportations of migrants from the hillsides around Ceuta and Melilla, the three activists drove out into the disputed territory of Western Sahara administered by Morocco in an attempt to monitor the movements of the deportees. In the course of this journey, they had a serious car crash in which two of her companions were seriously injured. Still bleeding, they were arrested by the Moroccan police and summarily deported back to Spain.

Today Garzón lives in Tangier and continues to work closely with migrant networks, particularly from sub-Saharan Africa. Her organization provides them with humanitarian assistance and works alongside other human rights organizations to bring the migrants' situation to the attention of the wider world. Like No Borders, Caminando Fronteras couples practical solidarity work with a radical critique of the policies and attitudes behind the exclusion of migrants. "There's a political discourse behind migration that interests us," Garzón says, "in the reasons why migrants left their countries and why they come here, breaking down and destroying borders, and with these points in common we work together to help realize our common aspirations."

For Garzón, "borders are the construction of an economic system that moves borders from one place to another depending on its interests, which open for one kind of immigrant and close for another." These ideas are heavily influenced by the Italian political scientist Sandro Mezzadra, for whom Europe's "migration regime" consists of selectively permeable barriers in which "each attempt to seal the borders will be accompanied by a series of exceptions" in response to specific labor needs and requirements. Even the name Caminando Fronteras is a play on words suggesting both the people who cross borders and Mezzadra's concept of "post-national border control" based on the "continuous undoing and re-composing of borders and boundaries." In Mezzadra's view, Europe's "deterritorialised" borders are simultaneously instruments of a "new apartheid" and sites of "battles for justice" where "incarcerated" migrants from the global South challenge their exclusion through their unauthorized crossings.[3]

Many of the support groups and networks that fall within the "no borders" framework share the belief that a borderless world is not only desirable but inevitable, and the same insistence, as Welcome to Europe puts it, that "the right of freely roaming the globe has to be fought for everywhere." For Gerardo Márquez, an Argentine member of the Casa Invisible (Invisible House) alternative arts collective in Málaga, which works closely with the Coordinadora de Inmigrantes de Málaga (Málaga Immigrants Coordinating Committee), both the repression and exploitation of Europe's migrants are part of a "Machiavellian exploitation game" that is being played in Spain and across the whole of Europe. I spoke to him in the splendid abandoned palace that the Invisible House has taken over in the center of the city, where its committee was planning the group's participation in Spain's first general strike under the Socialist government in the autumn of 2010.

Marquez sees Spain's migrants as victims of a "brutal regression" that is taking place across Europe and pushing both migrants and Europeans deeper into poverty and a common state of "absolute precarity." In this "stairway in which everyone goes down," the continent's financial elites have a common interest in promoting a struggle "between the poor and the poor." Like Mezzadra, he argues that "borders are not just territorial. There are many borders within every city, within every neighborhood, and we want to break down these borders and recognize ourselves as human beings."

Samaritans

Not everyone sees migrants as the de facto foot soldiers of a borderless world and an anticapitalist revolution. Whatever their political orientation, most organizations working with migrants find themselves involved in the practical tasks of helping people survive in extremely adverse circumstances, and churches have played a leading role in these activities. Numerous passages in the Bible refer to the need to welcome strangers and outsiders, and Christians of all denominations have applied these obligations to Europe's unwanted migrants. With his flowing robes, blue eyes, graying beard, and long black hair, Papa Stratis, the parish priest in the town of Kalloni on the island of Lesvos, is a striking and imposing figure who would not be entirely out of place in a novel by Kazantzakis or Dostoevsky, apart from the ever-present cigarettes and mobile phone.

Papa Stratis is the founder of a local NGO named Agayá (meaning "Hugging" or "Embracing"), which provides clothes, food, and medical assistance to migrants arriving on Lesvos. Initially created with the help of some of his parishioners as a spontaneous gesture, Agayá now works alongside a church NGO in Athens, and its warehouse is filled with new clothes, shoes, toys, and blankets, many of which have been donated by companies rather than individuals.

Such generosity is not universal in these islands. On the island of Patmos, the local council, with the support of much of the population, once turned back more than a hundred people who had been rescued from a shipwrecked boat off a nearby island. Why did Papa Stratis and his parishioners act differently? "I feel that our NGO is only doing what the Bible says we should be doing," he said.

Papa Stratis was prone to flights of biblical rhetoric and often referred to the religious imperative to welcome the "naked" refugees who came to Lesvos and the essential unity of human beings as divine creations from the womb to the grave. He is also a canny politician. When I asked if he thought that Greek officials on Lesvos were also operating according to the laws of the Bible, he replied diplomatically, "These officials are doing what their jobs tell them to do, but I'm a priest and I'm doing what God tells me to do. God says we should be compassionate and caring toward people, and since God loves all people, why shouldn't we?"

Not all members of the church are so willing to render unto Caesar, and the biblical imperative to welcome strangers does not preclude vigorous criticism of the policies that make such assistance necessary. Father Dionysius Mintoff is a Franciscan monk, brother of the former Maltese prime minister Dom Mintoff, and an outspoken critic of Malta's harsh treatment of undocumented migrants. In addition to providing homes for migrants, Father Mintoff has campaigned vigorously against Malta's detention and deportation policies in a country where the mainstream church has been largely silent on these issues. Before he became involved with the island's migrants, he was better-known for his work as a pacifist educator with the Peace Laboratory, which he founded in the early 1950s in the heart of the British military infrastructure in Malta and for which he has received numerous international awards.

Sandwiched between an army barracks and the Hal Far open center, the Peace Lab is an incongruous sight, with its sculptures of angels, its monument to the murdered Italian president Aldo Moro, and its busts of Gandhi and Martin Luther King Jr. I spoke to Father Mintoff in his sitting room, where Roosevelt, Churchill, and Molotov met on two occasions during World War II, including the 1945 preparation for the Yalta conference that paved the way for the division of Europe. Now in his eighties and walking with a stick, he is still a vigorous and passionate campaigner, whose lined, leathery features crease still further as he describes what he regards as the racist treatment of Malta's migrants.

Father Mintoff first came into contact with the island's *klandestini* in 2000, when he woke up one night to hear dozens of Eritreans shouting and screaming as they were herded into the detention center at the Lyster barracks. The police, he recalled, were "very unkind" toward their charges. Kindness is a key principle in Father Mintoff's vocabulary, and he found it noticeably absent when he was allowed to visit the Lyster detention center a few days later. "It was terrible," he recalled. "Men, women, children, babies in small rooms, all crowded together with one toilet closed behind bars."

These visits soon stopped when he began publicly denouncing conditions inside the center. In 2002 Father Mintoff witnessed some of the same Eritreans being driven away in handcuffs to the airport, part of the controversial mass deportations that began that year. Together with his close friend and collaborator Joe Abela, a Labour MP, he launched a landmark court case that halted the ongoing deportations. These activities have not made him popular. He frequently receives anonymous threatening phone calls, and racist graffiti has occasionally been painted on the Peace Lab walls, none of which seems to worry him.

Father Mintoff's moral opposition to Europe's exclusionary borders is not only based on the Christian duty of hospitality toward strangers but rooted in a broader commitment to the world's poor that recalls the Latin American liberation theologians of the 1960s. There is a surprising convergence between this radical Christian critique of Europe's exclusionary borders and the criticisms voiced by more-secular opponents. Sister Paola Domingo is a nun from the Carmelito Verdona order, and a tenacious advocate for the migrants coming to Ceuta. For more than twelve years migrants have made their way to her offices overlooking the city, where she and her colleagues have given them food, medical attention, and if possible a place to stay. Like José Palazón in Melilla, Sister Paola has been the object of smear campaigns accusing her of involvement with smuggling and the facilitation of illegal entry, charges that have never been brought to court.

Sister Paola is not the most obvious people smuggler. Slight, with short gray hair and glasses, she does not wear a habit and emanates a steely commitment and seriousness of purpose, broken by occasional bursts of laughter. The walls of her office are decorated with photographs of church missions in Africa in which she has participated, and there is a clear line of continuity between her commitment to Africa and her work in Ceuta. "I always say that the most important human right is to be able to stay in your own country," she says. "So why don't they? Because they can't. Because we have taken away their freedom, their wealth, everything, because the policies of their governments are controlled by Europe and America."

Having "suckled on Africa" for centuries, she argues, Europe is now embarked on a policy of exclusion based on "repression, fear, killing people," in an immoral and futile attempt to keep African migrants out. "You can't put gates on hunger, death, and injustice," she says. "You can kill them, but they're going to come anyway. They are very strong, and they need so little." She proposes instead a path of "mutual dialogue and negotiation" between Europe and Africa, in which European governments provide economic aid to immigrant-producing countries and adopt a "less aggressive attitude" toward migration in general. "I say we should build motorways between Europe and Africa, that way we'll all be younger and better-looking!" she says. She laughs, but I suspect that she is probably not joking.

Crimes of Solidarity

If governments are generally willing to tolerate certain forms of solidarity with Europe's excluded migrants, the smear campaigns directed at pro-migrant activists such as Sister Paola and José Palazón suggests that such tolerance sometimes has its limits. The fishing village of Marsaxlokk in southern Malta is one of Malta's picture-postcard ports, where large modern trawlers are moored alongside hundreds of brightly painted little wooden boats of the type that Maltese fishermen have used for centuries. Ray Bugeja is the secretary of the largest fishing cooperative in Malta. At his office near the port he describes what happened on June 28, 2007, when he received a radio message from the *Eyeborg*, an Icelandic fishing trawler subcontracted to his company. The captain informed him that he had encountered a sixteen-foot boat containing twenty African migrants that was in danger of sinking. Seven of its passengers had already died at sea and one woman was dead in the boat.

When the migrants climbed onto the *Eyeborg*'s tuna net and pleaded to be taken aboard, Bugeja informed the Maltese authorities so that they could facilitate a search-and-rescue operation, only to be told that the boat was in Libyan territorial waters and that he was not to bring it back to a Maltese port. Like most Maltese fishermen, Bugeja had personally encountered migrant boats in the Mediterranean, and he and his father had both rescued migrants on two separate occasions. A fervent believer in the "law of the sea," which obligates mariners to rescue people in distress whatever their circumstances, he was also aware of the treatment meted out to migrants sent back to Gaddafi's Libya. "I didn't believe that these people were going to get what they deserve there," he says. "And what they deserve is very simple—human rights."

Bugeja therefore took the unilateral decision to ignore these orders and instructed his captain to take the Africans on board and bring them back to Malta. A tense stand-off ensued, in which a Maltese army officer told Bugeja that he would be arrested unless he ordered the captain to return the migrants to their boat. Bugeja refused. Astutely taking advantage of the fact that the *Eyeborg* was flying an Icelandic flag, he informed the Icelandic government, which contacted the Red Cross in Italy and UNHCR. After three days, the Maltese authorities finally relented and agreed to allow the migrants to come to Malta.

Bugeja was not arrested, though he has subsequently been denounced as a "traitor" by the Maltese extreme right. The pressure that was exerted upon him nevertheless reflects a disturbing tendency in various European countries, in which governments have resorted to legal action or the threat of legal action in an attempt to prevent or discourage even the most elementary expressions of solidarity with irregular migrants. In 2007 seven Tunisian fishermen were tried in Sicily for aiding and abetting illegal immigration—a charge that carried a potential fifteen-year sentence—because they had rescued forty-four migrants whose boat was sinking off the coast of Lampedusa. The Tunisians were eventually acquitted in 2011, but their arrest and trial was not likely to inspire other fishermen to follow their example, which may well have been the whole point of the exercise.

In Philippe Lioret's powerful film *Welcome*, a French swimming instructor in Calais agrees to provide free lessons to a Kurdish migrant who wants to swim across the Channel to marry his girlfriend. Denounced by a neighbor, the swimming instructor is prosecuted for facilitating illegal immigration. This scenario did not spring entirely from the director's imagination. Article L622-1 of the French Code on Entry and Stay of Foreigners and Right of Asylum stipulates, "Any person who, by direct or indirect assistance, facilitates the entry or movement of a foreigner residing in France will be punished by five years' imprisonment and a fine of €30,000." In 2009, Claudine Louis, a Frenchwoman from the town of Foix, in southwestern France, was prosecuted for sheltering a sick and homeless Afghan teenager, though a local court subsequently found her actions to be lawful. In Calais in 2003, two members of the migrant solidarity collective C'Sur were fined more than €8,000 because they had taken migrants into their homes and allowed them to use their own names in order to receive money transfers from their families.

French volunteers have also been arrested in Calais for letting migrants charge their mobile phones or for accepting money transfers on their behalf. Despite the risk of arrest, some Calais residents have gone to extraordinary lengths to help migrants passing through the city. Philippe Longue is a thirty-seven-year-old architect who calculates that he has provided a temporary home to some three hundred migrants at his house in the village of Marc, just outside the city, including as many as ten or twelve people at the same time. A devout Catholic, Longue describes his activities on behalf of migrants as an "evangelical message" and a moral obligation that he first began to act upon in 2007, when he met a homeless thirty-seven-year-old Turkish woman in the street who was trying to rejoin her family in the United Kingdom, and put her up in his house. "I was very sad when I saw her," he says, "because I don't believe such things should be happening in the twenty-first century. I don't believe in borders."

Longue began to regularly visit the Calais food distribution center and started driving sick migrants to the hospital, where nurses sometimes asked him to take some of them home to convalesce. Some stayed only a weekend, to shower, rest, or microwave the meals they brought with them from the distribution center. Others came just to enjoy the simple pleasure of eating their food at a table instead of standing up or leaning on a trash bin. "After two or three weeks in Calais, they aren't human," he says. "They are broken, finished. They smell bad. Some of them have TB."

There were also those who stayed longer, such as the Eritrean who was shot while leaving his country and arrived in Calais with the bullet still in his leg. Longue found him lying under a bush, with the flesh turned blue from infection, and took him to the hospital to have the bullet removed; afterward the Eritrean convalesced at Longue's house. His other long-term houseguests included an Afghan teenager who was beaten about the head by three Frenchmen with iron bars and baseball bats, leaving him with permanent brain damage, and a teenage Eritrean girl called Fortuna who fell from the entrance to a truck depot in 2007 while being chased by police, and snapped off one of her fingers. After recovering in Longue's house, Fortuna eventually managed to get to the United Kingdom, where she now lives in Birmingham.

The continual flow of Eritreans, Ethiopians, and Afghans through a small French village of a few hundred inhabitants did not go unnoticed, and some of Longue's neighbors accused him of bringing "gangsters" to the village. His activities inevitably reached the attention of the gendarmerie. In 2010, police officers turned up at his house to arrest him and confiscated his computer. At the police station he was told that his phone had been tapped for six months and that he would be charged with trafficking offenses. These charges were subsequently dropped, but the arrest was sufficient to persuade him to cease his activities.

The threat of arrest has not deterred Longue's compatriot Pierre Falk, a Boulogne resident whose efforts on behalf of the migrants of Calais earned him the sarcastic title of "good Samaritan" in a 2009 article in the *Daily Mail* that accused him of "shamelessly" helping migrants "in defiance of the penal code." I met him in my hotel in Calais, where he came accompanied by Isabelle, the two-year-old daughter of his Nigerian live-in partner.

Fifty-five years old, short and portly, with a graying beard, dreamy eyes, and red cheeks, Falk looks like a cross between a sea captain and Santa Claus in his peaked blue hat, and he emanates a curious combination of innocence, vulnerability, and melancholy. He is a librarian in the music department at his local library in Boulogne, and his transformation into a migrant activist began in 2002, when he heard about the imminent closure of the Sangatte reception center and joined a church occupation to protest the closure. He has continued to help migrants ever since. "I always have migrants at my home and in my car," he says. "I know it's illegal, but I'm very naive, maybe stupid. But when I see people who are very cold, I say, 'Come on to my home.'"

A self-confessed depressive, Falk admits that the company of migrants has become an antidote to his loneliness and satisfies a need for affection inherited from his youth, when he was the neglected child of a large family. "For me it's like an addiction," he says. "I can't stop. I like to be among them. Always I'm searching for solutions for them. When I see teapots in the garbage I retrieve them for migrants. I can't say no—it's a problem."

One of the migrants he encountered in Calais was Kaihan, a fifteen-year-old Afghan boy who had spent four years in Europe as an unaccompanied minor trying to get to the United Kingdom. Falk persuaded Kaihan to apply for asylum in France and was eventually given legal permission to adopt him. For five years the boy lived in his house, sharing a room with his second son of the same age. Kaihan had never been to school, but he showed considerable artistic talent, drawing pictures mostly of bombings and explosions and Taliban. With Falk's help he went to art school in Boulogne, and today he works for a Paris company specializing in the restoration of ancient monuments.

This was one of numerous interventions that have made the home of "Mr. P." an obligatory port of call for many migrants coming through Calais. In certain periods Falk has had up to seventeen people staying at his little terraced house, and some of them have lived with him for months and even years. He has also made various trips to the United Kingdom, carrying the bags and belongings of migrants who made it across the Channel to London and as far north as Leeds and Manchester. He has even paid for a €160 monthly phone package that allows him to phone any country in Europe—an arrangement that was specifically designed to help migrants. In addition to taking his "public phone" around to squats in Calais so that migrants can call their friends and relatives for free, Falk often takes a boom box with him, on which he has recorded African music obtained through his library.

In the course of these activities, he has been arrested five times in three different countries on suspicion of trafficking and facilitating illegal immigration. On one occasion police came to the library where he worked, an episode that did not endear him to his employers. Falk has so far not been charged with any offense, but he openly proclaims his determination to continue what he regards as a humanitarian obligation. His passionate and even reckless engagement with the migrants of Calais is clearly due, at least in part, to his idiosyncratic personality. But solidarity is not synonymous with sainthood, and people have become involved with Europe's migrants for many different reasons.

Whatever their individual motivations, all of them have responded to Europe's undocumented migrants in ways that are at odds—sometimes radically—with the prevailing consensus demanding that migrants be separated and excluded. At a time when European governments are reimposing the distinctions between national citizens and aliens, between legality and illegality, many of them fulfill Oxfam's definition of the "global citizen" who is "aware of the wider world and has a sense of their own role as a world citizen" and is "outraged by social injustice." The political scientist Luis Cabrera has argued that the migrant solidarity activists at the U.S.-Mexico border, such as those involved with the No More Deaths campaign, represent a new global citizenship, characterized by a "moral cosmopolitanism" in which "right action in a global human community" takes precedence over purely national rights and obligations.[4]

Many of those who have shown solidarity with Europe's migrants also belong to this category. In the spring of 2011 migrants and Italians marched through the town of Gavardo to protest the Northern League's removal of public benches from the town, beating drums and carrying placards with slogans such as "Foreigners: Don't leave us alone with the Northern League!" and "If we sit on the ground will you tear up the asphalt?" In May that year I attended the weekly meeting of the Gavardo "bench committee" behind the protest. The restoration of public benches in a small Italian town may not seem like the most dramatic or significant political campaign, but in the Northern League–dominated Italian north, the bench committee was a powerful gesture of inclusiveness. Few of its members were seasoned activists. They were young and middle-aged, students, workers, and housewives, all of whom shared a similar indignation at the League's attempts to construct a de facto apartheid in Brescia province.

"We want to show that not all Italians are like the Northern League," said one woman. Another said that hospitality was an innate Italian quality that she believed was being violated by the League's "meaningless" removal of the benches. For these women, the struggle over Gavardo's public benches was part of a broader fight for the kind of society they wanted Italy to be: tolerant, inclusive, welcoming, and at ease with its newfound ethnic diversity. The Northern League's ordinances were intended to construct a very different Italy, and for many years it has been political forces such as these that have—directly or indirectly—dictated Europe's response to its uninvited guests.

11

Blurred Edges: Europe's Borderlands

The elimination of borders within the European Union signals recognition of the fact that all the citizens of the participating states belong to the same space and share the same identity.

—Bronislaw Geremek, Polish historian and politician, 2007

> the dark stain
> spreading on maps whose shapes dissolve their frontiers
> the way that corpses melt in a lime-pit or
> the bright mulch of autumn is trampled into mud

—Derek Walcott, "The Migrants"

In 2007 a short-lived bloc of 203 far-right members emerged in the European Parliament and called themselves Identity, Tradition, Sovereignty (ITS). They proclaimed a common opposition to non-European immigration based on a shared "commitment to Christian values . . . and the traditions of European civilisation." This attempt to unify the European far right did not last long, but its preoccupations have remained central to Europe's anti-immigration politics. The notion of an exclusive collective identity based on blood, race, or ethnicity and rooted in the national territory has always been intrinsic to the anti-immigrant discourse of the European right. In the last two decades established far-right parties and their newer populist and ultranationalist variants have scored significant political successes across Europe by depicting immigration as a mortal threat to "European civilization" and the national identities of its component parts.

These warnings are often—but not exclusively—directed toward Muslim immigrants, and they are often accompanied by a mood of crisis and alarm, along with dire warnings that Europe's identities are on the brink of a terminal collapse or transformation as a result of the unrestricted entry of incompatible and "unassimilable" foreigners. These warnings are not restricted to the far-right fringe. In 2009 Nicolas Sarkozy formed a new "ministry of immigration and national identity" in an attempt to generate a national debate regarding a "crisis" of French identity—which he attributed largely to the presence of Muslim immigrants. In January 2010, the former archbishop of Canterbury, George Carey, warned that "the sheer numbers of migrants from within Europe and elsewhere put the resources of Britain under enormous pressure and threaten the very ethos or DNA of our nation"—and identified British Muslims as a particularly grievous threat to Britain's "DNA." In August that year Thilo Sarrazin, a member of the German Social Democratic Party with a seat on the executive board of the Bundesbank, published a runaway bestseller entitled *Deutschland Schafft Sich Ab* (Germany Does Away with Itself), which predicted that Germans would soon be outnumbered by Turkish Muslims, whose allegedly low educational achievements were "making Germany stupid."

Identity has also become a recurring theme in the context of European integration. Long before the crisis in the euro zone, pro-European politicians were arguing that the European Union was failing to inculcate a common sense of belonging among its half a billion citizens, and some politicians spoke of a European crisis of identity that threatened to derail the project of European integration. These crisis narratives are to some extent a product of broader anxieties about the nation-state that are shared by many countries in the early twenty-first century, and they are often steeped in confusion and disagreement about what actually binds Europeans together.

Is a shared commitment to the laws, regulations, and political values of the European Union sufficient to define what it means to be European? Or is it the euro, which the European Commission once defined—with an optimism that now seems wildly premature—as "part of building a European identity among its citizens, alongside the national identities that preserve European diversity"? Do Europeans share a deeper connection to one another based on a common historical and cultural legacy? And if so, what components of that past are relevant to Europe today? Is Europe secular or religious? Is it Christian, Judeo-Christian, or Judeo-Christian-Islamic? Or is it merely a "geographical expression," as the German chancellor Bismarck once contended?

To some extent Europe's territorial borders are intended to answer these questions, but lines on a map rarely provide definitive answers. For centuries European geographers, intellectuals, and rulers have attempted to define the point where Europe begins and ends, and these debates are often reflected in shifting cartographical constructions. In the sixteenth century pro-Hapsburg cartographers drew up idealized maps of Europa Regina, depicting Europe in the shape of a queen, with the Iberian Peninsula at her head and Bohemia in her heart. Late eighteenth-century French maps described the Ottoman territories of southeastern Europe as "European Turkey." For some Renaissance geographers the boundary between Europe and Asia corresponded to the classical border of the Don River, while their successors later identified the Ural Mountains as Europe's eastern frontier with Russia.

These arguments continued into the twentieth century. In his December 1941 speech to the Reichstag declaring war on the United States, Adolf Hitler insisted, "There is no geographical definition of our continent, but only an ethnic-national [*volkliche*] and cultural one," and went on to argue "The frontier of this continent is not the Ural mountains, but rather the line that divides the Western outlook on life from that of the East."[1]

Today the European Union has redrawn the map of Europe on various occasions. In purely political terms, the boundaries of the EU include the "overseas countries and territories" left over from colonial rule in the Caribbean, the Indian Ocean, the Atlantic, and the South Pacific, from the French *départements d'outre-mer* of French Guiana, Guadeloupe, Martinique, and French Polynesia, which share the euro as their currency, to the Dutch Antilles and the former British outposts in the Pitcairn Islands, Bermuda, and Montserrat. Yet these territories rarely feature in the ongoing debates about European identity, which tend to focus on the continent itself.

Even when one limits the discussion to Europe, geographical or political boundaries do not provide clear-cut or definitive answers to old historical debates or newer arguments about European identity. Does the fact that Russia, Ukraine, and Moldova are not members of the EU mean that they are not European? Can Turkey be part of Europe, as many Turkish politicians insist? Or is it an intrinsically "Eastern" Islamic anomaly that has no place in a Christian continent, as opponents of Turkish EU membership often argue?

If the EU's elastic boundaries are not able to define what Europe is or should be, they nevertheless mark the territory within which some kind of collective European identity can be imagined and agreed upon. At a time when the very notion of the nation-state as a repository of cultural uniqueness is being challenged by globalization and migration, these borders constitute a fortified dividing line between them and us. Incompatible or alien people can be removed from the area inside these borders and prevented from entering it in the first place.

From a distance therefore, the image of Europe's compensatory borders is intended to transmit a comforting clarity and lack of ambiguity. But such clarity is not always so evident on closer inspection. The late Chicana poet Gloria Anzaldúa once defined the U.S.-Mexico border as *una herida abierta*, an open wound, where "the Third World grates against the first and bleeds. And before a scab forms it hemorrhages again, the lifeblood of two worlds merging to form a third country—a border culture."[2] For Anzaldúa, the physical border itself was only one component of a "vague and undetermined place created by the emotional residue of an unnatural boundary . . . in a constant state of transition," in which the overlapping of Anglo-American and Indian-Mexican cultural influences had forged a unique borderland identity that was both challenging and potentially liberating.

Europe's borders also dissect similarly "vague and undetermined" borderlands and border zones, whose complicated and often messy histories do not necessarily meet the expectations placed upon the border itself. In 2004 Michiel Smit, the founder of the Dutch Nieuw Rechts (New Right) political party, argued that the Netherlands required a "dominant culture" on the grounds that "if there is not one language, one history, and one value pattern, there is bound to be—there always is—chaos."[3] Europe's borderlands are filled with examples of such "chaos," where linguistic, religious, and ethnic categories merge and intermingle in unexpected and surprising ways. Intended—at least in the eyes of some governments—to preserve a certain notion of national homogeneity, these borderlands are often strikingly heterogeneous and impure places. Some of them have changed nationalities on various occasions. Some are inhabited by cultural and religious minorities that are specific to the borderland, and others have been the scene of bloody and catastrophic attempts to impose ethnic and national "order" on the diverse communities that once inhabited them.

Many of these borderlands are located alongside Europe's new fortified borders, and if we look at them more closely it is sometimes possible to detect different possible versions of European and national identity that are more in keeping with the European Union's own motto of "unity in diversity," and which reflect the realities of the twenty-first century rather than the reinvented "imagined communities" that the historian Benedict Anderson once saw as intrinsic to nineteenth-century nationalism.[4]

Hybrid Spaces

The distinctive feature of all borderlands is their location on the periphery and margins of nations, cultures, and civilizations, but the proximity of their inhabitants to their counterparts on the other side of the border can sometimes create its own specific relationships and cultural influences. Go to the village of Remerschen, which now forms part of the Schengen commune in Luxembourg, and you will find numerous headstones containing French and German names dating back into the eighteenth century, testifying to the long tradition of mixed marriages in the tripartite area. French, Germans, and Luxembourgers all have relatives on the opposite side of their mutual borders and share vineyards and farmlands that extend across the border, and the inhabitants of the borderland area in all three countries still speak the Moselle-Franconian dialect as well as their own national languages, while French and Luxembourgish citizens speak German, and Saarland Germans have incorporated French words into their everyday vocabulary.

"The borders here in this area have never been respected by the people," says Dominicus Rohde, the German-born founder and president of the Schengen Peace Foundation. "Therefore the culture is one, the language is one, the dialect is the same. These people are one family." Wine grower, art collector, and idealist, Rohde belongs to the same cosmopolitan borderland tradition that also produced Robert Schuman, the architect of the 1951 European Coal and Steel Community (ECSC), who was born only a few miles from Schengen in the French village of Evrange. For Schuman, the signing of the Statutes of the Council of Europe in May 1949 was the first step toward the transformation of Europe into "an organization putting an end to war and guaranteeing an eternal peace."[5]

In Rohde's opinion, these utopian aspirations have often been overlooked by the European Union's supporters and critics, and also by an excessive focus on monetary union. His decision to establish a new foundation dedicated to world peace in 2007 was partly intended to revitalize this tradition.

Every summer the foundation brings together some five thousand people from different nationalities to debate ways of putting these ideas into practice. For Rohde the dismantling of Europe's borders has been a giant step toward the establishment of a more peaceful continent. Though not unaware of the fortress-like consequences of Schengen, he insists that the Schengen area represents a model for the free movement of people that he would like to see extended across the world like a "virus, the Schengen seed."

Rohde's belief that "borders can become bridges" is clearly rooted in his own experience growing up in a hybrid borderland community for whom national frontiers have mostly been a bureaucratic inconvenience. But this hybridity is present even in some of Europe's more polarized borders. The continued tensions between Greece and Turkey do not prevent islanders from Samos from taking weekly trips on the ferry to Izmir to go shopping in the Izmir bazaar. Ever since Greece became independent in 1829, the Greek-Turkish land border has been a physical barrier against Ottoman/Turkish invasion and a symbolic boundary between Greek Christianity and Islam. The 1923 "population exchanges" agreed between the Greek and Turkish governments at Lausanne resulted in the transfer of more than a million ethnic Greeks from Turkey and another half a million Turks in the opposite direction, in what Bruce Clark has described as an attempt "to put a stop to all ambiguity over territory and over the fate of individuals" caught up in the conflict between the two countries.[6]

But the convention specifically excluded Turkish-speaking Muslims in western Thrace, and today Thrace is still home to an estimated 115,000 Muslims, including Turkish-speaking ethnic Turks, Roma Muslims, and Muslims of Bulgarian descent. Regarded as ethnic Turks by Turkey and as Greek Muslims by the Greek government, Thracian Muslims have become a permanently ambiguous community in Greece, with a limited communal autonomy that includes Turkish-language schools and the right to build mosques—a dispensation that has only just been extended to Athens itself.

Today Lampedusa is often depicted by the European far right as a beleaguered outpost of Europe. But the former feudal possession of the di Lampedusa family is also a Mediterranean island that has in the course of history been inhabited by Romans, Carthaginians, and Arabs, among others. In the late nineteenth and early twentieth centuries many Lampedusans emigrated to coastal towns and cities in North Africa to work in the sponge fishing industry, and there were weekly and sometimes daily ferries between Lampedusa and North African cities such as Tripoli, Tunis, and Benghazi.

Lampedusan and Tunisian fishermen still fish in each other's territorial waters, and these contacts meant that many Lampedusans did not regard the "biblical exodus" of Tunisians who came to the island in 2011 as alien invaders.

Even Europe's fortified frontiers at Ceuta and Melilla have not been able to eliminate the residue of the past. The history of these two exclaves is marked by colonial conquest and rebellion and often stark cultural and religious polarization, but prolonged proximity to Morocco has also generated mutual dependency on either side of the border. Ceuta and Melilla depend heavily on "atypical trade" and the import of Moroccan agricultural products, both of which also benefit Moroccan retailers and farmers, and the two exclaves also rely heavily on the daily flow of Moroccan workers across the border.

These relationships may be unequal and even exploitative, given the huge disparities in income on either side of the border and also within the two exclaves, but they also created religiously and culturally diverse societies that until a few decades ago would have been unimaginable on the Spanish mainland. Approximately 40 percent of the population of Ceuta is of Moroccan descent, and the figure is closer to 50 percent in Melilla. Both exclaves contain large Muslim neighborhoods, where the call to prayer alternates with the sound of church bells. During the daytime, Arabic—and Berber in the case of Melilla—are as common as Spanish in streets and buses, as thousands of Moroccans cross the border to work.

Melilla also has a small Jewish community, descended from Sephardic Jews who emigrated from Morocco in the last half of the nineteenth century, while some of the leading commercial firms in the two exclaves are owned by Indian families of Spanish descent. The administrations in the two exclaves often take pains to highlight this diversity to potential visitors. Ceuta proudly describes itself as a cosmopolitan "open city" and a meeting place between Europe, Africa, and Asia, while the Melilla tourist board similarly defines the city as a cultural melting pot.

This touristic promotion of multiculturalism may seem somewhat incongruous in fortified exclaves whose giant fences were specifically designed to keep Africans out of Europe, and it tends to gloss over the tensions between Spaniards and Muslims in both exclaves, which have erupted in periodic outbreaks of violence. But neither is it entirely illusory, and there is some truth in the Melilla Tourist Board's claim that "in speaking of four Melillas in a single city, we can also speak of one citizen." Though the right-wing

Spanish website Minutodigital recently described the changing Muslim demographics in Melilla as the beginning of a new Muslim reconquest of the Iberian peninsula, there is no indication that the Muslims of either exclave have any desire to give up their Spanish nationality and become part of Morocco.[7]

Moroccans living close to the two exclaves have also benefited from such proximity. At the northwestern corner of the Ceuta border, Moroccan villagers on the other side of the fence are allowed to work inside the exclave in return for allowing their Ceutan neighbors to access their water supply. In Melilla, Moroccan schoolchildren near the Moriguari checkpoint cross the frontier daily to attend school. Melillans of Moroccan descent are allowed to bury their deceased relatives in the Muslim cemetery on the Moroccan side, while Moroccan women in the villages adjoining both Ceuta and Melilla also take advantage of a dispensation in Spanish law that allows foreigners to access medical services in emergency cases, including birth, and some prefer to have their children in Spanish hospitals rather than in Morocco. Many of these *curiosidades fronterizas* (border peculiarities), as one Civil Guard officer in Ceuta described them to me, have been incorporated into Spain's Schengen accession agreements, in another indication that even at one of the hardest and most fortified of the EU's compensatory borders, the boundaries of "Europe" may sometimes have to accommodate themselves to the local realities of the borderland itself.

The Warrior Priest of Malta

It is tempting to believe that borderlanders have some special propensity for openness and inclusivity, as Dominicus Rohde does, but this is not always the case. Mention Norman Lowell's name to many Maltese of a liberal-left persuasion and they are likely to respond with a weary sigh or a grimace. Born in 1946, Lowell is a former bank employee and the founder of the extreme-right Imperium Europa, whose declared objective is to transform the "Sacred Island" of Malta into "the first liberated nation in the whole White world, liberated from the enemy within and the enemy without." He has publicly described Jews as "rodents" and in 2006 he was convicted of incitement to racial hatred and insulting the president and given a four-year suspended sentence.

Lowell has had a less-than-resounding endorsement from the Maltese electorate. In the 2008 parliamentary elections he received 84 votes. His party has been more successful in European parliamentary elections. In 2004 he received 1,603 votes and in 2009 the figure had more than doubled to 3,559. Nevertheless, Imperium Europa has had an undeniable impact on Maltese politics. Some Maltese argue that Lowell's extremism has enabled Malta's two main parties to justify punitive policies such as mandatory detention as a means of neutralizing his electoral appeal. This argument could also apply to other European governments, which present toughness on immigration as an antidote to the far right, and it seemed to me that Lowell was an expression of wider political tendencies that have had far more influence in other countries than they have in his own.

I spoke to Malta's self-styled "warrior-priest" in the Melita café in the elegant town of Attard, alongside the presidential palace. Lowell was an eccentric, self-regarding, and self-consciously messianic figure, with his wispy hair and beard, club-like walking stick, and trembling voice. He was mostly calm and polite, his fervid intensity broken by occasional bouts of slightly manic laughter as he outlined his plans to "set Europe ablaze" and create an empire of white "Europids" from South Africa to the Bering Strait.

Much of what he had to say was jaw-droppingly bizarre and outlandish, a mixture of racist pseudo-science, science fiction, fascist romanticism, and pagan mysticism that might have come from Heinrich Himmler on LSD or *The Turner Diaries*. One of his proposals entails the demolition of all buildings constructed in Malta after 1800 (when the industrial revolution began, according to him) following the triumph of his "organic empire" and the transformation of his country into the "Mecca of the white race," with no roads and a network of underground tunnels that connect a "circular city that circulates on its own axis" and will allow the pilgrims of the future to cavort freely in Malta's rediscovered temples. Lowell would also like to extend the U.S.-Mexico border as far as the Panama Canal in order to prevent the entry of racially inferior immigrants into the United States—a project that would require the removal by one means or other of millions of Hispanics.

Lowell is an admirer of Hitler but criticizes him for being "too ethnocentric" in declaring war on Slavic Russia and embroiling the white race in a divisive conflict that ultimately led to the Nazi defeat. Such wars are a luxury today's "Europids" can no longer afford, he insists, and racial survival can only be secured through the creation of an "organic empire of regions and peoples" led by a spiritually enlightened elite and purged of its racial impurities.

Enclosed within its "sealed borders," Lowell's Europid elite will then be able to abandon the planet altogether and "harness the solar system," since,

he confidently assures me, "the Moon is laden, Mars is laden with war materials. We don't need the earth." It was not surprising that these delirious
fantasies have made little electoral headway in Malta, but Lowell's contempt
for multiculturalism and multiracialism—which he considered a Jewish
invention—and his insistence that "Arabs and niggers" were responsible for
all crime on the island reflect a drearily familiar anti-immigrant discourse
that is hardly unique to Malta.

Lowell is a fan of Umberto Bossi and his proposals for dealing with
Malta's migrants echo those of the would-be president of Padania. "We just
have to shoot a few boats, that's all," he says cheerfully. "Just sink them. It's
no problem. You can't miss a boat from fifty yards with a bloody gunboat,
can you?" Immigrants already in Malta should be driven out through starvation (a favorite weapon in Lowell's arsenal) by issuing Maltese with ID cards
that give them—and only them—permission to buy and eat food. Migrants
will therefore die or leave.

Lowell's obsessive concern with the racial purity of his "sacred" homeland
is somewhat anomalous on an island where many Maltese, unlike him, are
dark-skinned, so much so that in 1915 Maltese cane cutters who emigrated
to Australia were regarded as "black" and subjected to Australia's notorious
dictation test in an attempt to exclude them. But for Lowell the authentic
indigenous Maltese consist of "European people coming from old stock"—a
formulation that skips over Malta's two centuries of Arab colonization and
its long history of foreign domination.

This selective interpretation of Maltese history is not the prerogative of
Imperium Europa. Phoenicians, Carthaginians, Romans, Arabs, Normans,
Sicilians, French, British, and the Knights of St. John have all left their mark
on this tiny archipelago of islands that the Romans called Melita, "the land
of honey," as well as a rich cultural mosaic that includes the paintings of
Caravaggio, British-style red telephone boxes and busts of King George,
Roman ruins and ubiquitous religious statues and shrines, some of the finest
baroque architecture in Europe, and the Maltese language itself—a unique
fusion of Arabic, English, and Italian.

But the cornerstone of Maltese national identity is its devout Catholicism
and particularly its history of holy warfare against Islam. "Being a boundary,
their whole political identity since the Great Siege under the Knights of
Malta, has been one of being a border zone, the Christian border, the Christian march," says Paul Clough, professor of anthropology at the University
of Malta, of the Maltese. In Clough's estimation this isolation on the Euro-

pean periphery and its history of domination and invasion by powerful foreigners has engendered a sense of "abroad" as something threatening and dangerous—and also an ambivalent attitude toward Europe itself.

Today Malta's conservative Catholic society is being transformed by a range of influences from Europe and the wider world that include consumerism, new sexual mores embodied by its belated legalization of divorce in 2011, the Internet, and online gambling (a major activity on the island). But as is the case in many European countries, it is immigration—specifically African and Muslim immigration—that has most often been singled out as a special threat to Maltese cultural and national identity. These threat narratives often ignore the extraordinary range of influences that have shaped Maltese history and culture.

"This diversity in our past is not part of our mind-set because we don't even acknowledge it," says Evarist Bartolo, a Maltese Labour Party MP who has campaigned for a more humane response to Malta's migrants. "It's as if we were a pure race that has developed apart from the rest of the world—especially apart from North Africa." In Bartolo's opinion Malta has yet to resolve these tensions between its history as a "bulwark of Europe" and the cultural influences stemming from its location as a Mediterranean border zone. "Although there has been talk during the last forty years or so that Malta should be a bridgehead between Europe and Africa, we're more of a bastion and a wall than a bridge because to be a bridge you have to be comfortable with different cultures," he says.

Lowell is the most extreme manifestation of this discomfort. For him, the Arab presence is an irrelevant and extraneous aberration and he insists that "only 2 percent" of Malta's original inhabitants mixed with Arabs—a surprisingly exact percentage that he claims can be proven through DNA testing, and which has left Maltese speaking a "shameful" and "unnatural" Semitic language "fit for slaves" and imposed by Arab colonists "with the whiplash."

At first sight Lowell's anti-Semitism and cartoon Nazism are out of kilter with the pro-Zionist and anti-Muslim sentiments of the more politically sophisticated European far right, which tends to focus on cultural and religious difference in its invocation of Europe's identity crises. But the distance between Imperium Europa and some of its ideological fellow travelers is more a question of rhetoric and presentation than substance. In the French author Jean Raspail's racist novel *The Camp of the Saints* (1973) the sudden arrival of millions of backward, parasitical, and impoverished Asian and African immigrants in boats brings about the collapse of European and

Western civilization. Raspail's nightmarish fantasy of racial engulfment has often been cited as a prophetic text in extreme-right circles, and it continues to underpin the new emphasis on culture, religion, and national values in defining Europe's immigrants as barbarian invaders.[8]

On July 22, 2011, a Norwegian anti-Muslim fanatic named Anders Breivik perpetrated one of the most horrendous acts of violence in recent European history when he exploded a car bomb outside the Norwegian government office buildings in Oslo, killing eight people, and then went on to massacre sixty-nine people, mostly young adults, who were attending at a Norwegian Labour Party summer camp on Utoeya Island. In a 1,500-page manifesto and a YouTube video, the self-styled "Knight Templar" justified these actions as a defensive response to "Cultural Marxists" and other "anti-nationalists . . . who want to deconstruct European identity, traditions, culture and even nation states."[9]

Breivik acted alone and of his own volition, but his views on Muslim immigration, multiculturalism, and European identity belong to a wider consensus that includes mainstream politicians and clerics, liberals, and media commentators as well as the newer street-level organizations such as the English Defence League that have sprung up to defend "our" culture from its imagined invaders.

Today the Internet is awash with videos like Breivik's, in which images of Mozart, Beethoven, cathedrals, and churches alternate with those of Muslims, Osama bin Laden, and veiled women, and invocations of Charlemagne and Richard the Lionheart set to the strains of Vivaldi call for acts of cultural "resistance." Stripped of its defensive pretensions, Breivik's murderous rage belongs to a dark tradition that has often had disastrous consequences in European history.

In the Shatter Zone

I thought of Norman Lowell on a bitterly cold morning in February 2011 when I visited the Majdanek concentration camp in the Polish city of Lublin, near the Ukraine border. Unlike most of the Nazi camps in eastern Poland, Majdanek is located on the outskirts of the city, right next to the road that once constituted the main Nazi supply line into Ukraine during World War II, and which now leads to the Poland-Ukraine border checkpoint at Dorohusk. Majdanek was originally built in 1941 as a labor camp for prisoners of war, and its inmates included Russian POWs, Polish political prisoners, farmers who failed to fulfill grain-requisitioning requirements, and Byelorussian peasants rounded up in operations targeting partisans. But most of its victims were Jews, some 59,000 of whom died there, out of an estimated 80,000 victims who were beaten, shot, or simply worked to death.

About half the original 670-acre site remains as a permanent monument and museum, surrounded by barbed wire and watchtowers, with further subdivisions into five fenced-off fields where different categories of prisoners were held. Many of the original wooden buildings are still intact, including the SS administrative offices and execution shed, a dormitory with wooden beds, a crematorium and gas chambers, and a former storehouse containing a permanent exhibit of tens of thousands of pairs of shoes taken from the camp inmates—a moving and terrible reminder of the humanity of the tens of thousands of men, women, and children who were destroyed within these wire fences. Not far from the crematorium, just behind the execution ditches where 18,400 Jews were shot on November 2, 1943, a large mausoleum encloses an enormous pile of human ashes retrieved from the fields where the SS spread them as compost and now shaped into a rounded and compact mound like the surface of a distant planet.

Majdanek was not designed as an extermination camp, but Lublin itself played a key role in the Final Solution. It was from here, in the autumn of 1941, that the psychotic SS chief of Lublin district, Odilo Globocnik, organized the construction of Belzec, Sobibor, and Treblinka along Poland's eastern borders in preparation for the extermination of Polish Jewry. In March 1942 the first shipments of Jews from the Lublin ghetto were transported by train to Belzec and gassed in the first phase of the mass killings of Jews known as Operation Reinhard.

This operation was intended as a prelude to an even more extensive campaign of genocide known as General Plan East, which the Nazis calculated would require the killing and expulsion of some 30 million Slavs and other "racially undesirable" elements by the 1970s. In this way Himmler hoped to establish a racial "border" made up of German soldier-farmers all along the Urals, whose settlements would be connected to Germany by vast motorways. This maniacal scheme was ultimately abandoned only because the tide of war began to turn against Germany.

The Nazi genocide was the bloodiest episode in a chain of ethnic wars, purges, massacres, and expulsions that spread up and down Europe's eastern borderlands during and immediately after World War II, from the Baltic

states in the north to Romania, Moldova, and Odessa in the south, and
ended in the massive refugee flights and population "exchanges" that followed the Nazi defeat. The scale and ferocity of the violence were partly a
response to the extraordinary cultural and ethnic complexity of the region
and its incompatibility with the national and racial boundaries that were being
established in the period. For centuries the borderlands of eastern Europe
constituted a shifting march between the Latin and Byzantine Churches,
between Catholic Europe and the Eastern Orthodox Church, between Christendom and Islam, where different religious, ethnic, and national groups
overlapped and mingled. Jews, Ukrainians, ethnic Germans, Poles, Catholics,
Orthodox, and Protestant Christians, plus various religious cults and sub-
groups, all made up the multicultural fabric of the Polish/Ukrainian *kresy*
(borderlands).

The cultural and ethnic mosaic of Europe's "shatter zone" or "crush
zone"—as English geographers once described the weak states of central and
eastern Europe—was not easily incorporated within the new nation-states
that emerged in the nineteenth and twentieth centuries.[10] In *A Biography of
No Place*, her meticulous re-creation of the lost world of the *kresy* in the first
half of the twentieth century, the historian Kate Brown has traced the attempts by Soviet officials and Nazi racial theorists to impose their own ideological, national, and racial "order" on borderland communities that were
often difficult if not impossible to categorize.[11]

In the aftermath of the Nazi invasion of the Soviet Union, German eth-
nologists and racial specialists were dispatched to the *kresy* to identify ethnic
Volksdeutsche and "redeem" them for the Reich, only to find that it was difficult if not impossible to distinguish these "amphibians" from the supposedly
inferior Slavs who surrounded them.

Today these borderlands have been purged of many of the peoples who
once inhabited them. In Lublin's immaculately reconstructed city center
there are few traces of the "Polish Jerusalem" where Isaac Bashevis Singer
once described "bearded Jews, dressed in long cloaks and wearing white
beads, mov[ing] through the streets on their way to evening prayers" in his
tribute to his mother's hometown, *The Magician of Lublin*. Less than a hundred yards from the Judenrat, the Jewish offices during the Nazi occupation,
a sign at the Grodska Gate identifies the "border" between the Jewish and
Christian communities that existed until the Jewish Emancipation Act of
1862 and which now forms part of a Jewish heritage trail and a "multicultural trail" established by the Lublin tourist office.

The cobblestone streets and elegant pink and yellow buildings where Nazi racial fanatics once organized genocide are now filled with trendy art galleries, lively bars, and pubs full of young people, and the once remote world of the *kresy* has been fully incorporated into the new digital age. One evening in my hotel room I counted more than 225 channels on my hotel television; these included Sexy Arab TV, the Pentagon Channel, Christian television programs such as Heaven TV and God TV, TRT Turk, TV Coran, the Berber TV channel Tamazight, and a succession of national TV channels such as Armenia TV, Sri Lanka One, Assadissa, and the Iranian Saamen TV.

As I watched this media-driven Babel of languages, cultures, and religions zip past, it occurred to me that technology has transformed the whole world into a kind of cultural borderland. Whether we live on the edges of nations or in the heart of modern cities, we all inhabit peripheral zones in which we are bombarded by competing cultural messages and influences. In this context the whole idea of an overarching and exclusive "national" identity rooted in a particular territory becomes questionable—or at least can be considered only one of the many different ways that individuals and communities can define themselves.

Rusyn Blues

The firestorm of violence that spread through the eastern borderlands in the first half of the twentieth century did not succeed in eradicating its cultural and ethnic complexities entirely. The Slovakia-Ukraine border dissects a wider region known as Subcarpathia, Transcarpathia, or Ruthenian Carpathia, which includes parts of Slovakia, Ukraine, Poland, and Hungary, and a variety of ethnic groups: Roma, ethnic Hungarians, Bulgarians, Bogomils, Orthodox Hungarians (known as Csango), Slovaks who have been Ukrainians, and Ukrainians who have been Slovaks.

These borderlands are also home to one of eastern Europe's oldest and least-known ethnic minorities, the Rusyns or Ruthenians. The origins of the Rusyns are obscure, but they are believed to be the descendants of Russian-speaking Slavic settlers who came to these borderlands in the early Middle Ages. Divided into further ethnic and regional subdivisions, Rusyns speak their own language, write in the Cyrillic script, and have their own distinct folk traditions.

For centuries they have existed on the fringes of more powerful societies that often refused to recognize their language and ethnicity and which sometimes actively sought to suppress them. On March 15, 1939, the Rusyns in what is now the Ukrainian oblast of Zakarpatia seized the opportunity presented by the Nazi dismemberment of Czechoslovakia and declared an independent state, Carpatho-Ukraine, which was snuffed out in less than three days by a Hungarian invasion.

Today some 24,000 Rusyns live in the remote highlands of eastern Slovakia, out of an estimated 1 million Rusyns scattered across Poland, Slovakia, Hungary, Ukraine, and Romania, in addition to a diaspora community that extends to the United States. Travel up toward the Polish border and you enter a world that might have been culled from the classic Czech movie *Closely Observed Trains*, with its corpulent train conductors stuffed into ill-fitting blue uniforms, tiny railway stations no bigger than bus shelters in empty fields, Legoland Communist-era towns and neat rural villages, World War II tanks, and immaculately constructed wooden churches.

These wooden churches are a legacy of the 1681 Congress of Sopron, when the Hapsburg emperor Leopold I permitted the construction of evangelical and Calvinist churches in imperial territory—on the condition that they used no nails or metal and that each church had to be constructed in the same year. Nine Rusyn wooden churches of different denominations have become UNESCO World Heritage Sites, and they are exquisite constructions, incorporating Gothic spires, crosses, or Orthodox domes into cascading layered rooftops built on a log-cabin-style base in keeping with the rural foundations of Rusyn society.

Following World War II Slovak Rusyns were subjected to a repressive campaign of assimilation in Communist Czechoslovakia. Since the end of the Cold War Rusyn culture has undergone something of a revival that is evident in the codification of the Rusyn language, the publication of periodicals and newspapers, the creation of a Rusyn academy, and official recognition as ethnic minorities in Ukraine and Slovakia.

One of the most striking expressions of this cultural resurgence can be found in Medzilaborce, a small town of some 6,500 inhabitants in northeast Slovakia near the Polish border. Situated in a forested valley reminiscent of Vermont or Appalachia, this remote corner of Europe is not the most obvious setting for a world-class modern art museum. A few hundred yards up from the sleepy railway station in Medzilaborce, however, past the flatcars piled with logs and the tree-lined slope beyond them, a large Campbell's soup can

announces a unique tribute to the most famous Rusyn of all—Andrew Warhola, better known as Andy Warhol.

Directly opposite a domed Orthodox church, in a ponderous three-story
building with painted symmetrical rectangular slabs that was once destined
to become a Communist "palace of culture," the strains of the Velvet Underground's "Venus in Furs" and "Sunday Morning" accompany a comprehen-
sive exhibition of paintings and prints by Warhol and his brother Paul. The
Andy Warhol Museum of Modern Art also contains a number of artifacts
and memorabilia donated by the Warhol family, including the "singing
book" written in Cyrillic script and used by Warhol's devoutly religious
mother, Julia.

Warhol liked to say that he came from "nowhere," but his parents came
from the nearby village of Mikova, and the museum was the brainchild of its
chief curator, Michal Bycko, who became a fan of Pop Art and the New
York School as a student in the 1970s, when such artists were regarded by
the Communist authorities as "bourgeois decadent imperialists." In 1991
Bycko established the museum with the collaboration of Warhol's brother
John. This project was not initially popular, either with the authorities or
with the local population.

Today, the museum attracts some seventeen thousand visitors every year
and Warhol's enigmatic face in sunglasses is plastered all over the town. One
large mural can be seen directly behind a statue of a Red Army soldier near
Andy Warhol Avenue—a juxtaposition that certainly would have amused
the connoisseur of surfaces, whose work found room for Lenin and the ham-
mer and sickle as well as ketchup bottles and Ingrid Bergman. Warhol died
before the museum was opened and never visited the country that his parents left in the 1930s, but Bycko insists that his Rusyn childhood influenced
both the artist and the man, both through the visual influence of religious
iconography and in the devout Catholicism of his mother.

It is salutary to consider the remarkable survival of one of Europe's "invisible nations" on the European periphery alongside the paranoid narratives of
Europe's imminent cultural extinction. Such fantasies invariably construct
monolithic collective identities in the first person plural that are presented as
more homogeneous than such identities actually are, and tend to depict culturally dominant and entrenched majorities as marginalized and victimized
groups, besieged by supposedly privileged ethnic or cultural minorities. The
Rusyns have experienced real marginalization in the midst of powerful nations that at best ignored them and at worst set out to absorb and eradicate

them. Yet not only have they survived, but they have also evolved and absorbed new influences.

Michal Bycko himself embodies that adaptability. Having been Czech, he has now become Slovak, without ever ceasing to be Rusyn. A former dissident student in the Czech Communist underground, he is also an art critic and aficionado of Pop Art, and a blues guitarist with a collection of a hundred guitars, some of which once belonged to John Lee Hooker, Buddy Guy, and Eric Clapton. Bycko nevertheless remains fervently committed to Rusyn culture, with its Cyrillic prayer books, wooden churches, and rural folk traditions, and even insists that there is a musical genre called "Rusyn blues."

We need to remember that such transactions are possible. Perhaps the Rusyns can remind Europeans that cultural identities cannot be quarantined and ring-fenced within territorial boundaries, and that it is possible to acquire many different identities in the course of a lifetime, without losing the ones we started out with, and that, like Andyho Warhola (as he is known in Rusyn), the migrant from "nowhere" whose parents left this borderland world of singing books, icons, and wooden churches and who went on to celebrate the advent of a ubiquitous consumer culture long before anyone had heard of globalization, it is possible to be many different people at the same time.

Czeslaw Milosz's Borderlands

Today there are signs that some of Europe's eastern border states are beginning to reappraise the borderland regions that were once seen as so problematic in the first half of the twentieth century. Since 2007 the Polish and Slovak governments have cooperated in a project based on the "meeting of seven cultures" in their common borderlands region in the eastern Tatra Mountains, which aims to promote local artists whose work is born in "the multicultural setting of the borderlands." Farther north, in the isolated and sparsely populated borderlands of northeast Poland near the Kaliningrad oblast, Lithuania, and Belarus, the administrative district of Sejny county has become the location for a unique experiment with cultural bridge building that draws its inspiration from the history of the borderlands.

Sejny is not the easiest place to get to. The quickest route is by road from the Lithuanian capital, Vilnius, some 107 miles farther north. Cross the border and you pass through the deserted checkpoints and customs platforms that preceded Poland and Lithuania's accession to the Schengen area in 2007. During the Cold War this border was a heavily guarded frontier between Poland and the Soviet Union. Following Lithuanian independence in 1991, it became a national border between Lithuania and Poland. Now traffic moves back and forth between the two countries without checks or controls, subject to nothing more than a cursory glance from the Lithuanian border guards.

Just a few miles from this ghost border, in a rustic landscape of undulating hills, lakes, and tall forests, lies the hamlet of Krasnogruda, the former home of the family of Poland's Nobel Prize–winning poet Czeslaw Milosz. The Polish parliament officially designated 2011, the Milosz centennial, as "Milosz Year," with a series of national and international events. On June 30, exactly one hundred years since Milosz's birth, more than a thousand guests sweltered in the hot sun to hear speeches from the Polish president, Bronisław Komorowski, the Lithuanian minister of culture, and Milosz's son Tony Milosz at the inauguration of the Milosz family home as a museum and "international dialogue center" to coincide with the Polish presidency of the European Union.

For the next three days philosophers, translators, academics, and literary critics from Poland, the rest of Europe, Russia, and the United States gathered at a former synagogue in the nearby town of Sejny to debate Milosz's autobiographical *Native Realm* and its relevance to contemporary Europe. All this was conducted with a very Mitteleuropean intensity and rigor, leavened by poetry readings at the Europa Café, an art exhibition, a concert by the Sejny klezmer orchestra, and the first international performance of a specially written oratorio, based on Milosz's poem "Return," by the New York–based composer Wlad Marhulets.

There are not many countries where a poet would generate this level of attention, and fewer still where a national cultural event would take place in a rural border town of seven thousand inhabitants. All this is due to the Fundacja Pogranicze (Borderland Foundation), a remarkable Sejny-based organization dedicated to "the craft of international dialogue on the world's borderlands," which has been based in the town for more than twenty years. Milosz's writings and his personal connection to the Polish-Lithuanian borderlands were instrumental in the unusual decision by a Warsaw-based group of artists, actors, and writers to relocate to Sejny in 1990.

Though he spoke and wrote in Polish, Milosz was born in Lithuania and attended university in Vilnius, and these formative years in a border zone of overlapping cultures, religions, and languages had a lasting impact on his life and work. In *Native Realm* Milosz once wrote of his desire to "connect the marchland of Europe where I was born, with its mixture of languages, religions, and traditions, not only to the rest of the continent but to our own age—which has long since become intercontinental."[12]

The Borderland Foundation shares the same philosophy. Its driving force is Krzysztof Czyzewski, a poet, essayist and the foundation's president, who accompanied Milosz on his return to Krasnogruda after a fifty-year exile in 1989. Czyzewski and his colleagues were attracted to Sejny partly because of the region's association with Milosz, and also because of its diverse cultural heritage, which includes Lithuanians, former Ukrainian Poles, Roma, Tartars, Catholics, Lutherans, and Orthodox "Old Believers." Until World War II, some 40 percent of Sejny's population were Jews; they fled the town following the 1939 Nazi invasion for Vilnius, where most of them were subsequently killed during the annihilation of the Jewish ghetto.

For Czyzewski and his colleagues, the rich multicultural past—and present—of this borderland periphery constituted a more appealing location for their experiment with cultural bridge building than the capital itself. In an evocative and suggestive essay, Czyzewski once described the region as a ruined "Atlantis" littered with the relics of "the historical cataclysms and totalitarian ideologies of the 20th century," in which a hypothetical traveler finds that

> everything was destroyed. The area was full of traces of the end of the world, the end of the "old civilization" . . . devastated manors, empty cloisters, temples made into taverns or storehouses for fertilizers, trading routes suddenly disappeared in the face of borders freshly drawn after World War I, huge spans of bridges lost in the woods, connecting nothing and leading nowhere, abandoned cemeteries with engravings in lost languages.[13]

The physical evidence of this "old civilisation" was still present in Sejny itself, in the abandoned public buildings in the former Jewish shtetl, which the foundation was given permission to use for its activities. "We were searching for a space that could be like a borderland center," says Czyzewski, "and the Jewish quarter was located in the very center of the town between the Polish and Lithuanian cultural centers. So there you had space for a cultural center that could reach all sides."

The arrival of these unknown artists and writers from Warsaw was initially greeted with suspicion and hostility by some locals who believed—

inaccurately—that the foundation's members were Jews coming to reclaim their property. Czyzewski and his colleagues eventually overcame these reservations through their long-term presence in the town, and through their patient recruitment of the youth of Sejny in their creative excavation of the lost history of the borderlands. In 1999 the youth section of the foundation's local theater company premiered a work called *The Sejny Chronicles*, under the direction of Czyzewski's multitalented wife, Malgorzata Sporek-Czyzewski, and Wojciech Szroeder. In a combination of oral history and performance, local children told the town's history by collecting stories and songs from their parents, grandparents, and other relations, and also by learning prayers, songs, and dances in Yiddish, Polish and Lithuanian. Lithuanian- and Polish-speakers were also encouraged to step outside their own cultural and linguistic "borders" and immerse themselves in the cultural histories of their counterparts.

This play is the cornerstone of the foundation's work in Sejny, and it has toured nationally and internationally, garnering rave reviews in New York. The foundation's activities also include filmmaking, education, and community arts projects, a local café and performance space, an archive and documentary center containing more than 4,500 films and documentaries, a library of books and documents on ethnic groups and national minorities in the eastern European borderlands, and its own publishing house, Pogranicze (Borderland). In 2000 the foundation published the groundbreaking *Neighbours* by the Princeton historian Jan Gross, a searing account of the wartime massacre of the Jewish population of Jedwabne, a small village within an hour's reach of Sejny, by their Polish neighbors, which presented many Poles for the first time with the reality of Polish anti-Semitism during World War II.[14]

In Czyzewski's opinion, all this has had a transformative and cathartic impact on Sejny itself. "Borderlanders were the losers of the twentieth century," he says. "If you were a borderlander with mixed family roots, it was something to hide. Now it is an honor and dignity to be a borderlander in Sejny, and it sounds very positive, and when you ask the mayor of the city or local government what is the promotional strategy of the region, they say borderland." In 2002 a memorial stone was laid in the local Jewish cemetery bearing the simple inscription "In memory of the Jews of Sejny—[from] the inhabitants of Sejny," a belated commemoration that was largely due to the foundation's influence. The foundation has also exported its philosophy and methodology to former conflict zones in Mostar, Georgia, Azerbaijan, and Aceh in Indonesia.

The notion of cultural dialogue has been very much in vogue in contemporary Europe in recent years, from the Alliance of Civilizations initiative proposed by the Spanish prime minister José Luis Zapatero in 2005 to the 2008 Council of Europe white paper on intercultural dialogue. These efforts are often limited to worthy declarations of principle and discussions between like-minded intellectuals. What makes the foundation so different is its grassroots cultural activism and its exploration of the eastern European borderland as a paradigm for its search for a "connective tissue" capable of binding seemingly polarized cultures and nations together.

Czyzewski defines himself and his colleagues as the "Bosnia generation," whose ideas were shaped by the destruction of Bosnia's multicultural society in the 1990s. As he sees it: "We didn't have tools, we didn't have strong ideas to keep Bosnia together. We understood the language of Karadzic, who wanted to divide, and it was very clear to Western politicians that this was logical. So we didn't have the power, language, or communities to counter it, and our prediction was that sooner or later we'll have this in Paris and London and Berlin as well, and in Warsaw."

It is particularly poignant that these ideas have emerged from a region where the imposition of exclusionary ethnic and national borders has been the cause of so many tragedies, crimes, and disasters. Nor are these forces absent from the contemporary Polish borderlands. During President Komorowski's speech at Krasnogruda, a busload of Polish nationalists tried to enter the grounds to protest what they regarded as discriminatory legislation by the Lithuanian government against Polish-speaking Lithuanians, and Lithuanian nationalists are prone to similar accusations regarding the treatment of Lithuanians on the other side of the border.

In September 2011 a protest march took place in Bialystok, just over an hour from Sejny, following a series of anti-Semitic and racist incidents that included the desecration of a monument to the Jews of Jedwabne, swastika graffiti in a local Jewish cemetery, and the vandalism of a local Islamic center. These developments are another manifestation of the resurgent extreme-right and ultranationalist populism in eastern Europe that has variously declared Jews, Muslims, Roma, Turks, and other ethnic or linguistic minorities to be enemies of the nation or usurpers of their national territories. In this context the Borderland Foundation's pedagogy of bridge building represents a challenge to the new politics of exclusion—and not only in eastern Europe. In recent years mainstream politicians such as David Cameron and Angela Merkel have joined in the backlash against multiculturalism and made coded speeches that depict Europe's newfound cultural and ethnic diversity as alien and dangerous. These condemnations of "multi-kulti" are invariably accompanied by strident and authoritarian demands that immigrants must become "like us" or leave—even if it has yet to be defined who "we" actually are—and the identity threats that they invoke often act as a further justification for tougher enforcement at the border. In these circumstances it is more urgent than ever for Europeans who oppose these exclusivist tendencies to construct more generous and fluid "imagined communities" that reflect the reality of the borderland rather than the border itself.

12

The Western Borders

What the Western allies face is a long, sustained and proactive defence of their societies and way of life. To that end, they must keep risks at a distance, while at the same time protecting their homelands.

—*Towards a Grand Strategy for an Uncertain World*, NATO REPORT, 2008

For all their specific features, Europe's borders are not an isolated or anomalous phenomenon in the early twenty-first century. Across the world states have reinforced their national borders with walls, fences, and other barriers. India is close to completing a 2,429-mile fence along its border with Bangladesh. In the last ten years more than a thousand migrant workers, mostly Bangladeshis, trying to cross this frontier have been shot dead by the Indian Border Security Force. In 2003 Botswana began the construction of a three-hundred-mile electrified fence along its border with Zimbabwe, ostensibly to prevent the spread of foot-and-mouth disease, but which the Zimbabwean authorities believe is intended to prevent its own nationals from crossing the border in search of work. Despite this barrier, tens of thousands of impoverished Zimbabweans work in Botswana every year, where they have been attacked by local vigilantes and are routinely arrested, beaten, and deported by police.

Similar events have taken place along the Zimbabwe–South Africa border. In January 2009 UNICEF reported that thousands of Zimbabwean migrants, including unaccompanied children, were living in makeshift camps at the South African border town of Musina, where they were routinely attacked and robbed by predatory gangs that patrol the border zone. In Malaysia irregular migrants are punished by detention and whippings with canes, in addition to arbitrary raids, extortion, and violence from the Malaysian police and the paramilitary citizens group the People's Volunteer Corps (RELA).

In December 2010 Israel began building a 130-mile fence along its 155-mile desert border with Egypt in response to what Benjamin Netanyahu had earlier called a "flood of illegal workers infiltrating Israel from Africa" that represented "a concrete threat to the Jewish and democratic character of the country."[1] In recent years migrants trying to cross Israel's borders in the Sinai have routinely been shot at by Egyptian security forces. In 2008 the Israeli NGO Hotline for Migrant Workers claimed that hundreds of migrants had been shot by Egyptian security forces trying to cross the border. In 2010 Human Rights Watch reported that thousands of migrants in the Sinai had been kidnapped and tortured by smugglers who demanded a ransom for their release, and that as many as five thousand women had been smuggled across the desert (and most of them raped in the course of these crossings) to work in Israeli brothels.[2]

In terms of their policies, methods, and objectives—and the political forces that underpin them—there is a striking convergence between Europe's anti-migrant borders and the border enforcement model adopted by the United States and Australia in the same period. In all these countries, democratic governments have used their formidable powers to keep out irregular migrants who are perceived as threats to their security, their identity, and their prosperity. To some extent, Fortress Europe is only one component in a wider wall or series of walls that have been erected across the industrialized West in the last twenty years, primarily in order to lock out the world's poor, though those barriers have also served to lock them in.

La Frontera

Border security has been an obsessive concern in American politics for more than two decades, and as in Europe, these concerns have been largely driven by anxieties and phobias regarding immigration. From the last decade of the twentieth century onward, a stream of books by U.S. conservatives has depicted Latino immigration as a threat to America's security and cultural identity; their essential preoccupations are reflected in titles such as *Alien Nation*,

State of Emergency: The Third World Invasion, and *Illegals: The Imminent Threat Posed by Our Unsecured U.S.-Mexico Border*.

In *Who Are We? The Challenge to America's National Identity* (2005) the late political scientist Samuel Huntington argued that the United States was being inexorably transformed into "Mexamerica" as the result of a mass influx of unassimilable Hispanic immigrants whose culture was inimical to the values that defined the American melting pot. In his fanatically anti-Hispanic polemic *In Mortal Danger: The Battle for America's Border and Security* (2006), the Republican congressman and anti-immigrant demagogue Tom Tancredo similarly warned that the "cult of multiculturalism" and unrestricted Hispanic immigration were turning America into "a vague, confusing collection of ethnic groups or religious sects" pockmarked with "immigrant cesspools"—a process facilitated by the "illegal aliens," drug gangs, and terrorists with Arab or al Qaeda connections who Tancredo insisted were routinely slipping across the border.[3]

Even more than in Europe, irregular immigration across the U.S.-Mexico border tends to be described in military terms. Both mainstream conservatives and far-right border vigilantes have depicted Mexican immigration as the advance guard of a new "reconquest" of the territories annexed by the United States in the nineteenth century, which aims to transform the American Southwest into a de facto Mexican colony known as Aztlán.[4] The paleo-conservative military theorist William Lind has described the U.S.-Mexico border as a battleground against a "mestizo invasion" that is "more dangerous than invasion by a foreign army."[5] And the former head of the Ku Klux Klan, David Duke, once described his desire to transform the border into an unbreachable "Maginot Line" as part of his policy on immigration.[6]

More mainstream politicians and commentators have advocated a similarly militarized approach to border security, which tends to weave Hispanic migrants, drug smugglers, and terrorists into a common narrative of a violated and porous border. In June 2010, Texas congressman John Carter urged the government to deploy between 25,000 and 50,000 troops to defend the "lawless southern border" against an array of threats that included illegal aliens, drug cartels, and al Qaeda.[7]

Such solutions are often presented as an essential antidote to a perceived softness on the part of the federal government, even though over the better part of two decades successive administrations have engaged in a sustained and largely futile attempt to transform America's southern border into an impregnable security barrier. In the early 1990s the Clinton administration took a decisive step toward the militarization of the border when it boosted the numbers of border personnel and used decommissioned metal landing strips from the first Gulf War to construct fortified barriers at El Paso and San Diego in an attempt to reduce the traffic of irregular migrants in both cities. By closing the more accessible urban migratory routes, U.S. officials calculated that migrants would cross in more remote desert areas whose harsh conditions would act as a natural deterrent.

These initiatives coincided with the coming into force of the North American Free Trade Agreement in 1994 and were to a large extent a preemptive attempt to prevent the entry of irregular migrants from Mexico. Since then the border has been continually reinforced with new physical barriers, additional personnel, and an array of surveillance and detection technologies. In the wake of the September 11 attacks, the U.S.-Mexico border was seen as a symptom of American vulnerability in the new era of "homeland security." On one hand, immigration—particularly from Muslim countries—was singled out as a potential security threat to be dealt with through arrests, deportations, and new checks and restrictions. At the same time, expenditures on border enforcement in general—and the U.S.-Mexico border in particular—soared to unprecedented levels.[8]

In 2004 the U.S. Bureau of Customs and Border Protection introduced a new surveillance program along the U.S.-Mexico border called America's Shield Initiative in an attempt to obtain "operational control" against "illegal aliens, potential terrorists, weapons of mass destruction, and other contraband." Between 2001 and 2006, border security funding rose from $4.6 billion to $10.4 billion and the number of Border Patrol agents climbed to just over 21,000, supported by periodic deployments of the National Guard to assist the Border Patrol with logistics and surveillance.

By 2011 Customs and Border Protection had constructed 643.3 miles of pedestrian and vehicle fences along the border, and anti-immigration lobbyists have campaigned for the construction of a "Great Wall of Mexico" stretching from coast to coast—a project that has received little official support on the grounds of cost and practicality. These efforts have often been presented by American officials as an essential corollary of homeland security, regardless of the fact that no known terrorist has ever been caught trying to cross the U.S.-Mexico border. But the dominant concern behind the militarization of the frontier is immigration enforcement, and these efforts are not limited to the territorial frontier. In some border states, the U.S. Border Patrol has introduced permanent inland checkpoints and mobile "tactical checkpoints" up to thirty miles inside U.S. territory, similar to the patrols established in Poland and Slovakia.

As in Europe, American governments have presented their ability to remove illegal immigrants as a litmus test of their ability to control the border. In a ten-year period the number of deportations more than doubled, from just over 150,000 in 1999 to upward of 350,000 in 2008, according to Department of Homeland Security statistics. Deportations reached a new peak under Barack Obama. In the first two years of the Obama administration, Immigration and Customs Enforcement (ICE) shifted its focus away from the mass raids on factories and workplaces and the neighborhood sweeps that characterized the Bush years, concentrating instead on removing irregular migrants with a record of violence or criminality, defined as "the worst of the worst."

In March 2010 the *Washington Post* published internal ICE memos that predicted a steep drop in the numbers of deportations that year, to 310,000—well below ICE's annual target of 400,000.[9] In October 2011, however, ICE announced that it had deported a staggering 396,906 people during the previous fiscal year—an exodus of unprecedented magnitude in U.S. or world history that brought the total number of migrants expelled under the Obama administration to more than 1 million. This increase took place at a time when irregular migration was actually falling, and these figures were achieved by widening the detention net so that even irregular immigrants charged with minor infractions of the law could be depicted as criminals and transformed into deportable migrants.[10]

As in Europe, the enforcement of the U.S. border has become extraterritorial, extending beyond the United States into southern Mexico, where Mexican police routinely intercept U.S.-bound migrants as they cross the border from Guatemala. In Central and even South America, U.S. immigration officials collaborate with local police in an attempt to cut off undocumented migration at its source or in transit countries, where migrants believed to be heading for the United States have been detained and deported.

Despite these efforts, tens of thousands of Mexican and Latino migrants attempt to reach *el otro lado* (the other side) each year via remote desert areas such as the eighteen-mile desert cauldron, known as "the Devil's Highway," on the Tohono O'odham reservation in Arizona. These journeys have massively increased the death toll along the frontier. Estimates of the numbers of migrant deaths since 1994 range between 3,861 and 5,607, but there is a direct correlation between the "prevention and deterrence" strategy adopted by the U.S. Border Patrol in the early 1990s and the rise in casualties from 23 in 1994 to a peak of 827 in 2007.[11] Many of these deaths are the result of hypothermia, exposure, heatstroke, or drowning. But migrants also have been killed by *bajadores* (criminal gangs) during border crossings, massacred by drug cartels, thrown off trains, robbed, assaulted, kidnapped, and raped by criminal gangs and police long before they even reach the border.[12]

If the militarization of the border has failed to prevent these crossings, it has nevertheless provided a rich seam of government funding for defense contractors such as Boeing and Lockheed Martin, which have been tasked with developing border surveillance technologies, and also for the private security corporations that run many U.S. immigrant detention facilities.

Some 400,000 illegal aliens are now detained in the United States every year, while the average number of migrant detainees on any given day in U.S. jails and immigrant detention centers is 32,000. In January 2006 KBR, the engineering and construction subsidiary of the Halliburton group, was awarded a $385 million contract by the U.S. Department of Homeland Security to expand the Enforcement and Removal Operations facilities of ICE as a contingency for what the company described as a hypothetical "emergency influx of immigrants into the U.S." from a destabilized Mexico.

In 2007 the Boeing Corporation won a $2.5 billion contract with the U.S. Department of Homeland Security to construct a seven-hundred-mile "virtual fence" along the U.S.-Mexico border, consisting of 1,800 towers fitted with sensors, video cameras, and stadium lights. In January 2011, however, the Department of Homeland Security was obliged to cancel the much-vaunted Secure Border Initiative (SBInet) as a result of spiraling budget costs and technical inadequacies in an eighty-mile pilot scheme along the Arizona-Mexico border.

Faced with continued evidence of the government's inability to seal the border, politicians and paramilitary vigilantes have undertaken their own enforcement efforts, with ad hoc armed patrols and new surveillance programs. In 2008 Texas governor Rick Perry authorized the Virtual Border Watch program, in which ordinary Texans were invited to observe twenty-four-hour live footage of the 1,250-mile Texas-Mexico border transmitted from twenty-one hidden surveillance cameras. Described by its architect, Blue Servo Inc., as an attempt "to empower the public to proactively participate in fighting border crime," the program enabled viewers to become "virtual deputies" in their own living rooms and report any unauthorized border crossings to local sheriffs.

The invitation for Americans to become "armchair deputies" was more effective as political spectacle than enforcement. Despite receiving more than 50 million hits and reports of sightings from "border guards" as far afield as Australia and New Zealand, the site generated only twenty-six arrests, mostly for drug smuggling, between November 2008 and March the following year. Such initiatives are another consequence of a hyperbolic national debate about immigration and borders in which the wildest fantasies are often propagated without challenge. During the Republican presidential candidates' debates in November 2011, for example, Perry himself claimed that Hamas, Hezbollah, and Iran had all infiltrated Mexico and were preparing to come into the United States—a ridiculous claim that has never been backed up by any credible evidence.

Such fabrications have done little to calm public anxieties about the "vanishing border." From the point of view of security, the U.S.-Mexico border undoubtedly provides legitimate grounds for concern. In recent years the border has become a terrifyingly dystopian frontier between two countries where the average annual income is $30,000 and $4,000, respectively; where armed right-wing vigilantes with racist and white supremacist affiliations talk of "engaging illegal aliens" as if they were military encounters; where retirement homes, golf courses, and prosperous suburban towns are located only a few miles from savage territorial battles between Mexican drug cartels for control of the lucrative American drug market, which have resulted in more than 40,000 deaths in the last three years; and where sophisticated Gaza-like tunnels provide conduits for marijuana and cocaine shipments into the United States and for automatic weapons being sent in the opposite direction.

The militarization of the border has had little impact on these developments, but as in Europe, it has tended to present irregular migration as another form of criminality and reinforced xenophobic and racist depictions of Latino migrants as a collective threat. The political obsession with the border has also coincided with the increased victimization of the estimated 9 million to 12 million irregular Hispanic migrants inside the United States. In April 2010 the state of Arizona passed SB 1070, an act that authorized police to check the immigration status of anyone suspected of being an illegal alien—a category that applied almost exclusively to the state's Hispanic population, many of whom fled the state to avoid arrest and deportation. Since then other states have enacted similar laws. In Alabama in 2011, hundreds of Hispanic families withdrew their children from school after a new law mandated schools to check the immigration status of their pupils. Others ceased going to work or moved to other states, for fear of being stopped by police and deported. These tendencies have clearly been exacerbated by America's economic doldrums. But they also demonstrate once again how exaggerated and unrealistic notions of border security and exclusionary enforcement policies that punish and criminalize irregular immigrants tend not to make societies feel more secure, open, or amenable but instead legitimize instincts that liberal democracies normally would seek to keep in check.

Australia's Refugee Emergency

The public debate about America's "vanishing border" is to some extent a continuation and a reprise of older fears of racial and cultural infiltration that have underpinned previous American attempts to limit immigration in the late nineteenth and early twentieth centuries. Such fears have also been a recurring theme in Australian history, from the various dictation tests introduced in the late nineteenth century to restrict Chinese and Indian migrants to the "white Australia" immigration policy that was not abandoned until the early 1970s.[13]

Australia's historical nervousness because of its geographical proximity to Asia was a key contributing factor to its extraordinarily hard-line response to the relatively low numbers of asylum seekers who began arriving in the 1990s across the Pacific Ocean. In the course of the decade, the number of "unauthorized boat arrivals" seeking asylum in Australia rose from almost nothing to 4,174 in 1999–2000. These developments took place at a time when Australia's relatively recent adoption of a more integrationist and multicultural immigration policy was coming under intense political pressure from the maverick Pauline Hanson's anti-immigrant party One Nation, which argued that Australia was being "swamped by Asians" and that multiculturalism had diluted its Anglo-Saxon identity.

Mainstream Australian politicians were prone to similar rhetoric, and in the closing years of the century the asylum seekers coming to Australia by sea were increasingly depicted as a mortal threat to Australian identity and security.[14] A transformative moment in Australia's refugee "emergency" took place in August 2001 when a Norwegian oil tanker called the *Tampa* rescued 435 asylum seekers, mostly Afghans, from a stricken fishing boat in which they were attempting to travel from Indonesia to Christmas Island in Australia.

The *Tampa* tried to land on the island, where Australia had a reception center cum detention camp for asylum seekers. The government of John Howard was then in the middle of a closely fought electoral campaign and refused to allow the passengers to disembark on Australian soil, in a calculated attempt to gain political advantage through a display of toughness at the border. For eight days the refugees remained on deck, under the vigilance of an Australian Special Air Service boarding party, before Australia finally managed to cajole Papua New Guinea and the tiny island republic of Nauru into accepting them. Bolstered by this unedifying episode, the Howard government authorized the Australian navy to intercept future asylum seekers on the high seas and prevent them from landing on Australian territory.

In addition to funding detention centers on Nauru and Papua New Guinea, the government introduced a new policy known as "excision," which effectively reclassified some five thousand Australian islands, including Christmas Island, as "offshore excised places," in which "offshore entry persons" would be considered "unlawful citizens" and subject to mandatory detention, without access to the asylum procedures available on the mainland.

In a radio interview shortly before his reelection, Howard rejected suggestions that the "Pacific Solution" breached Australia's human rights commitments under the Geneva Convention, insisting that such measures were necessary to ensure that Australia did not become "thick with asylum seekers." In October that year his administration demonstrated how far it was prepared to go to prevent this outcome, reporting that an SIEV (suspected illegal entry vessel) carrying 233 refugees had been intercepted by the Australian navy in the Indian Ocean. According to Howard and his ministers, after being intercepted the asylum seekers had thrown their own children into the sea in an attempt to blackmail the navy into taking the children on board, This episode was presented to the Australian public as proof that people who behaved in this way could not be "genuine refugees" and were not worthy of admission into Australia.

This story quickly unraveled when two photographs of the incident showed six people, including adults, in the sea, wearing life jackets. It then emerged that the Australian frigate HMAS *Adelaide* had fired more than forty rounds across the boat's bow in an attempt to make it turn back to Indonesia, and that these photos had in fact been taken only *after* the Australian navy was finally obliged to rescue the passengers because their boat was sinking.

The "children overboard" affair was followed by a horrific tragedy on October 19 when a boat carrying more than four hundred refugees sank in international waters after leaving Indonesia en route for Australia. At least 353 people drowned, with 45 survivors rescued after spending more than a day in the water. This disaster increased the political pressure on the Howard government from human rights activists and refugee advocates and also from the executive director of the Australian Defence Association, who claimed in November that Australian sailors were demoralized by an ongoing operation against asylum seekers that "goes against their sense of humanity."[15]

The government shrugged off these criticisms, and opinion polls suggested that its tough stance enjoyed public support. According to its own criteria the Pacific Solution appeared to have worked, since few boats reached Australia. But this "victory" was achieved by diverting asylum seekers to remote Pacific processing centers, where they had little or no access to the screening or appeal procedures available inside Australia itself. Many of the migrants were eventually transferred to the mainland, where they found themselves in one of the harshest detention regimes in the Western world.

Even more than the United States, Australia has relied almost exclusively on private security corporations to run its detention facilities, and companies such as GSL Australia, G4S, and Serco have presided over an inhumane detention regime in which detainees, including young children, have been held for two to seven years.

Australia's centers have been the subject of reports of abuse and neglect of detainees and incidents of self-harm. Some of the worst allegations were directed at the Woomera Immigration Reception and Processing Centre in the South Australian outback, which was run by Australian Correctional Management (ACM), a subsidiary of the U.S. security giant Wackenhut. Built with a capacity of four hundred, in 2002 Woomera had a population of more than one thousand detainees, who were incarcerated under an astonishingly dysfunctional system in which detainees were mocked by their guards while self-harming or trying to kill themselves, doped with strong antipsychotic drugs, or had the doors to their cells drilled shut. Dr. Glenda Koutroulis, a psychologist in Woomera, told a newspaper how she saw fifty Iraqi asylum seekers dig mock graves in protest against their detention and then lie dehydrating for hours in the heat.[16]

In 2002 and 2003 Australia's seven centers were set on fire during riots and protests, and Howard's successor, Kevin Rudd, eventually closed the worst facilities following the Labour Party election victory in 2007. The Rudd government also ended the Pacific Solution and closed the reception center on Nauru. Over the next few years, however, the numbers of boat arrivals began to increase once again, reaching an all-time high of 118 boats with 5,609 asylum seekers in 2009–10. In 2009, Australia's Department of Immigration and Multicultural and Indigenous Affairs awarded a $370 million contract to Serco to manage its immigration detention facilities, and by 2011 the numbers of detention centers had increased to twenty-four and the number of detainees had risen from 1,000 to 6,700.

That year, according to the *New York Times*, "riots, fires and suicidal protests left millions of dollars in damage at Serco-run centers from Christmas Island to Villawood and self-harm by detainees rose twelvefold."[17] The Labour government also embarked on an offshore processing program not very different from that of its predecessors, in that it aimed to involve other states in the region, particularly Indonesia, in cutting off smuggling routes and detaining and screening asylum seekers before they reached Australia. After various unsuccessful attempts to develop an "East Timor solution" and an "Indonesia solution," Rudd's successor, Julia Gillard, finally concluded an agreement with the Malaysian government in August 2011, in which Malaysia agreed to accept eight hundred asylum seekers from Australia in return for an Australian pledge to resettle 4,000 of Malaysia's 92,000 refugees.

Fear of a Migrant Planet

As in Europe and the United States, Australia's "refugee emergency" has fueled a constant search for new forms of exclusion that reach beyond the border in an attempt to intercept and identify unwanted travelers before they reach the border itself. Australia's panoply of preentry border controls includes the use of Advance Passenger Processing databases; the Movement Alert List, which contains travel documents, biographical details, and biometric data on travelers who the Australian government considers "may pose a serious threat to the Australian community"; and the deployment of airline liaison officers at foreign airports, who categorize travelers as "OK to board" or "not OK to board" at the moment when they present their documents for inspection.

American and European governments have also attempted to fix the identities of unwanted travelers by amassing an ever-widening array of biometric data that includes not just fingerprints but iris, face, gait, and vein recognition. In 2004 the U.S. Department of Homeland Security introduced its Smart Border Alliance, which collates information from various biometric databases on all travelers entering and leaving the United States through the United States Visitor and Immigrant Status Indicator Technology (US-VISIT) program in order to eliminate what the Department of Homeland Security calls "criminals and immigration violators."

According to the company Accenture, which created many of these data-bases, the collation of this information will make "US border inspectors the last line of defense, not the first," through a detection and enforcement program that is potentially limitless.[18] Australia and Europe have a similar concept of deterritorialized border enforcement. In theory at least, this ac-cumulation of data will one day extend borders to the most far-flung airport or travel agency, flagging unwanted travelers the moment they make an online booking, so that the process of buying a ticket or obtaining a visa will be dependent on biometric information that cannot be forged or evaded.

Proof of identity may still not justify entry at the border. In September 2010 the U.S. Department of Homeland Security announced that it was testing iris scanner technology on immigrants caught by Border Patrol offi-cers at the U.S.-Mexico border. In October the following year the Depart-ment of Homeland Security began testing a "pre-crime" system known as Future Attribute Screening Technology (FAST), which aims to detect po-tentially harmful behavior by measuring changes in people's breathing rate, temperature, and other bodily indicators. The technology is intended to be used at airports, borders, and public events.

The European Union is researching similar technologies. More than €1.5 billion has been earmarked by the European Commission for new security research projects, which include the development of a video and audio sur-veillance network called Automatic Detection of Abnormal Behaviour and Threats in Crowded Spaces (ADABTS) for use at public events and border entry points.[19]

In February 2008 the European Commission announced proposals to create a European Border Surveillance System (EUROSUR), which pro-poses to integrate satellite and radar systems into a "system of systems" that will provide complete "situational awareness" at Europe's land and maritime borders in order to "reduce the number of illegal immigrants entering the EU undetected."[20]

The EU also plans to make increased use of robotics in border surveillance. In 2010 Frontex invited expressions of interest in an R&D workshop on

"Small UAVs and Fixed Systems for Land Border Surveillance," systems that would be used at Europe's "green borders." In 2012 the European Union is set to deploy the Autonomous Maritime Surveillance System at various maritime borders. Consisting of a chain of buoys equipped with visual and acoustic sensors, this early warning system is being constructed by a consortium led by Carl Zeiss Optronics, whose prediction that it will lead to "safer, more secure borders" is accompanied by a photograph of a border guard attempting to turn back a *cayuco* filled with African migrants.

The European Union's research projects also include the Transportable Autonomous Patrol for Land Border Surveillance (TALOS) consortium, which is currently testing "a mobile network of ground robots, drones and the command centers from which they are run" at the EU's eastern borders. The TALOS consortium includes many giants from the security-industrial complex, including the French company Sagem, Thales Security Systems, Israeli Aerospace Industries and the Polish company PIAP, the last of which manufactures combat robots.[21] A 2010 article in *New Scientist* described a hypothetical European border at which

> a migrant makes a furtive dash across an unwalled rural section of a national border, only to be confronted by a tracked robot that looks like a tiny combat tank—with a gimballed camera for an eye. As he passes the bug-eyed droid, it follows him and a border guard's voice booms from its loudspeaker. He has illegally entered the country, he is warned, and if he does not turn back he will be filmed and followed by the robot, or by an airborne drone, until guards apprehend him.[22]

This sci-fi scenario may not be far away. In 2004 the U.S. Border Patrol began testing unmanned aerial vehicles along the border, and U.S. Customs and Border Protection currently has six Predator drones in operation along the border. Armed robots have already been deployed by the South Korean government at the DMZ, and Israel has used a similar device at its border with the Gaza Strip. Current U.S. research into military robotics makes it highly likely that autonomous land robot sentries designed for "area denial" will be deployed to monitor the U.S.-Mexico border.

Other area denial technologies under development by the U.S. military include taser mines, which shoot out electrified darts; remote-controlled guns; directed-energy systems that project extreme heat, unbearable noise, or strong unpleasant smells; and a mobile truck-mounted projector that directs disabling heat at adversaries. All these technologies have potential applications for militarized border enforcement in a century that may well be dominated by even larger migratory movements.[23] The United Nations has predicted that 50 million people may become "climate refugees" in the next thirty years, and other estimates are considerably higher. According to the UN, 10 million people worldwide have already been displaced by environmental degradation and other weather-related disasters, and some politicians and environmentalists have called upon governments to widen the criteria for refugee protection to include them.

These demands have not met with a positive response from governments that are already keen to limit the numbers of political refugees. In 2003 a scenario-planning report commissioned by the U.S. Department of Defense, entitled "An Abrupt Climate Change Scenario and Its Implications for United States National Security," analyzed the potential repercussions of a global cooling event occurring by 2030, which ushers in a cascade of catastrophic events including global famine, riots, nuclear war, and mass migrations. One scenario raised the possibility that

> the United States and Australia are likely to build defensive fortresses around their countries because they have the resources and reserves to achieve self-sufficiency. . . . Borders will be strengthened around the country to hold back unwanted starving immigrants from the Caribbean islands (an especially severe problem), Mexico, and South America.[24]

This possibility was one of various scenarios, but given the current mood, the notion that "unwanted starving immigrants" might one day be turned back at the border is not an especially outlandish prospect. In the Mexican film director Rodrigo Plá's dystopian parable *La Zona*, a middle-class gated community in Mexico City retreats from the poverty and corruption of the metropolis behind barbed wire and high walls. With its entrances and outer perimeter permanently monitored by closed-circuit cameras and security guards, the well-heeled residents of the Zone inhabit a seemingly placid and insulated bubble of fortified privilege, with manicured lawns, four-wheel drive vehicles, expansive suburban houses, and a golf course under the supervision of the all-powerful neighborhood committee. But their obsession with security and their paranoia about the dysfunctional world outside also trap them in a state of perpetual fear and hatred of what lies outside. When three petty criminals break into the compound and murder a rich woman during a botched robbery, the Zone's crust of well-heeled civility crumbles and its residents turn into a vengeful and lawless lynch mob.

For the last two decades, some of the most powerful nations on earth have attempted to transform themselves into insulated and protected zones in an attempt to limit and restrict the unwanted movement of people from the global South. There is no indication that these efforts have made those who live inside them feel more secure—to say nothing of their impact on those who have been excluded. Faced with the fortified world order that has been constructed, and the prospect of even worse to come, it is necessary to return to Europe once again and consider how things might be done differently.

Beyond the Border

More than twenty-five years after the signing of the Schengen Agreement, Europe's attempts to manage irregular migration cannot be listed among the European Union's most sterling achievements. In their determination to limit or at least slow down the pace of irregular migration, European governments have created an extraordinarily elaborate and complex system of exclusion and control that is simultaneously ruthless, repressive, devious, chaotic, and dysfunctional, with consequences that are often strikingly at odds with its stated rationalizations and objectives. Presented as a moral or humanitarian crusade to combat "immigration crime" and save migrants from death and exploitation, this border enforcement regime has spawned a transnational smuggling industry and contributed to a shocking death toll that surely would be considered intolerable if white Europeans were dying in the same numbers. Intended to harmonize asylum procedures across the continent and share the refugee "burden" more evenly between member states, legal instruments such as the Dublin Convention have transformed border countries such as Greece, Italy, and Malta into migrant traps, where men, women, and children remain for months and sometimes years in legal limbo with little or no possibility of becoming productive members of any society. If the harsh post-entry asylum measures such as detention and destitution adopted by various governments over the last two decades have made life harder for asylum seekers, there is no evidence that these policies have worn down their resolve to remain in Europe. In Greece the destruction of the Patras migrant camps in 2009 merely dispersed their occupants to Athens, Igoumenitsa, and other parts of the country. After nearly two years of unrelenting police repression in Calais, new migrants continue to pass through the city's squats or less visible camps up and down the French coast.

Nor is it clear that these measures have reduced the number of people coming to Europe to seek asylum. The impact of border enforcement is always difficult to quantify, because the intensity of irregular migration is invariably influenced by a variety of factors. In 2010, Frontex noted a 30 percent decrease in the numbers of detections of illegal border crossings since the previous year—a decline that it attributed to the reduced pull factor of employment opportunities and what it called the "strong deterrent effect" of naval patrols in the Mediterranean. In July 2011, on the other hand, the Frontex Risk Analysis Unit recorded a steep rise in the number of illegal crossings in the central Mediterranean in the first quarter of the year that was "almost exclusively due to Tunisians arriving in Lampedusa following civil unrest that spread across North Africa" since the beginning of the year, suggesting that this "deterrent effect" was not necessarily a decisive factor in determining levels of irregular immigration.[1]

There is no doubt that the concentration of resources and personnel has sometimes succeeded in closing migratory routes across specific borders, but these "victories" have usually been followed by the emergence of new routes elsewhere. What is clear is that despite deportations and refusals of entry, pushbacks and towbacks, externalized border partnerships, preentry border controls and punitive postentry policies, and immigration raids, men, women, and children have continued to find their way to Europe in search of asylum and work, sometimes by extraordinarily convoluted and dangerous routes.

All this constitutes a political and moral failure on a massive scale. It is shameful and contemptible that one of the richest trading blocs in the world should depict migrants as criminal intruders and potential invaders. It is a gross violation of the EU's moral and political values for governments to reduce rejected asylum seekers to homelessness and destitution in order to make them leave, place children in detention, or provide a home to unaccompanied minors only to deport them when they reach eighteen.

Such policies not only have had disastrous consequences for migrants themselves but also have a chilling effect on the societies that introduced them. Democratic principles of accountability, transparency, and the rule of law are not compatible with cultures of impunity in which even the most grievous violations of migrant rights—including the right to life—are neither investigated nor punished. Governments cannot proclaim their commitment to refugee protection and human rights yet do everything possible to deny these rights in practice. The European Union's laudable determination to enshrine human rights as the cornerstone of its political identity does not sit easily with an enforcement agenda that intimidates victims of rape and sexual violence into silence, outsources the repression of its unwanted migrants to foreign governments, and then turns a blind eye to the results.

Such practices have become so routine and seemingly natural that many Europeans have become inured to their inherent brutality and inhumanity, enabling unscrupulous governments to engage in squalid political competitions over the numbers of migrants they detain and deport as proof of their ability to secure their borders and protect the public. Although some European politicians have argued that enforcement is a precondition for social cohesion and integration, this morbid and mutually reinforcing dynamic involving governments, the media, and the public has stigmatized immigration in general and legitimized the most xenophobic and racist anti-immigrant politics of ultranationalists and the extreme right in ways that threaten to derail the entire European project.

Even from the viewpoint of Europe's own self-interest, this enforcement regime is counterproductive and irrational. It benefits no one—except some employers—to have some 5 million to 8 million people scattered across the continent in a state of permanent illegality. If detention and deportation have brought lucrative contracts to some private security companies, they have also created a constant drain on the public purse that is out of all proportion to their negligible impact on migration. Last but not least, Europe's persistent attempts to keep immigrants out is at odds with the continent's increasing need to bring immigrants in.

Numerous economists and analysts have pointed out that for a continent whose population is both decreasing in number and aging, a continued flow of immigration from outside the European Union is essential to maintain its standard of living, pay for its social services, and fund its pensions. In December 2010 the European commissioners Cecilia Malmstrom and László Andor argued that "Europe will not survive without immigration" and predicted that Europe's working-age population would shrink by as many as 50 million people between 2013 and 2050. The authors calculated that between 384,000 and 700,000 IT workers and 1 million to 2 million health care workers from outside the EU would be required by 2015 and 2020, respectively, in order to fill a skills shortage across the continent.[2]

Other analysts have made similar predictions. In May 2007 Christopher Johnson, former chief economic adviser for Lloyd's Bank, argued that the

United Kingdom would require 7 million immigrants over the next half century in order to pay its pensions and maintain the Treasury's modest predicted growth rate of 2 percent.[3] In May 2011 Frank-Jürgen Weise, the German labor agency chief, claimed that Germany needed 2 million immigrants to address a national labor shortage—in spite of the ongoing European debt crisis.[4] According to the *Economist*, the Italian population would have fallen by 750,000 in 2009 had it not been for immigration. Instead it rose by 295,000, despite the Berlusconi government's boasts of having "stopped the invasion" that same year.[5]

Many governments recognize the economic importance of immigration in private but too many politicians lack the courage to explain it to their electorates, preferring instead to engage in crowd-pleasing promises of tougher border enforcement, regardless of the ineffectiveness of these efforts—or the accusations of "softness" that invariably rebound on them when these crackdowns fail to achieve their targets. The result is that Europe remains locked into a fortress model of border enforcement that will never be able to do anything more than slow down the pace of migration—unless European governments are prepared to escalate the current level of surveillance and enforcement in ways that would effectively seal the continent off from the outside world and transform much of the continent into panoptic police states of the kind that were only recently thought to have passed into historical obsolescence.

A Borderless World?

There are—at least in theory—alternatives to this model. European governments could dismantle the detention gulag inside the continent and beyond it. They could end the brutal and ineffective policy of enforced destitution. They could reform the Dublin Convention, so that asylum seekers would be able to make their appeals in the country of their choice, rather than the first one they come to. If this meant that some countries received more asylum seekers than they were able to absorb, then incoming migrants could be offered choices from a wider list of countries. Instead of negotiating readmission agreements with countries that have poor or nonexistent human rights commitments, European governments could work with the countries that migrants pass through in order to ensure that the human rights of those trying to reach the continent are protected throughout their journeys.

If Europe seriously wishes to "ensure the full and inclusive application of the Geneva Convention on Refugees," as Commissioner Cecilia Malmstrom insisted in a speech in 2011 to commemorate the convention's sixtieth anniversary, then European governments could make it easier for refugees to claim asylum in or close to the countries they come from without having to risk their lives or run the current gauntlet in order to achieve it.[6] Ultimately commitments to refugee protection are dependent not just on the obligations contained in formal treaties but on the willingness of governments and their populations to actually implement them.

After decades of misrepresentation and vilification of "bogus" asylum seekers by the media and politicians, such generosity is conspicuously absent in many European countries, and it would require a major educational effort and a significant raising of awareness to reverse this situation. Individual governments and the European Union could take a major step toward this process by detaching the issue of irregular migration from questions of security and criminality. Governments have the right and the obligation to ensure the security of their citizens, but this objective is not served through spurious and ultimately meaningless rhetoric that identifies migrants and asylum seekers as "harmful" people and places them in the same category as gangsters, human traffickers, and terrorists.

Instead of restricting the principle of solidarity to pan-European cooperation in border enforcement and Frontex-style joint operations, EU member states could engage in a collective effort to create a genuine "Europe of asylum," according to their different capabilities and resources. A more generous attitude toward refugees should not be predicated on the vilification of economic migrants. If people fleeing war, violence, and persecution deserve priority, this should not mean that those coming to Europe to escape poverty or support their families should be regarded as parasitical intruders or "bad migrants." Such aspirations are an inevitable consequence of the fractured and divided world that we now inhabit, but they also need to be placed in perspective. Contrary to media representations, Europe is not facing an irresistible and limitless influx of the world's poor and dispossessed. In 2010 the total number of third-country nationals in the twenty-seven countries of the European Union was 20.2 million, 6.5 percent out of a total population of nearly half a billion.[7]

Of these the largest number were Turkish citizens, at nearly 2.5 million, followed by Moroccans (1.8 million) and Albanians (1 million). Morocco and Algeria were the only African countries included in the top ten non-EU nationalities, despite the fears of an African invasion that have so often accompanied Europe's attempts to harden its southern borders. These statistics do not reveal the many different types of migration, which include both permanent and temporary workers as well as students. Nor do they include irregular migrants.

But they do not bear out the fantasies of a continent inundated by immigration to the point of collapse. Contrary to the way it is often represented, migration is a surprisingly rational phenomenon, in which choices and expectations change according to geopolitical and economic circumstances. In 2009 statistics published by the Latin American airlines Aersur and Avianca revealed that 25,000 Latin American immigrants with residency papers in Spain had bought one-way tickets back to their countries of origin—a development that suggests that illegal migrants without papers may be equally disinclined to seek jobs or economic opportunities. According to the Spanish Office of National Statistics 232,000 migrants left Spain in 2008, compared with 120,000 in 2006. By March 2009, more than half the 1.8 million migrants who had arrived in Britain from eight eastern European countries (the A8 nations) since 2004 had returned home. Within months of the "biblical exodus" of Tunisians in the spring of 2011, many Tunisians had begun to return to Tunisia because there was no work available in Europe.

Recognizing the inherent rationality of migration not only allows for a less fearful and more rational response to it but also makes it possible to seek policies that take its variants into account. Many migrants come to Europe to work seasonally or temporarily but, like the greenhouse workers I met in Almería, choose to remain there even when work is not immediately available rather than return home and risk having to make the same dangerous journey. European governments could devise programs that recognize the phenomenon of "circular migration" through less stringent visa restrictions and temporary or multiple-entry visas, based on a realistic assessment of the numbers of migrants who come to their countries each year.

They could also offer coherent pathways to citizenship or legality to the 5 million or so irregular migrants already in the continent, many of whom have been in Europe for years. They could sign the United Nations Convention on the Protection of the Rights of All Migrant Workers and Members of their Families and take steps to ensure that these rights are enforceable. Europe could undoubtedly do more to improve conditions that drive migrants to leave their countries—not least by not waging wars in them. The European Union and individual member states have made attempts to promote trade and economic development in immigrant-producing countries, particularly in North Africa, but these efforts have been largely piecemeal and their impact on migration is likely to be negligible, at least in the short term.

The idea that development can prevent migration by addressing its root causes tends to overlook the contribution that migrants themselves make to their countries of origin in the form of remittances, the acquisition of new skills, and higher wages.[8] Immigration from poor to rich countries always creates the risk of a brain drain of skilled personnel, such as nurses and doctors, but these effects could be mitigated through negotiation between European governments and immigrant-producing countries aimed at balancing the needs of both.

These alternatives do not necessarily mean a borderless Europe that anyone can enter "without anyone asking you questions about who you are," as one German No Borders activist put it to me in Calais. As long as the nation-state remains the dominant political unit in global society, there will be borders and dividing lines between one country and another, and governments will insist on the right to monitor who crosses them and restrict or grant admission.[9] But national borders do not have to be "walled" antimigrant barriers. If borders can be hardened, they can also be softened and made more open and accessible. The fact that there are no checkpoints on the frontier between Poland and Lithuania does not mean there is no border or that Poland and Lithuania have ceased to exist.

It may seem outlandish to think of extending similar arrangements to other countries in today's security-obsessed and xenophobic climate, but the European Union managed to achieve something that until a few decades before had been thought impossible: the removal of national border controls and the extension of free movement across the continent to all its citizens. This transformation was achieved through years of complicated and arduous negotiations, and often in the teeth of fierce opposition from northern European countries that feared a flood of impoverished migrants from southern Europe.[10] There is no reason to believe that similar agreements could not be concluded one day with some of the countries Europe's migrants come from, and that new arrangements could be made allowing nationals from non-EU countries the same right to sell their labor that Europe has now created for its own citizens.

Such a world might not be entirely borderless, but the absence of borders cannot be considered a panacea for every problem. Even within Europe, the new movement of European workers from east to west has not been without tensions and problems, and dismantling Europe's antimigrant borders will not be an entirely painless process. But accepting the inevitability of migration and seeking to maximize its benefits both for migrants and for the receiving countries would nevertheless be a considerable improvement on the brutal system that has been constructed over the last few decades. The search for such a better way cannot be confined to Europe alone. Migration is a global phenomenon that requires international attention and cooperation, but the European Union's successful dismantling of its national border controls—however tentative this experiment may seem at present—nevertheless offers a potential model that could be widened outward.

Some of these proposals are contained in the European Commission's "Global Approach to Migration and Mobility," a strategy paper that was presented to the European Parliament in November 2011. In it the commission noted, "European countries are facing labor market shortages and vacancies that cannot be filled by the domestic workforce in specific sectors, e.g. in health, science and technology," and that "long-term population ageing in Europe is expected to halve the ratio between persons of working age (20–64) and persons aged 65 and above in the next fifty years."[11]

The paper called for new efforts to facilitate the entry of non-EU nationals to fill the continent's skills shortages through less stringent visa requirements; for the development of "migration and mobility dialogues" with neighboring countries such as Morocco, Tunisia, and Egypt, and also farther afield in China and India; and for new rules to extend employment and social security protection rights to non-EU citizens working in the continent. Though driven primarily by European economic priorities, the paper also proposed to transform migration into a mutually beneficial process for its partner countries, based on the recognition that "migration governance is not about 'flows,' 'stocks' and 'routes,' it is about people."

At first sight these recommendations represent a positive alternative to the restrictive policies of the last two decades and a significant step toward the less aggressive attitude toward migration advocated by many NGOs and human rights activists. But the commission also tied these proposals to a continuation and intensification of the fight against illegal immigration, with the same emphasis on restrictions, barriers, return and readmission policies, and outsourced border controls, as well as the same arid linkages between irregular migration, security, and crime—all of which call into question the paper's insistence that "the dialogue and cooperation with partners should strive to protect the human rights of all migrants throughout their migration process."

Nowhere in this document is there any recognition of the disastrous impact that Europe's attempts to prevent irregular migration have had on the human rights of migrants for more than two decades, nor does it define how these rights might be protected or even what they actually consist of. In the current climate it is difficult to imagine that even its more progressive proposals are likely to be accepted—and they are more likely to be presented by Europhobic politicians as another example of Europe's "democratic deficit" and an attempt from Brussels to foist an open-border policy on an unwilling continent.

Fortress Europe is unlikely, therefore, to be dismantled from the top down. A transformation in Europe's response to undocumented migration and migration in general requires a wider political transformation from below, which challenges the current enforcement model and the fear, racism, and paranoia that drives it, which replaces exclusion with solidarity and inclusiveness and sets out to create a genuine European "area of freedom, security and justice" that is not dependent on denying all three conditions to others.

All over Europe undocumented migrants are challenging their exclusion and marginalization with the limited instruments and means available to them, from hunger strikes, demonstrations, and protests to riots and insurrections in detention centers. In some cases they have won significant individual battles, but these mobilizations cannot by themselves change the policies that have been developed over the last two decades—or the attitudes that underpin them. In the current age of austerity, Europe's anti-immigrant politics are dragging the continent toward a very bleak and dangerous future. With the European dream tarnished by economic crisis and incompetent leadership, with a public increasingly fearful and resentful of the impact of the economic crisis on jobs, pensions, and lifestyles, the nihilistic hatreds and identity politics promulgated by the far right have an attractive and simplistic appeal, and even supposedly progressive politicians have propagated populist slogans such as "British jobs for British workers" in order to distract attention from their own failings.

If Europe is to avoid falling into something that may not be fascism but may not be far removed from it, it is imperative that Europeans resist these tendencies and develop a response to migration that reflects its best traditions rather than its worst. Years ago, Ronald Reagan demanded that Mikhail

Gorbachev tear down the Berlin Wall as proof of his commitment to perestroika. Today it is incumbent on Europeans to take down the "walls" that have been constructed over the last two decades in order to demonstrate their commitment to the principles on which the union was founded, and to prevent their fears, prejudices, and hatreds from corroding these ideals.

Notes

Introduction

1. United Against Racism, *Death by Policy: The Fatal Realities of Fortress Europe*, www.unitedagainstracism.org/pages/underframeFatalRealitiesFortressEurope.htm.

2. Transcript of interview taken from http://news.bbc.co.uk/1/hi/world/europe /2995084.stm.

3. "Beware: The New Goths Are Coming," *Sunday Times*, June 12, 2006.

4. Medical Foundation for the Victims of Torture, *Harm on Removal: Excessive Force Against Failed Asylum Seekers*, 2004, 55–58, www.statewatch.org/news/2004 /oct/Harm-on-Removal.pdf.

1. A Gated Continent

1. M. McLuhan, *Understanding Media: The Extensions of Man* (MIT Press, 1964), 3.

2. Friedrich Ratzel, *Politische Geographie* (1897), quoted in Malcolm Anderson, *Frontiers: Territory and State Formation in the Modern World* (Polity Press, 1996), 14.

3. Quoted in Duncan Salkeld, "Alien Desires: Travellers and Sexuality in Early Modern London," in Thomas Beveridge, ed., *Borders and Travellers in Early Modern Europe*, 35–51 (Ashgate, 2007).

4. Quoted in Peter Fryer, *Staying Power: The History of Black People in Britain* (Pluto Press, 1992), 12.

5. The best history of the advent of the passport is John Torpey, *The Introduction of the Passport: Surveillance, Citizenship and the State* (Cambridge University Press, 2000).

6. Stefan Zweig, *The World of Yesterday* (Pushkin Press, 2009), 436.

7. Quoted in Adam M. McKeown, *Melancholy Order: Asian Migration and the Globalization of Borders* (Columbia University Press, 2008), 190.

8. Zweig, *World of Yesterday*, 436–37.

9. For a detailed discussion of the Nansen passport initiative, see Torpey, *Introduction of the Passport*; and M. Marrus, *The Unwanted: European Refugees in the Twentieth Century* (Oxford University Press, 1985), 51–121.

10. International Organization for Migration, *World Migration 2003: Managing Migration Challenges and Responses*, 177, http://publications.iom.int/bookstore/free /WMR_2003.pdf.

2. Postcards from Schengenland

1. Statistics from Migration Office, Ministry of Interior of the Slovak Republic, February 2010.

2. "Slovak Asylum System 'Discourages' Refugees," *Slovak Spectator*, November 15, 2004, http://spectator.sme.sk/articles/view/17808/1.

3. Human Rights Watch, *Ukraine: On the Margins, Rights Violations Against Migrants and Asylum Seekers at the New Eastern Border*, November 2005, www.hrw.org /sites/default/files/reports/ukraine1105webwcover.pdf. See also Border Monitoring Project Ukraine, *Access to Protection Denied: Refoulement of Refugees and Minors on the Eastern Borders of the EU—The Case of Hungary, Slovakia and Ukraine*, http:// bordermonitoring-ukraine.eu/2010/11/18/access-to-protection-denied-refoule ment-of-refugees-and-minors-on-the-eastern-borders-of-the-eu-%E2%80%93-the -case-of-hungary-slovakia-and-ukraine.

3. Policing the Spanish Frontier

1. Javier Bauluz, *Dead Body by an Umbrella: The Story of a Controversial Picture*, www.ha-ka.dk/kf/tarifa.htm.

2. Defensor del Pueblo, *Informe annual 2005 y debates en las Cortes Generales*, Publicaciones del Congreso de los Diputados, 288, www.defensordelpueblo.es/es/Docu mentacion/Publicaciones/anual/Documentos/INFORME2005informe.pdf.

3. Ibid., 292.

4. Defensor del Pueblo, *Informe annual 2006 y debates en las Cortes Generales*, Publicaciones del Congreso de los Diputados, 296, www.defensordelpueblo.es/es/Doc umentacion/Publicaciones/anual/Documentos/INFORME2006informe.pdf.

5. For an analysis of the development of the Euro-Med partnership and the "Barcelona process" in the 1990s, see Russell King, "The Mediterranean: Europe's Rio Grande," in Malcolm Anderson and Eberhard Bort, eds., *The Frontiers of Europe* (Continuum, 1998).

6. Médecins Sans Frontières, *Sexual Violence and Migration: The Hidden Reality of Sub-Saharan Women Trapped in Morocco En Route to Europe*, March 2010, www.doc torswithoutborders.org/publications/reports/2010/MSF-sexual-violence.pdf.

7. UN Office on Drugs and Crime, *The Role of Organized Crime in the Smuggling of Migrants from West Africa to the European Union*, 2011, 20, www.unodc.org/doc

uments/human-trafficking/Migrant-Smuggling/Report_SOM_West_Africa_EU
.pdf.

4. Mare Schengen

1. Jack Shenker, "Aircraft Carrier Left Us to Die, Say Migrants," *The Guardian*, May 8, 2011, www.guardian.co.uk/world/2011/may/08/nato-ship-libyan-migrants.

2. "The Third Great Siege?" *Sunday Times of Malta*, August 21, 2005, www .timesofmalta.com/articles/view/20050821/opinion/the-third-great-siege.80456.

3. *Frontex-Led EU Illegal Immigration Technical Mission to Libya: 28 May–5 June 2007*, 10, www.statewatch.org/news/2007/oct/eu-libya-frontex-report.pdf.

4. There are a number of reports that deal with the dire conditions facing migrants in Libya. See Fortress Europe, *Escape from Tripoli: Report on the Conditions of Migrants in Transit in Libya*, www.statewatch.org/news/2007/nov/fortress-europe -libya-report.pdf; and Sara Hamood, *African Transit Migration Through Libya to Europe: The Human Cost*, American University in Cairo, Forced Migration and Refugee Studies Program, 2006, www.aucegypt.edu/GAPP/cmrs/reports/Documents/Afri can_Transit_Migration_through_Libya_-_Jan_2006_000.pdf.

5. *La Repubblica*, March 9, 2010, quoted in Migreurop 2009/10 Report, *European Borders: Controls, Detentions and Deportations*, 4, www.migreurop.org/IMG/pdf /rapport-migreurop-2010-en_-_2-121110.pdf.

5. The Greek Labyrinth

1. "Undercover Officer Explains How He Trawls Border Looking for Immigrants," Agence France-Presse, June 16, 2009, http://archive.ekathimerini.com/ 4dcgi/_w_articles_ell_0_16/06/2009_108089.

2. For an account of this episode, see Amnesty International, *Turkey/Greece: Fear for Safety, Torture, Ill-Treatment*, July 25, 2001, www.amnesty.org/en/library/ asset/EUR44/045/2001/en/5979d410-fb29-11dd-9486-a1064e51935d/eur440452 001en.pdf.

3. The European Committee for the Prevention of Torture offered a more positive account of conditions at Filakio in a 2008 report that concluded it was clean but overcrowded. See "Report to the Government of Greece on the Visit to Greece Carried Out by the European Committee for the Prevention of Torture and Inhuman or Degrading Treatment or Punishment (CPT)," September 2008, www.cpt.coe.int /documents/grc/2009-20-inf-eng.htm.

4. Human Rights Watch, *Stuck in a Revolving Door: Iraqis and Other Asylum Seekers and Migrants at the Greek/Turkey Entrance to the European Union*, November 2009, 71, www.hrw.org/sites/default/files/reports/greeceturkey1108web_0.pdf.

5. Group of Lawyers for the Rights of Migrants and Refugees, press release for the rebellion in Venna detention center, March 15, 2010, http://omadadikigorwneng lish.blogspot.com/2010/03/press-release-for-rebellion-in-venna.html.

6. Pro Asyl, "The Truth May Be Bitter but It Must Be Told: The Situation of Refugees in the Aegean and the Practices of the Greek Coast Guard," 2007, www .proasyl.de/fileadmin/proasyl/fm_redakteure/Englisch/Griechenlandbericht_Engl .pdf. The Iranian author Behzad Yaghmaian has also interviewed a survivor who claims that the boat he was on was rammed and sunk by the Greek Coast Guard, killing twelve of his fellow passengers near the island of Hios. See Behzad Yagh-maian, *Embracing the Infidel: Stories of Muslim Migrants on the Journey West* (Dela-corte Press, 2005), 83.

7. Ibid., 13.

6. Small Island: British Borders

1. Behzad Yaghmaian, *Embracing the Infidel: Stories of Muslim Migrants on the Journey West* (Delacorte Press, 2005), 91.

2. Ibid., 109.

3. Quoted in Campaign Against Racism and Fascism, "Learning the Lessons of Dover," CARF 52 (October/November 1999), www.irr.org.uk/carf/feat31.html. For a wider analysis of the policy repercussions of Dover, see V. Robinson et al., *Spreading the Burden? A Review of Policies to Disperse Asylum Seekers* (Polity Press, 2003), 103–46.

4. Quoted in Tony Kushner and Catherine Knox, *Refugees in an Age of Genocide* (Frank Cass, 1999), 23. For a discussion of British anti-immigrant sentiment at the turn of the twentieth century and the political context surrounding the Aliens Act, see Robert Winder, *Bloody Foreigners: The Story of Immigration to Britain* (Abacus, 2005).

5. For an analysis of the political background to this legislation, see Paul Foot, *Immigration and Race in British Politics* (Penguin Books, 1965).

6. In a special report on the vilification of asylum seekers worldwide, UNHCR singled out the British media for their "derogatory and inflammatory language." See "Victims of Intolerance," *Refugees Magazine* 142, no. 1 (2006), www.unhcr.org /44508c182.html.

7. Home Office, *Secure Borders, Safe Haven: Integration with Diversity in Mod-ern Britain*, 2002, www.archive2.official-documents.co.uk/document/cm53/5387 /cm5387.pdf.

8. Secretary of State for the Home Department, *Controlling Our Borders: Making Migration Work for Britain: Five Year Strategy for Asylum and Migration*, February 2005, 33, www.archive2.official-documents.co.uk/document/cm64/6472/6472.pdf.

9. "UK to Tighten Border Controls Even Further," WorkPermit.com, March 29, 2007, www.workpermit.com/news/2007_03_29/uk/new_initiative_border_control .htm.

10. *Fairer, Faster and Firmer: A Modern Approach to Immigration and Asylum* (HMSO, 1998), www.archive.official-documents.co.uk/document/cm40/4018/4018.htm.

11. For an indication of the tone of these allegations, see Melanie Phillips, "The Secret Plot to Destroy Britain's Identity," *Daily Mail*, February 24, 2010.

7. The Internal Border

1. *An Opportunity and a Challenge: Migration in the European Union*, European Commission Directorate-General, May 2009, ec.europa.eu/publications/book lets/move/81/en.doc.

2. For a detailed analysis of these new quota-driven deportations, see Liz Fekete, *A Suitable Enemy: Racism, Migration and Islamophobia in Europe* (Pluto Press, 2009), 135–56.

3. Amnesty International, *Spain: Briefing to the UN Committee on the Elimination of Racial Discrimination: 78th Session February 2011, Article 3.4*, www.amnesty.org /en/library/asset/EUR41/003/2011/en/249396f2-dacb-43e9-86a8-83b7a8f311f2 /eur410032011en.html.

4. The Eritreans were deported on September 30 and October 3, 2002, despite prior warnings from Amnesty International that they risked punishment beforehand. "Borg Had Been Warned About Danger Days Before Deportation," *Times of Malta*, May 25, 2004, www.timesofmalta.com/articles/view/20040525/local/borg-had -been-warned-about-danger-days-before-deportation.122150. See also Amnesty International, *Eritrea: You Have No Right to Ask, Government Resists Scrutiny on Human Rights*, May 18, 2004, www.amnesty.org/en/library/asset/AFR64/003/2004 /en/d5063e29-d5f6-11dd-bb24-1fb85fe8fa05/afr640032004en.pdf.

5. Medical Foundation for the Victims of Torture, *Harm on Removal: Excessive Force Against Failed Asylum Seekers*, 2004, www.statewatch.org/news/2004/oct/Harm -on-Removal.pdf.

6. Operation Melilla received a lot of criticism from Spanish human rights organizations and in the Spanish press, but Spain's prime minister, José Maria Aznar, was unapologetic, declaring that "we had a problem and we solved it."

7. "Staff Played 'Russian Roulette' with Lives," *The Guardian*, February 8, 2011, http://www.guardian.co.uk/uk/2011/feb/08/staff-deportation-flights-g4s. See also "Dangerous Deportation Techniques May Still Be in Use, MPs Warn," *The Guardian*, January 26, 2012, www.guardian.co.uk/uk/2012/jan/26/deportation-techniques -mps-warn.

8. UN High Commissioner for Refugees, *Alternatives to Detention of Asylum Seekers and Refugees*, April 2006, www.unhcr.org/cgi-bin/texis/vtx/refworld/rwmain ?docid=4472e8b84&page=search.

9. Jesuit Refugee Service, *Becoming Vulnerable in Detention: Civil Society Report on the Detention of Vulnerable Asylum Seekers and Irregular Migrants in the European Union (The DEVAS Project)*, June 2010, www.jrseurope.org/publications/JRS-Europe _Becoming%20Vulnerable%20In%20Detention_June%202010_PUBLIC_updated %20on%2012July10.pdf.

10. Home Office, *Enforcing the Rules: A Strategy to Ensure and Enforce Compliance with Our Immigration Rules*, March 2007, 17, www.medact.org/content/refugees/En forcementStrategy.pdf.

11. PAFRAS, *Underground Lives: An Investigation into the Living Conditions and Survival Strategies of Destitute Asylum Seekers in the UK*, 2009, 6, www.irr.org .uk/pdf2/Underground_Lives.pdf.

12. Amnesty International, *Down and Out in London: The Road to Destitution for Rejected Asylum Seekers*, November 2006, 8, www.amnesty.org.uk/uploads/documents /doc_17382.pdf.

13. House of Lords/House of Commons Joint Committee on Human Rights, *The Treatment of Asylum Seekers:Tenth Report of Session 2006–07*, 42, www.publications. parliament.uk/pa/jt200607/jtselect/jtrights/81/81i.pdf.

14. Questions asked in House of Lords, March 19, 2009, available at www.publi cations.parliament.uk/pa/ld200809/ldhansrd/text/90319-0002.htm.

8. Difficult Journeys

1. Emmanuel Mayah, "Europe by Desert: Tears of Migrants," *Sun News*, February 20, 2010, www.nigeriavillagesquare.com/articles/guest-articles/europe-by-desert -tears-of-african-migrants.html.

2. These efforts were described by the *Daily Mail* as a "sinister development" ("Calais Migrants Mutilate Fingertips to Hide True Identity," *Daily Mail*, July 22, 2009). But they are not usually successful, since detained migrants with mutilated fingerprints are usually held until their fingers have healed sufficiently to be matched against the Eurodac database, whereupon they are liable to be sent back to the countries in which their prints were originally taken.

3. Gazmend Kapllani, *A Short Border Handbook* (Portobello Books, 2009).

4. Cruz Roja Española, *Migraciones africanas hacia Europa. Estudio cuantitativo y comparativo: Años 2006–2008*, www.cruzroja.es/pls/portal30/docs/page/cancre/ copy_of_accioninternacion/documentacinternac/infodocus/docutec/migraciones_ final.pdf.

5. Lucy Ash, "Portugal's Jobless Graduates Flee to Africa and Brazil," BBC News, August 31, 2011, www.bbc.co.uk/news/world-14716410.

6. Quoted in Shahram Khosravi, *"Illegal" Traveller: An Auto-Ethnology of Borders* (Palgrave Macmillan, 2010), 108. Khosravi's short book is a brilliant and personalized analysis of "illegality" from the point of view of a refugee who became an anthropologist, and it contains a long interview conducted with Heidari in prison.

7. I tried to interview Sakhizada in prison to hear his perspective. Though he agreed, the prison authorities refused my request.

9. Traffic

1. "A Borderless World," address to the OECD Ministerial Conference, Ottawa, October 7, 1998, www.wto.org/english/news_e/sprr_e/ott_e.htm.

2. "Tampere Summit Conclusions, 15–16 October 1999," www.statewatch.org /news/2003/sep/tamp.htm.

3. European Commission, *Draft Internal Security Strategy for the European Union*, February 23, 2010, http://register.consilium.europa.eu/pdf/en/10/st05/st0 5842-re02.en10.pdf.

4. Tobacco multinationals have always denied such allegations. In 2000, however, the European Commission sued the Philip Morris and R.J. Reynolds companies for collusion with smuggling that it claimed had cost the European Union billions of euros in lost tax revenues. BBC News, "EU to Sue Tobacco Giants," July 21, 2000, http://news.bbc.co.uk/1/hi/business/844966.stm. The lawsuit eventually resulted in an agreement with Philip Morris to make a "voluntary contribution" of $1.2 billion in July 2004—a decision that was not well regarded by antitobacco campaigners. See Yesmoke, "Cigarette Smuggling," http://yesmoke.eu/big-tobacco /cigarette-smuggling.

5. El Khiari's sentence does not seem to have deterred him from political activity. Today he has resumed his activities as head of the Association for Human Rights in the Rif and continues to campaign against Morocco's treatment of migrants, as his brother predicted that he would.

6. In Article 3 of the 2000 Anti-Trafficking Protocol, which came into force in 2008. See UN High Commissioner for Refugees, *Refugee Protection and Human Trafficking. Selected Legal Reference Materials*, December 2008, 22, www.unhcr.org/ref world/docid/498705862.html.

7. Council of Europe Convention on Action Against Trafficking in Human Beings, 2005, in UN High Commissioner for Refugees, *Refugee Protection and Human Trafficking. Selected Legal Reference Materials*, December 2008, 261, www.unhcr.org/ refworld/docid/498705862.html.

8. European Commission, "Protecting the Weakest," March 29, 2010, http://ec .europa.eu/news/justice/100329_en.htm.

9. "New Fight to Stop Sex Trade," *Athens News*, April 9, 2009, www.helleniccom serve.com/archivedgreeknews33.html.

10. ECPAT International, *Sex Trafficking of Children in Malta*, http://ecpat.net/ EI/Publications/Trafficking/Factsheet_Malta.pdf.

11. Anti-Trafficking Monitoring Group, *Wrong Kind of Victim? One Year On: An Analysis of UK Measures to Protect Trafficked Persons*, June 2010, www.antislavery.org /includes/documents/cm_docs/2010/a/1_atmg_report_for_web.pdf.

12. Médecins Sans Frontières, *Sexual Violence and Migration: The Hidden Reality of Sub-Saharan Women Trapped in Morocco En Route to Europe*, March 2010, 7, www .doctorswithoutborders.org/publications/reports/2010/MSF-sexual-violence.pdf.

13. Bridget Anderson and Ben Rogaly, "Forced Labour and Migration to the UK," COMPAS and Trades Union Congress, 2005, www.tuc.org.uk/international/tuc -9317-f0.pdf.

14. For a useful summary of this concept by a sociologist, see Klaus Dörre, "Precarity—the Causes and Effects of Insecure Employment," Goethe Institut, November 2006, www.goethe.de/ges/soz/dos/arb/pre/en1870532.htm.

15. For a detailed comparative analysis of the politics of immigration and official policies toward irregular migrant labour in Spain and Italy, see Kitty Calavita, *Immigrants at the Margins: Law, Race, and Exclusion in Southern Europe* (Cambridge University Press, 2005).

16. International Convention on the Protection of the Rights of All Migrant Workers and Members of Their Families, Adopted by UN General Assembly of 45/158 of 18 December 1990, full text available at www2.ohchr.org/english/law/cmw .htm.

17. J. Goytisolo, *Campos de Níjar* (Grant & Cutler, 1985).

10. Hands Across the Border

1. A similar "day without us" took place on the same date the following year, but it was not as successful. I witnessed a demonstration in the Brescia town square where the numbers were less than two hundred, compared with thousands the previous year. Other Italian cities had a similarly weak turnout, with the exception of Bologna, for reasons the organizers themselves were at a loss to explain.

2. Paco Cuevas, *Solidaridad directa con Marruecos: Crónica de un viaje* (Indymedia, 2004).

3. Sandro Mezzadra, "Battles for Justice at the Borders: The Search for a New Political Subject in the Global Age," paper delivered at second Critical Studies Conference, Kolkata, 2007. English translation available at www.mcrg.ac.in/Spheres /Sandro.doc. See also Manuela Bojadzijev and Isabelle Saint-Saens, "Borders, Citizenship, War, Class: A Discussion with Etienne Balibar and Sandro Mezzadra," *New Formations* 58, no. 1 (June 1, 2006), 10–30, www.newformations.co.uk/abstracts/nf 58abstracts.html.

4. Luis Cabrera, *The Practice of Global Citizenship* (Cambridge University Press, 2010).

11. Blurred Edges: Europe's Borderlands

1. "Germany's Declaration of War Against the United States, December 11, 1941," *Journal of Historical Review* 8, no. 4 (Winter 1988–89): 389–416 (revised October 2007), www.ihr.org/jhr/v08/v08p389_Hitler.html.

2. Gloria Anzaldúa, *Borderlands: La Frontera* (Aunt Lute, 1987), 3.

3. Quoted in Rebecca Larsen, "Immigrants as a Convenient Security Threat in Western Europe," paper presented at International Studies Conference, Honolulu,

Hawaii, 2005, 12, PDF available at http://citation.allacademic.com/meta/p_mla_apa_research_citation/0/7/0/9/9/p70990_index.html.

4. Benedict Anderson, *Imagined Communities: Reflections on the Origin and Spread of Nationalism* (Verso, 1991).

5. R. Schuman, *The Coming Century of Supranational Communities*, speech at Strasbourg, Festival Hall, May 16, 1949, www.schuman.info/Strasbourg549.htm.

6. Bruce Clark, *Twice a Stranger: How Mass Expulsion Forged Modern Greece and Turkey* (Granta, 2006), 221.

7. "Melilla supera el 50% de población musselmana," MinutoDigital.com, February 2010, www.minutodigital.com/actualidad2/2009/11/16/melilla-supera-el-50-de-poblacion-musulmana.

8. Jean Raspail, *The Camp of the Saints* (Social Contract Press, 1994), available online at www.jrbooksonline.com/PDFs/Camp_of_the_Saints.pdf.

9. Andrew Berwick, *2083: A European Declaration of Independence*, 2011, www.kevinislaughter.com/wp-content/uploads/2083+-+A+European+Declaration+of+Independence.pdf.

10. The notion of a "shatter zone," "shatter belt," or "crush zone" is not exclusively applied to central Europe. It has been used in various ways by geographers and geostrategists to describe zones of small states perceived as inherently unstable and subject to rival claims of their more powerful neighbors. In his book *The Problem of Asia* (1900), Alfred Thayer Mahan of the U.S. Naval War College placed a group of states between the 30th and 40th parallels in Asia in this category in the context of the ongoing competition between Britain and Russia. The British geographer James Fairgrieve coined the term "crush zone" to describe states "with sufficient individuality to withstand absorptions, but unable or unwilling to unite with others to form any larger whole" that were located between the sea powers and the Eurasian heartland (*Geography and World Power* [1919], 329–30). Others have since applied these terms more specifically to the states that came into existence in central and eastern Europe after World War I.

11. Kate Brown, *A Biography of No Place: From Ethnic Borderland to Soviet Heartland* (Harvard University Press, 2004).

12. Czeslaw Milosz, *Native Realm: A Search for Self-Definition* (University of California Press, 1981), 3.

13. Krzysztof Czyzewski, "The Borderland: The Atlantis," in *Limes—Pontes—Agora* (Fundacja Pogranicze, 2010), 85–87.

14. Jan Gross, *Neighbors: The Destruction of the Jewish Community in Jedwabne, Poland, 1941* (Arrow Books, 2003).

12. The Western Borders

1. "Netanyahu: Illegal African Immigrants—A Threat to Israel's Jewish Character," *Haaretz*, July 18, 2010, www.haaretz.com/news/national/netanyahu-illegal-african-immigrants-a-threat-to-israel-s-jewish-character-1.302653.

2. Human Rights Watch, *Sinai Perils: Risks to Migrants, Refugees and Asylum Seekers in Egypt and Israel*, November 2008, www.hrw.org/sites/default/files/reports /egypt1108webwcover.pdf.

3. Tancredo presents himself as a concerned patriot and the voice of the silent majority in his invocation of America's "broken" border, but his virulently anti-immigrant message overlaps seamlessly with that of the more overtly extremist border vigilante groups whose gatherings he has sometimes addressed. See Deepa Fernandes, *Targeted: Homeland Security and the Business of Immigration* (Seven Stories Press, 2007), 223–29; and Tom Barry, "Tom Tancredo: Leader of the Anti-Immigrant Populist Revolt," Rightweb, December 29, 2005, http://rightweb.irc -online.org/articles/display/Tom_Tancredo_Leader_of_the_Anti-Immigrant_ Populist_Revolt.

4. For example, a documentary by the vigilante group American Border Patrol entitled "Conquest of Aztland" has accused the Mexican government of "sponsoring the invasion of the United States with hostile intent." See Anti-Defamation League, "Border Disputes: Armed Vigilantes in Arizona," 2003, 3, www.adl.org/ex tremism/arizona/arizonaborder.pdf.

5. William Lind, "War on the Home Front," LewRockwell.com, December 2, 2004, www.lewrockwell.com/lind/lind49.html.

6. Quoted in Fernandes, *Targeted*, 211.

7. "Border security: What Works and What Doesn't," *Texas Insider*, June 15, 2010, www.texasinsider.org/?p=28433.

8. For a detailed analysis of the impact of the September 11 attacks on U.S. border security and immigration policy, see Edward A. Alden, *The Closing of the American Border: Terrorism, Immigration and Security Since 9/11* (HarperCollins, 2008). For analysis on the overlap between border security and conservative politics, see Fernandes, *Targeted*; and Adrian I. Reynolds, "US-Mexico Border Securitization: The Conservative Pursuit to Privatize Security," 2010, University of Alberta Department of Political Science, available online at www.politicalscience.ualberta.ca/en /InnovativeTeachingandLearning/~/media/University%20of%20Alberta/Facul ties/Arts/Departments/Political%20Sc.

9. "ICE Officials Set Quotas to Deport More Illegal Immigrants," *Washington Post*, March 27, 2010, www.washingtonpost.com/wp-dyn/content/article/2010/03/ 26/AR2010032604891.html.

10. The boom in immigrant detention was already under way well before Obama. See Mark Dow, *American Gulag: Inside U.S. Immigration Prisons* (University of California Press, 2004).

11. See María Jiménez, "Humanitarian Crisis: Migrant Deaths at the US-Mexico Border," ACLU/Mexico National Commission of Human Rights, October 1, 2009, www.aclu.org/pdfs/immigrants/humanitariancrisisreport.pdf.

12. See Amnesty International, "Invisible Victims: Migrants on the Move in Mexico," 2010, www.amnesty.org/en/library/info/AMR41/014/2010.

13. For a history of Australia's dictation tests, see Adam M. McKeown, *Melancholy Order: Asian Migration and the Globalization of Borders* (Columbia University Press, 2008).

14. For examples of the "invasion" rhetoric used by Australian politicians and the dehumanisation of the refugee "enemy" that accompanied it, see Michael Grewcock, *Border Crimes: Australia's War on Illicit Migrants* (Institute of Criminology Press, 2009), 152–95.

15. Jack H. Smit, "Uninvited and Unheard: Australia's Case of Post-*Tampa* Boat Arrivals," *TAMARA: A Journal for Critical Organization Inquiry* 8, no. 2 (September 2009): 207–24.

16. "Blowing the Whistle on Hidden Suffering at Woomera," *The Age*, April 24, 2002, www.theage.com.au/articles/2002/04/23/1019441244295.html.

17. Nina Bernstein, "Companies Use Immigration Crackdown to Turn a Profit," *New York Times*, September 28, 2011.

18. Accenture, "U.S. Department of Homeland Security Awards Accenture-Led Smart Border Alliance the Contract to Develop and Implement US-VISIT Program," press release, June 1, 2004, newsroom.accenture.com/article_display.cfm?article_id=4112.

19. This project is being developed under the European Commission's Seventh Framework Programme for Research (FP7) 2007–2013. For a list of ongoing research currently being carried out under the auspices of FP7, see *Investing into Security Research for the Benefits of European Citizens*, European Commission, September 2010, ftp://ftp.cordis.europa.eu/pub/fp7/security/docs/securityresearch_catalogue2010_2_en.pdf.

20. European Commission, "European External Border Surveillance System (EUROSUR)," February 13, 2008, http://europa.eu/legislation_summaries/justice_freedom_security/free_movement_of_persons_asylum_immigration/l14579_en.htm.

21. For an overview of new European technologies and research programs pertaining to border enforcement and immigration, see Ben Hayes, "Arming Big Brother: The EU's Security Research Programme," Transnational Institute, 2006, www.statewatch.org/analyses/bigbrother.pdf.

22. "Robot Border Guards to Patrol Future Frontiers," *New Scientist*, January 8, 2010.

23. Steve Wright, "Sub-Lethal Vision: Varieties of Military Surveillance Technology," *Surveillance and Society* 4, no. 1–2 (2006): 136–53, www.surveillance-and-society.org/Articles4(1)/sublethal.pdf.

24. Peter Schwartz and Doug Randall, "An Abrupt Climate Change Scenario and Its Implications for United States National Security," Global Business Network, October 2003, www.gbn.com/articles/pdfs/Abrupt%20Climate%20Change%20February%202004.pdf.

Epilogue

1. *FRAN Quarterly*, no. 1 (January–March 2011), www.frontex.europa.eu/situa
tion_at_the_external_border/art25.html.

2. "EU Must Remain Open to Immigration," *European Voice*, December 9, 2011,
www.europeanvoice.com/article/imported/eu-must-remain-open-to-migration/69
669.aspx.

3. "Aging UK Needs 7m Immigrants to Survive," *The Observer*, May 13, 2007,
www.guardian.co.uk/business/2007/may/13/immigrationasylumandrefugees.im
migrationandasylum.

4. "Job Center: Germany Needs Two Million Skilled Immigrants," *The Local:
Germany's News in English*, May 14, 2011, www.thelocal.de/national/20110514-35023
.html.

5. "Benvenuto, up to a Point: The World Comes to Italy," *The Economist*, June 9,
2011, www.economist.com/node/18780903.

6. Speech by Cecilia Malmström, European Commissioner responsible for home
affairs, at the roundtable discussion "Protection Challenges and Opportunities—
Where Will We Be in Ten Years?" UN intergovernmental event, Geneva, December
7, 2011, http://eeas.europa.eu/delegations/un_geneva/documents/press_corner/news
/2011/20111207_01_en.pdf.

7. Katya Vasileva, "6.5 Percent of the EU Population Are Foreigners and 9.4 Percent Are Born Abroad," Eurostat: Statistics in Focus, July 2011, http://epp.eurostat
.ec.europa.eu/cache/ity_offpub/ks-sf-11-034/en/ks-sf-11-034-en.pdf.

8. For a more critical view of the "development versus migration" idea, see Hein
de Hass, *Turning the Tide? Why "Development Instead of Migration" Policies Are
Bound to Fail*, working paper, International Migration Institute, University of Oxford, 2006, www.imi.ox.ac.uk/pdfs/imi-working-papers/wp2-development-instead
-of-migration-policies.pdf.

9. Not everyone thinks they should have this right. See, for example, T. Hayter,
Open Borders: The Case Against Immigration Controls (Pluto Press, 2000).

10. For a discussion of these negotiations, see Willem Maas, *Creating European
Citizens* (Rowman & Littlefield, 2007), 11–29.

11. European Commission, *The Global Approach to Migration and Mobility*, Brussels, November 18, 2011, http://ec.europa.eu/home-affairs/news/intro/docs/1_EN_
ACT_part1_v9.pdf.

Index

ABCDS. *See* Association Beni Znassen for Culture, Development, and Solidarity (ABCDS)

Abd el-Krim, 50–51

Abela, Joe, 73, 200

Accenture, 241

ADABTS. *See* Automatic Detection of Abnormal Behaviour and Threats in Crowded Spaces (ADABTS)

Afghanistan, 48, 121, 159

Afghan migrants, 237–38
    Calais, 116–23, 203, 204
    Greece, 90, 92, 97–99, 100, 104
    Rome, 141
    United Kingdom, 162

African American travelers, 186

African migrants, 150, 153, 174, 249–50
    France, 119–20, 202
    Greece, 86, 91–92, 99, 101
    Italy, 148, 181
    Malta, 70, 150
    Morocco, 163, 197
    Spain, 45–63, 129, 134, 150, 177–81, 186
    Turkey, 86, 87
    See also Eritrean migrants; Kenyan migrants; North African migrants; Somali migrants; West African migrants; Zimbabwean migrants

Agayá, 198

agriculture, 177–81, 213

airline passenger screening, 240, 241

air travel, charter. *See* charter flights

Alabama, 237

Albania, 153

Albanian migrants, 22, 86, 249

Algeciras, Spain, 47, 168

Algeria, 2, 57–62, 150. *See also* Maghnia, Algeria

Algerian migrants, 125, 130–32, 249

Aliens Act of 1905 (U.K.), 18, 110

Alleanza Nazionale, 69

Alliance of Civilizations, 228

Almeria, Spain, 48, 177–81, 250

al-Shabaab, 41, 42

America's Shield Initiative, 233

amnesties, 176, 182

Amnesty International, 138

ancient Greece, 15

Andalusia, 177–81

Andor, László, 247

Andy Warhol Museum of Modern Art, 223

anti-Semitism, 18, 110, 214, 228. *See also* Jewish Holocaust

Anzaldúa, Gloria, 210

Arab Spring, 76, 172

Arizona, 234, 236

arms smuggling. *See* weapons smuggling

arrest quotas. *See* police: arrest quotas

Association Beni Znassen for Culture, Development, and Solidarity (ABCDS), 58, 191–92

Associazione Askavusa (Barefoot Association), 82

asylum seekers, 22, 66, 75, 129, 158–60, 249
    Australia, 237–40
    Ceuta, 134

asylum seekers (*cont.*)
  databases, 28
  economic exploitation, 175
  France, 118, 121, 160
  Germany, 129, 135, 160
  Greece, 87, 88, 95–98, 102, 159, 160
  Italy, 7, 75, 79, 140–41
  Malta, 69–70, 127, 160
  Melilla, 53–56
  Poland, 31, 32
  Slovakia, 36, 160
  Turkey, 106
  Ukraine, 41–44
  United Kingdom, 109, 111, 113, 130–42
  See also Dublin Convention; gay and
    lesbian asylum seekers
Ataturk, Kemal, 90
Athens, 102–5, 158, 186, 198
Australia, 17, 23, 85, 160, 216, 231, 237–41,
  243
Austria, 168
Automatic Detection of Abnormal
  Behaviour and Threats in Crowded
  Spaces (ADABTS), 241
Autonomous Marine Surveillance System,
  242

Baghdad, 12–13
Bangladeshi migrants, 54, 55, 79, 105
Bangladesh-India border. *See* India-
  Bangladesh border
Baraka, Hicham, 58, 60, 191
Barefoot Association. *See* Associazione
  Askavusa (Barefoot Association)
Barej, Artur, 29
Bari, Italy, 99, 100
barriers. *See* fences, walls, etc.
Bartolo, Evarist, 217
Bauluz, Javier, 45–46
Belarus, 29–34, 128, 168–69
Belgium, 21, 25–26, 78, 129, 184
  Spaniards in, 46, 157
  See also Zeebrugge, Belgium
Ben Ali, Zine el-Abidine, 73, 75, 76, 78
Berlin Wall, 3–4, 11, 27
Berlusconi, Silvio, 74–75, 77, 183
Besson, Eric, 116
A Biography of No Place (Brown), 220
biometric identification systems, 114,
  240–41. *See also* fingerprinting
Birmingham, England, 186, 203
Bismarck, Otto van, 17

Blunkett, David, 113, 115
boat people, 4, 46–49, 61, 148–50, 239
  Canary Islands, 48, 49, 55
  Greece, 90, 92–93, 94, 98, 157–58, 192
  Italy, 5, 64–66, 71, 78–79, 128, 148
  Malta, 64–66, 71–72, 148
  Melilla, 53, 55
  Turkey, 9, 192
  See also drownings
Boeing Corporation, 235
Boer War, 110
Boldrini, Laura, 66, 78
border-control technology. *See* technology,
  border-control
Borderland Foundation, 225–28
The Borderless World (Ohmae), 11
Border Monitoring Project Ukraine, 191
Bosnia, 228
Bossi, Renzo, 74
Bossi, Umberto, 5
Botswana-Zimbabwe border, 230
Boulghassoul, Caron, 142
Bratislava, 36, 130
Breivik, Anders, 218
Breschia, Italy, 181–84, 186–87
bribery, 149, 151
Brindisi, Italy, 99, 100
Britain. *See* United Kingdom
British Brothers League, 110
Brown, Kate, 220
Brussels, 184
brutality, 52, 128–29, 141. *See also* rape;
  torture
Bugeja, Ray, 201–2
Bugri, Ahmed, 70, 71
Bug River, 29, 31, 34, 35, 36, 168
Bulgaria, 33
Burmese migrants, 150
Bycko, Michal, 223, 224
Byrne, Liam, 115, 124

Calabria, Italy, 181
Calais, 116–24, 152–58, 163, 193–96, 202–5
cameras, 29, 30, 38, 47, 51, 235
  "not allowed by Islam," 42
Cameron, David, 24, 228–29
Cameroonian migrants, 160
Caminando Fronteras, 196–97
Campeciano, Angelo, 82
The Camp of the Saints (Raspail), 217–18
Canada, 72, 160
Canary Islands, 48–49, 55, 151, 153

Carey, George, 208
Caribbean islands, 243. *See also* West Indian
  migrants
Caritas, 154, 188
Carl Zeiss Optronics, 242
Carpatho-Ukraine, 222
Carter, John, 232
cartography. *See* mapmaking
Casa Invisible, 197–98
Catholicism, 67, 216, 217, 220, 223
Ceuta (Spanish exclave), 1–3, 50–52, 56, 57,
  150, 196–97, 213–14
  drug trade, 171
  duty-free goods traffic, 169–70
  immigrant reception center, 133–35
  Sr. Paola Domingo in, 200–201
charter flights, 128
Chechen migrants, 4, 31, 43
Channel Tunnel, 108, 111–12, 116, 120
children, 59, 60, 153, 158, 238, 239
  in detention centers, 31–32, 91, 132, 200,
    239, 246
  Dover, England, 131
  Greece, 91–92, 100, 104
  Lampedusa, 79
  Melilla, 52, 189–91
  See also disabled children
China, 171
Chinese Exclusion Act, 17
Chinese migrants, 16, 18, 114, 150, 162,
  175, 237
Christmas Island, 238, 240
Chrysi Avgi (Golden Dawn), 104
Christianity, 105, 140, 199, 200, 212, 220,
  222. *See also* Catholicism
Christian migrants, 59, 255
churches, looting of. *See* religious icon
  looting
churches, Rusyn, 222
cigarettes
  selling of, 41
  smuggling of, 30, 167, 168–69
citizenship, 250
Clark, Bruce, 212
Clarke, Charles, 127
"climate refugees," 243
Clough, Paul, 216–17
cockle pickers, 175
Cold War, 21, 22, 166, 222, 225
colonies and colonization, 17, 111, 154, 201,
  209, 213. *See also* Ceuta (Spanish
  exclave); Melilla (Spanish exclave)

Commonwealth Immigrants Act (U.K.), 111
Communist bloc. *See* Eastern Europe
  (Communist bloc)
Conakry, Guinea, 54, 150
concentration camps, 132, 218–19. *See also*
  detention centers
Congolese migrants, 138–40
Congress of Sopron, 222
corruption, 42, 149, 151, 161, 180
Corsini, Paolo, 182
Council of Europe, 172, 174, 211, 228
Crete, 158
crime, "cross-border," 164–84
crime, organized. *See* organized crime
"crush zone" (term), 220, 263n10
C'Sur, 202–3
Cuesta, Violeta, 188–89
Ćwikła-Sztembis, Joanna, 35
Czechoslovakia, 36, 222, 224
Czech Republic, 32, 36, 109
Czyzewski, Krzysztof, 226–28

Darfur, 120, 130, 150, 157
death of migrants, 3–5, 28, 38–39, 61,
  65–66, 192, 201, 245
  Dover, England, 160
  in forced deportation, 129–30
  Greece, 86, 99–100
  Morocco-Melilla border, 52
  Sahara Desert, 71, 151
  Spain, 45–46, 188
  statistics, 3–4, 47
  Strait of Gibraltar, 47
  U.S.-Mexico borderlands, 234–35
  See also drownings; murder; suicide
The Death Ship (Traven), 147–48
Democratic Republic of Congo (DRC),
  138–40
Department of Defense (U.S.). *See* U.S.
  Department of Defense
Department of Homeland Security (U.S.).
  See U.S. Department of Homeland
  Security
deportees and deportation, 43, 158
  Algeria, 57–58, 59
  brutal incidents, 128–29
  Ceuta, 57, 191, 196–97
  England, 5–6
  in fiction, 147
  France, 127
  Germany, 4, 16, 17, 18
  Great Britain, 101

deportees and deportation (*cont.*)
  Greece, 87
  Greece (ancient era), 15
  Lampedusa, 76, 128
  Libya, 74
  Malta, 127–28, 200
  Melilla, 57, 129, 191, 196–97
  Morocco, 3, 57–60, 191, 196–97
  Poland, 32
  sexual exploitation, 174
  United Kingdom, 118, 127–31, 141, 175
  United States, 234
  See also fear of deportation
detention centers, 28
  Australia, 238–40
  France, 121, 195
  Greece, 88–91, 96–97
  Lampedusa, 76
  Libya, 74
  Malta, 69–71, 73, 199–200
  Mauritania, 62
  Poland, 31–32
  Spain, 55
  Turkey, 185
  Ukraine, 40, 42, 43
  United Kingdom, 133
  United States, 235
Deutschland Schafft Sich Ab (Sarrazin), 208
De Villiers, Melius, 18
direct action, 76. See also uprisings
disabled children, 125–26
disasters, weather-related. See weather-
  related disasters
displaced persons. See internally displaced
  persons; refugees
Domingo, Paola, 200–201
Don River, 209
Dorohusk, Poland, 34–36
Dover, England, 108–10, 113–16, 124, 173
drones, 242
drownings, 4, 5, 45–48, 65, 79–80, 92–94,
  149, 161
  England, 175
  Greek-Turkey border, 86
  Indian Ocean, 239
  Malta, 72
drugging. *See* forced drugging
drug smuggling, 167, 168, 170–72
Dubai, 42
Dublin Convention, 32, 36, 69, 97, 105,
  141, 245, 248
Dublin II, 32, 130

Duke, David, 232
duty-free goods traffic, 169–70, 213

Eastern Europe (Communist bloc), 21, 22,
  33, 223
Economic Community of West Africa
  (ECOWAS), 62
education access, 186, 187
Education Sans Frontières, 187
Efficiency and Empire (White), 18
Egypt, 82, 231
el-Khiari, Amine, 171
el-Khiari, Chekib, 171–72
Enciso, Juan, 180
England, 4, 16, 101, 173. *See also*
  Birmingham, England; Dover,
  England; Nottingham, England;
  Wakefield, England
English Channel, 111–12, 202. *See also*
  Channel Tunnel
English Defence League, 218
Ercoban, Piril, 192
Eritrean migrants, 66, 70, 100, 119,
  127–28, 150, 199–200, 203
Estonia, 32, 33
eugenics, 18
euro (currency), 208, 209, 211
Eurodac, 28, 152
Euro-Mediterranean Partnership, 56
European Border Surveillance System
  (EUROSUR), 67, 241
European Coal and Steel Community
  (ECSC), 211
European Commission, 64, 67, 75, 165,
  241, 252
European Convention on Human Rights, 127
European Council, 132, 165
European emigration, 46, 156–57. *See also*
  intra-European migration
European identity. *See* identity, European
European Neighborhood Policy, 40, 56
European Parliament, 132, 207
European Social Forum, 185
European Union, 245–54
  African migration control, 47–49, 62,
  63, 73
  border-control technology, 241–42
  Belarusian relations, 30
  eastern frontier, 32–44, 105–6, 128,
  218–29, 242
  enlargements, 24, 32, 38, 68, 105
  identity issues, 208–11

Italy relations, 77
Libyan relations, 73, 75
as promised land, 152–53
Return Directive, 132–33
Schengen Agreement, 26, 28
security architecture of, 23
SIVE, 47–48
southernmost border, 76
Turkish relations, 106
U.K. relations, 107–8, 115
Ukrainian relations, 43
Voluntary Assisted Return and
   Reintegration Program, 130
See also Dublin Convention; European
   Commission; European Council;
   European Neighborhood Policy;
   European Parliament; Frontex
EUROSUR. See European Border
   Surveillance System (EUROSUR)
Eurotunnel. See Channel Tunnel
evictions, 106, 116, 117, 120, 180, 181
Evros River, 84, 86, 90, 93, 106, 155
exclaves, Spanish. See Ceuta (Spanish
   exclave); Melilla (Spanish exclave)
expulsion. See deportees and deportation
extortion, 42, 149, 151

Fairgrieve, James, 263n10
Falk, Pierre, 204–5
farmworkers, 177–81, 250
far right, 212, 217–18, 247, 253
   eastern Europe, 228
   European Parliament, 207–8
   France, 77, 117
   Greece, 103–5
   Italy, 77
   Malta, 69, 202, 214–17
   Netherlands, 210
   Sweden, 186
   United Kingdom, 77, 109, 111, 218
   See also Northern League
FAST. See Future Attribute Screening
   Technology (FAST)
favelas, 12
fear, 6, 104, 108, 243, 253
fear of deportation, 4–5, 139, 173, 175, 237
fear of Islam, 95, 208
fear of migrants, 102, 108, 111, 116, 250
fear of terrorism, 35
fences, walls, etc., 12–13, 38, 230
   Eurotunnel, 112
   Greece, 99, 106

Israel, 231
Melilla, 1–2, 51–53
U.S.-Mexico border, 233, 234
   See also Berlin Wall
Fernández, Gil Arias, 85
ferries, 99, 101, 112, 113, 115, 116, 212
fingerprinting, 28, 97, 99, 152
Fiore, Roberto, 77
fishing and fishermen, 201–2, 212–13
forced drugging, 129, 239
forced labor, 167, 175–76
Forced Labour and Migration to the UK, 175
forgery, 35, 40, 100, 131
France, 21, 77, 78, 115–18, 155, 160, 186
   arrest quotas, 127
   asylum laws, 202
   British relations, 116
   German/Luxembourgish borderlands,
      211
   history, 16–18, 116
   internment camps, 132
   island territories, 209
   Italian immigrants, 18, 156
   migrant workers, 176, 184
   in Morocco, 50, 57
   Muslim immigrants, 208
   Schengen Agreement, 25–26, 27
   solidarity work in, 187, 202–5
   See also Calais; Paris
Franco, Francisco, 50
Frattini, Franco, 77, 83
Frontex, 23, 67, 93–96, 128, 165–67, 241–42
Fundacja Pogranicze. See Borderland
   Foundation
Future Attribute Screening Technology
   (FAST), 241

Gaddafi, Muammar, 73, 75, 76, 79, 82
Gambia, 62
Gangmasters Licensing Act, 175
Garzón, Helena Malena, 196, 197
gated communities, 12, 13, 243–44
Gavardo, Italy, 182, 206
gay and lesbian asylum seekers, 159–60
Gaza, 95, 103, 107, 242
general strikes, 186, 198
Geneva Convention on Refugees, 20, 36,
   56, 97, 159, 238, 249
   "European clause," 106
   non-signatories, 74
"Geneva Convention passports," 70
Georgian migrants, 31, 130

Geremek, Bronislaw, 207
Germany, 31, 32, 78, 129, 135, 160
    history, 4, 15–23
    labor shortage, 248
    No Borders movement, 195
    Poles in, 17, 18, 156
    Schengen Agreement, 25–26
    smuggled goods market, 168
    Spaniards in, 46, 157
    Turks in, 208
Germany-Luxembourg border, 211
G4S, 129, 239
Gibraltar Strait. *See* Strait of Gibraltar
Gillard, Julia, 240
Giscard d'Estaing, Valéry, 185
Glasgow, 189
Globocnik, Odilo, 219
Golden Dawn. *See* Chrysi Avgi (Golden
    Dawn)
Gonzi, Lawrence, 75
Gosden, Terry, 70–71, 156
Goytisolo, Juan, 177
Great Britain. *See* United Kingdom
Greaves, Steven, 86, 119, 122, 155
Greece, 84–106, 118, 153, 155, 162, 173,
    192, 258n6. *See also* ancient Greece;
    Athens; Crete; Igoumenitsa, Greece;
    Lesvos; Samos
Greece-Turkey border, 4, 84–99, 212
Greek Council for Refugees (GCR), 102–3
Greek migrants, 85, 90, 157, 212
Green, Andrew, 112
greenhouse agriculture, 177–81, 250
Griffin, Nick, 77
Gross, Jan, 227
Guatemala, 234
gun smuggling. *See* weapons smuggling
Guterres, António, 82
"Gypsies." *See* Roma (people)

Hague, William, 80
Hanson, Pauline, 237
Hapsburg Empire, 14, 19, 222
hashish trade, 168, 170–71
health care, 103, 126, 176, 192, 247
    Italy, 183
    Morocco, 61
    right-wing views, 111
    Spain, 176, 186
Heidari, Amir, 161–62
Himmler, Heinrich, 219
Hitler, Adolf, 209, 215

Holocaust, Jewish. *See* Jewish Holocaust
Homeland Security Department (U.S.). *See*
    U.S. Department of Homeland
    Security
homelessness
    Calais, 119–21
    Greece, 91, 92, 102–4
    Melilla, 190
    Rome, 140–41
    United Kingdom, 4, 137, 139, 142
Howard, John, 238
Hudson, Nick, 109
humanitarian rescue. *See* rescue
human trafficking, 167, 172–74
Hungary, 14, 32, 36–42, 221, 222
hunger strikes, 91, 106, 117, 133, 195, 253
Huntington, Samuel, 232
Hurd, Jessica, 5–6
hybridity and multiculturalism. *See*
    multiculturalism

Iceland, 201, 202
icon looting. *See* religious icon looting
identification documents, 18–19. *See also*
    passports
identification systems, biometric. *See*
    biometric identification systems
identity, European, 208–11
Identity, Tradition, Sovereignty (ITS), 207
Igoumenitsa, Greece, 99–102, 106, 156,
    158, 163, 186
Immigration and Asylum Act (U.K.),
    110, 115
Immigration and Customs Enforcement
    (ICE). *See* U.S. Immigration and
    Customs Enforcement (ICE)
Imperium Europa, 69, 214–16
India-Bangladesh border, 230
Indian migrants, 16, 17, 54, 237
Indonesia, 238, 239, 240
inequality of income, 152, 213
informal economy, 175
In Mortal Danger (Tancredo), 232
insurrections. *See* uprisings
internally displaced persons, 159
*Internal Security Strategy for the European
    Union*, 165
International Convention for the Protection
    of the Rights of All Migrant Workers,
    176, 250
International Convention on Search and
    Rescue, 65–66

International Organization for Migration (IOM), 40, 62, 78, 130
international police, 23
Internet, 153, 217, 218
internment camps. *See* concentration camps
intra-European migration, 16, 18, 46, 68, 90, 156–57, 252
Invisible House. *See* Casa Invisible
Iran, 97–98, 138
Iranian migrants, 117–21, 136–37, 159–62
Iraq, 12–13, 129, 161
Iraqi migrants, 100–101, 129, 158, 160
Irish migrants, 157
Islam, 14, 95, 208, 212, 216, 220. *See also* Muslims
Islamist militias, 41, 42
islands. *See* Canary Islands; Caribbean islands; Christmas Island; Lampedusa; Lesvos; Malta; Nauru; Samos; Sicily
island territories, 209
Israel, 231, 242
Italian migrants, 18, 21, 156
Italy, 5, 22, 26, 64–65, 69, 98, 118, 139
    amnesties, 176, 182
    coast guard, 65, 66, 79, 80, 168
    Greek relations, 100
    Libyan relations, 73–74, 75, 83, 128
    migrant workers, 181–84
    population stabilization, 248
    promised land to Albanians, 153
    rescues, 148
    solidarity marches, 206
    Tunisian relations, 76
    See also Bari, Italy; Brindisi, Italy; Breschia, Italy; Lampedusa; Milan; Rome; Sicily
Italy-Albania border, 167–68
Izmir, Turkey, 192, 212

Jesuit Refugee Service, 140–41
Jewish Holocaust, 219, 226, 227
Jews, 15, 18, 20, 110, 161, 162
    Melilla, 213
    Poland, 219, 220, 226, 227
    "warrior-priest" Lowell's contempt for, 214, 216
Johnson, Christopher, 247–48
Jordan, 160
Juan Carlos I, 190

Kaliningrad, 29, 168, 224
Kapllani, Gazmend, 153

Kashmiri migrants, 54–55
KBR, 235
Kenyan migrants, 154–55
kidnapping, 139, 140, 231, 235
Knights Hospitaller of St. John, 67–68
Komorowski, Bronislaw, 225, 228
Kosovan migrants, 100, 109–10, 113
Kosumi, Vebi, 131–32
Koulocheris, Spyros, 102
Krasnogruda, Poland, 225, 226, 228
Kurdish migrants, 4, 22, 92, 99–101, 142, 158, 161–62, 202

labor, forced, *See* forced labor
labor market shortages, 21, 247, 248, 252
Labour Party (Australia), 239–40
Labour Party (U.K.), 21–22, 109, 110, 112–15
Laitinen, Ilkka, 166–67
Lampedusa, 66, 75–83, 202, 212–13, 246
Lalumière, Catherine, 27
land mines, 4, 85, 86, 150, 242
language, 43, 88, 95–96, 221, 227
    hybridity, 211, 216
    laws, 182, 228
    tests, 17, 216, 237
LAOS. *See* Popular Orthodox Alarm (LAOS)
Latin American migrants, 177, 232, 234, 250
Latinos, 236–37
Latvia, 32
League of Nations, 19, 20
least developed countries (LDCs), 152
Leeds, 136–40
Leopold I, 222
Le Pen, Marine, 77, 117
Lesvos, 90–93, 198–99
Liberian migrants, 65, 156
Libya, 5, 59, 64–83, 128, 148, 150, 201–2
Libya-Niger border, 151
Libyan migrants, 78–79
Liebetezou, Zoe, 94
Lind, William, 232
Lioret, Philippe, 202
Lisbon Treaty, 6
Lithuania, 29, 33, 224–28
Lithuanian migrants, 5–6, 112
Logathetes, George, 88
Longue, Philippe, 203–4
looting, 168
Louis, Claudine, 202–3
Lowell, Norman, 214–17

Lublin, Poland, 218–21
Luca, Silvana, 81
Lukashenko, Alexander, 29, 30
Luxembourg, 25–26, 27, 211

Maastricht Treaty, 24
mafia. *See* organized crime
Mafia (Italy), 181
Maghnia, Algeria, 57, 60, 163, 174
The Magician of Lublin (Singer), 220
Mahan, Albert Thayer, 263n10
Majdanek concentration camp, 218–19
Málaga, Spain, 129, 197–98
Malawi, 140
Malaysia, 231, 240
Mali, 55, 150, 156, 178
Malian migrants, 150
Malmstrom, Cecilia, 77, 105, 247, 249
Malta, 64–75, 148, 150, 156, 160, 199–202, 214–17
  deportation from, 127–28, 200
  human trafficking, 173
Maltese migrants, 216
Mandela, Nelson, 57
maps and mapmaking, 14, 209
Maritsa River. *See* Evros River
Maroni, Roberto, 5, 83
Márquez, Gerardo, 197–98
Martín, Jorge, 61, 62, 193
Mauritania, 55, 62, 150, 153
McLuhan, Marshall, 12
Médecins Sans Frontières (MSF), 3, 60–62, 78, 82, 88, 104, 193
media, 2, 4, 81, 116, 123, 158, 161, 176. *See also* Internet; press; television
medical care. *See* health care
Mediterranean islands. *See* Lampedusa; Lesvos; Malta; Samos; Sicily
Melilla (Spanish exclave), 1–3, 49–57, 135, 150, 189–91, 196–97, 213–14
  doping of African migrants in, 129
  drug trade, 171
  duty-free goods traffic, 169–70, 213
  immigrant reception center, 53–55
Mexico, 234, 243–44. *See also* U.S.-Mexico border
Mezzadra, Sandro, 197
Miaris, Vassilios, 101–2
Middle Ages, 15
Mignonet, Philippe, 119, 120
migrant camps and shantytowns, 58–61, 69, 82, 100–106, 116, 117, 162

migrant detention centers. *See* detention centers
migrant workers, 49, 101, 118, 153, 175–81, 213, 250, 251
  growing market for, 247
  history, 16, 21, 111
  intra-European, 16, 17, 18, 46, 156–57, 252
MigrationWatch, 112
Mikromastoras, Apostolos, 95
Milan, 101, 184
militarized border control, 242–43
militias, Islamic. *See* Islamic militias
Milosz, Czeslaw, 225–26
Mine Ban Treaty, 86
minefields. *See* land mines
Mintoff, Dionysius, 72, 73, 199–200
Mitilini, Greece, 90–93
Mohamadi, Aminullah, 4
Mohammed I University, 58
Moldova, 3, 33, 35, 152, 168, 173, 220
Moldovan migrants, 35
Molinario, Barbara, 79
Morana, Antonio, 80
Moroccan Auxiliary Forces ("Alis"), 52
Moroccan migrants, 46, 101, 127, 179, 180, 188–91, 249
Morocco, 1–3, 5, 46–64, 150, 153, 162, 193
  drug trade, 168, 170–72
  per capita income, 152
  villages, 188–89
  See also Oujda, Morocco; Tangier
Moscow, 42
MSF. *See* Médecins Sans Frontières (MSF)
Multecilerle Dayanism Demegi (Multeci Der), 192
multiculturalism, 211–14, 221–29, 239
murder, 130, 138–39, 161, 180, 235, 243
Muslims, 23, 48, 50, 67, 208, 213–14

Nanclares Mendía, José, 189
NAFTA. *See* North American Free Trade Agreement
"Nansen passports," 19
Naruhana, Germain, 138–40
Natal (British colony), 17
National Alliance (Italy). *See* Alleanza Nazionale
National Front (U.K.), 109
National Guard (U.S.), 233
National Health Service (U.K.), 175
Native Realm (Milosz), 226

NATO, 66, 76, 80, 82, 83, 109, 230
Natta, Pierfrancesco Maria, 36–37
Nauru, 238, 240
Nazar, 65
Nazis, 209, 215, 218–21, 222
Neighbours (Gross), 227
neo-Nazis, 23
Netanyahu, Benjamin, 231
Netherlands, 21, 25–26, 105, 158, 160, 210
 island territories, 209
Niger, 62, 150, 151
Nigerian migrants, 58–59, 129, 154, 163, 172
No Borders, 118–19, 122, 194–96, 251
North African migrants, 21, 46–47, 55,
 184. *See also* Algerian migrants; Libyan
 migrants; Moroccan migrants;
 Tunisian migrants
North American Free Trade Agreement,
 233
Northern League, 5, 74, 81, 83, 182,
 183, 206
Norway, 30, 98, 105, 158, 218, 237
Nottingham, England, 111, 142, 187

Obama, Barack, 234
Oder-Neisse line, 32
Ohmae, Kenichi, 11
Olympic Games, 12
One Nation (Australian party), 237
Operation Poseidon, 95
Operation Reinhard, 219
Operation Seahorse, 48–49
Orange Free State, 18. *See also* Boer Wars
Organisation for the Integration and
 Welfare of Asylum Seekers (OIWAS),
 70, 72
organized crime, 160–63, 165
Ostrovany, Slovakia, 12
Ottoman Empire, 19, 67–68, 209, 212
Oujda, Morocco, 57–62, 162, 191
Oxfam, 205–6

PAFRAS. *See* Positive Action for Refugees
 and Asylum Seekers (PAFRAS)
Pakistani migrants, 41, 79, 84, 89, 150, 155,
 181–84
Palazón, José, 52, 54, 189–91
Palestinian migrants, 89, 95, 97, 103, 106,
 120, 130, 160
Papua New Guinea, 238
Paris, 4–5, 167, 184
Parry, Chris, 5

passports, 16–19, 27, 149, 175. *See also*
 "Geneva Convention passports";
 "Nansen passports"; visas
Peace Laboratory, 72, 199, 200
people smugglers and smuggling 4, 55, 57,
 93, 94, 150–51, 160–63. *See also*
 human trafficking
pepper spray, 51
Perry, Rick, 235
Pisani, Maria, 69
Pisanu, Giuseppe, 128
Plá, Roberto
 La Zona, 243–44
Poland, 29–37, 130, 152, 218–28, 234. *See
 also* Polish migrants
Poland-Belarus border, 29–31, 168
Poland-Ukraine border, 34–36, 218
police, 28
 arrest quotas, 127
 brutality, 129, 141
 Calais, 116–23, 194, 195, 204
 Ceuta and Melilla, 1, 2, 134
 databases, 39–40
 France, 118
 Greece, 86–106, 118, 186
 Italy, 141, 182
 Lampedusa, 81
 Malta, 199–200
 Morocco, 60, 61, 62
 Turkey, 185
 Ukraine, 42, 43
 See also international police
Polish migrants, 17, 18, 156
political prisoners, 76, 136, 171–72, 219
Popular Orthodox Alarm (LAOS), 104, 105
Portugal, 26, 49
Portuguese migrants, 157
Positive Action for Refugees and Asylum
 Seekers (PAFRAS), 136, 138
press, 110, 112, 116
Priecel, Bernard, 36
prisons and prisoners. *See* concentration
 camps; detention centers; political
 prisoners
Prodein, 190
prostitution, 173, 174, 179, 231
Protecting Our Border, Protecting the Public,
 164
protests, 133
 Australia, 239, 240
 Belgium, 184
 Calais, 117–18, 204

protests (*cont.*)
  Democratic Republic of Congo, 139
  France, 184
  Iran, 136
  Italy, 183–84, 186–87, 206
  Melilla, 54
  Poland, 228
  Turkey, 185
  United Kingdom, 4, 109, 129
  See also hunger strikes
Protocol on the Free Movement of
    Persons, 62
Punjabi migrants, 54, 55

Quadt, Mattheus, 14
Quiroz, Rafael, 188–89

racial violence, 69, 105, 113, 137, 180
racism, 18, 69, 105, 111, 112, 253
  Greece, 103, 105
  Malta, 200, 215
  United Kingdom, 137
  See also anti-Semitism
rape, 60, 138, 139, 151, 161, 231, 235, 247
Rapid Border Intervention Teams
    (RABIT), 23, 106
Raspail, Jean
  The Camp of the Saints, 217–18
Ratzel, Friedrich, 15
Raytheon, 114
reality television programs, 124
rebellions. *See* uprisings
Red Cross, 202
Refugee and Migrant Justice (RMF), 142
refugees, 19–22, 66, 157–60, 249
  Afghan, 90, 97–99, 104, 118, 121
  in Australia, 240
  in England, 109–10
  "European clause," 106
  in Greece, 97, 104
  Greek, 90
  Iraqi, 160
  Liberian, 65
  in Malawi, 140
  Malaysian, 240
  in Malta, 70
  Palestinian, 160
  in Poland, 31
  in Rome, 140–41
  Russian, 19–20
  in Slovakia, 36, 37
  statistics, 7, 36

Sudanese, 157–58
Turkish, 90
in United Kingdom, 115
World War II, 220
See also asylum seekers; "climate
    refugees"; Geneva Convention on
    Refugees; United Nations High
    Commissioner for Refugees
    (UNHCR)
religious icon looting, 168
remittances, 153, 251
Repington, Charles, 108
rescues, 49, 65–66, 80, 94–95, 201–2,
    237–39
  asylum seeking and, 75
  Greece, 92, 198–99
  Italy, 148
  Sahara Desert, 3
Rif Mountains, 170, 171
Rif nationalism, 50–51
right-wing extremists. *See* far right
Rio de Janeiro, 12
riots, 111, 167, 181, 239, 240, 253
Rivera, Juan Antonio Martin, 52
robotics, 241–42
Rohde, Dominicus, 211–12
Roma (people), 12, 15, 37, 212, 221,
    226, 228
Roman Catholicism. *See* Catholicism
Roman Empire, 13–14, 67
Romania, 33, 220, 222
Romanian migrants, 173, 177
Rome, 140–41
Romero, Alejandro, 135
rubber bullets, 52, 53
Rudd, Kevin, 239
Ruggiero, Renato, 164–65
Russia, 18, 19, 33, 42, 110, 173, 209
Russian migrants, 19–20, 31, 35, 43
Rusyns (Ruthenians), 221–24
Ruthenian Carpathia. *See* Subcarpathia

Sahara Desert, 3, 150–51, 178
St. John, Joseph, 68
Sakhizada, Abdul, 162
Sakhizada, Ahmed, 162
Samos, 93–99, 212
Sanchez, José Alonso, 52–53
San Isidro, Spain, 177–79, 189
Sarkozy, Nicolas, 77, 117, 208
Sarrazin, Thilo, 208
Schengen, Luxembourg, 25, 27, 211

Schengen Agreement, 25–28, 46, 77, 110, 119, 212
Schengen Borders Code, 33, 56
Schengen Information System (SIS), 28, 30, 40
Schengen Peace Foundation, 211, 212
Schonaraius, Emmaniou, 94
Schuman, Robert, 25, 211
Scotland, 189
screening of airline passengers. *See* airline passenger screening
Secours Catholique, 150, 187
Secure Border Initiative, 235
Secure Borders, Safe Haven, 113
Sejny, Poland, 224–27
The Sejny Chronicles, 227
Senegal, 150, 156
Senegalese migrants, 181
September 11, 2001, terrorist attacks, 113, 233
Serco Group, 114, 240
sexual exploitation, 151, 174. *See also* human trafficking
sexual violence, 59–60, 247. *See also* rape
Sferlazzo, Giacomo, 82
shantytowns. *See* migrant camps and shantytowns
"shatter zone" (term). *See* "crush zone" (term)
Shiri, Israfil, 4
Sicily, 65, 79
Sierra Leonean migrants, 141–42
Sinai, 231
Singer, Isaac Bashevis, 220
Sistema Integrado de Vigilancia Exterior (SIVE), 47–48, 64, 170
Slovakia, 27, 32, 36–40, 41, 109, 160, 224
    mirrored in U.S., 234
    per capita income, 152
    Rusyns in, 222–223
    walling off of Roma, 12
    See also Bratislava
Slovakia-Ukraine border, 37–40, 221
Slovenia, 32, 33
Smit, Michiel, 210
smuggling of goods, 30, 167–70. *See also* drug smuggling; weapons smuggling
smuggling of people. *See* people smugglers and smuggling
Sobrance, Slovakia, 37–38
Solh, 161
Solidaridad Directa, 189
solidarity, 186–94

Somalia, 138, 159
Somali migrants, 38–44, 138
    Calais, 119, 120
    Ceuta, 135
    Greece, 100, 103
    Malta, 70–73
    Rome, 141
South Africa, 115. *See also* Boer Wars; Natal (British colony); Orange Free State
South Africa–Zimbabwe border, 230–31
sovereignty, 11, 12, 14, 20, 24, 127
Soviet Union, 11, 19, 37, 168, 220, 225
Spain, 26, 45–64, 150, 153
    African migrant workers, 101
    amnesties, 176
    arrest quotas, 127
    duty-free goods traffic, 169–70
    Latin Americans in, 177, 25
    per capita income, 152
    prostitution, 173
    Schengen Agreement, 214
    solidarity work in, 188–89, 196–97
    See also Almeria, Spain; Ceuta (Spanish exclave); Málaga, Spain; Melilla (Spanish exclave); San Isidro, Spain; Vic, Spain
Spanish Foreign Legion, 1, 50, 52
Spanish migrants, 46, 156–57
Spindler, William, 193–94
squatters and squatting, 119–20, 195
Sri Lankan migrants, 22, 114
statistics, 6–7, 16, 22–23, 127, 247–50
    comparative income, 152
    Greece, 85, 97
    Italy, 74, 76, 248
    Libya, 74, 82
    Malta, 68, 73
    Poland, 30–31
    Slovakia, 36
    Tunisia, 82
    United Kingdom, 138
    United States, 233–35
    use of by right-wing media, 112
stowaways, 4, 99–101, 114, 149
    detection, 30, 35, 38
Strait of Gibraltar, 46–48, 168
Stratis, Papa, 198–99
Straw, Jack, 161
Subcarpathia, 37, 41, 221
Sudan, 128
Sudanese migrants, 119, 120, 130, 150, 154
suicide, 4–5, 54, 130, 133, 142–43, 239, 240

sunken treasure ships, 168
surveillance, 47–48, 67, 93, 241–42
  Melilla, 51
  Poland-Belarus border, 29, 30
  Slovakia, 38
  U.S.-Mexico border, 235
Sweden, 152, 154, 160, 161, 186
Syria, 160

Talbi, Mohammed, 191–92
Taleb family, 125–26
Tancredo, Tom, 232
Tangier, 57, 150, 153, 156, 170, 188,
  196–97
Tarifa, Spain, 45–48
Tatra Mountains, 4, 224
technology, border-control, 35, 47–48, 67,
  241–43
  Greece, 85
  Melilla, 51
  Poland, 29–30
  Slovakia, 38, 40
  United Kingdom, 114
  United States, 35, 235, 241–43
television, 153, 185, 221. *See also* reality
  television programs
Terespol, Poland, 29–31, 168
territories, island. *See* island territories
terrorism, 33, 35. *See also* September 11,
  2001, terrorist attacks
Texas, 235
Thatcher, Margaret, 111
Thrace, 212
torture, 94, 128, 139, 157, 158, 231
tourists and tourism, 76, 81, 90, 123
trains, 30, 111, 168
Transcarpathia. *See* Subcarpathia
Transnistria, 33
Transportable Autonomous Patrol for Land
  Border Surveillance (TALS), 242
Traven, B., 147–48
treasure ships. *See* sunken treasure ships
Treaty of Amsterdam, 26
Tunisia, 64, 73–82, 212
Tunisian fishermen, 202, 213
Tunisian migrants, 77–82, 213, 246, 250
Turkey, 48, 87, 90, 98, 106, 118, 162
  potential EU membership, 24
  solidarity work in, 192
  See also Greece-Turkey border; Izmir,
    Turkey; Ottoman Empire
Turkish migrants, 21, 22, 90, 160, 203, 249

U.K. Border Agency (UKBA), 113–16,
  124–26, 142, 143, 186
  *Protecting Our Border, Protecting the
    Public,* 164
  rejection of trafficking claims, 174
UK Border Force, 124
Ukraine, 24, 29, 33, 34, 40–44, 128
  human trafficking, 173
  per capita income, 152
  Rusyns in, 222
  smuggling, 168–69
  See also Slovakia-Ukraine border;
    Uzhgorod, Ukraine
Ukrainians in Poland, 31, 35
Ungar, Hungary, 41
United Kingdom, 24, 80–81, 98, 103,
  107–43, 158, 203–5, 247–48
  anti-Muslim sentiment, 208
  colonies, 17, 154
  entry restrictions, 21–22
  French relations, 116
  gay and lesbian asylum seekers, 159–60
  Greek relations, 105
  history, 16–21
  human trafficking in, 173–74
  island territories, 209
  migrant returnees from, 250
  *Proposals for a New European Border
    Guard,* 11
  See also England; Scotland; U.K. Border
    Agency (UKBA)
United Nations High Commissioner for
  Refugees (UNHCR), 20, 56, 66, 75,
  80, 82, 193–96, 202
  Greece, 96, 103, 105
  Lampedusa, 78, 79
United Nations International Convention
  for the Protection of the Rights of All
  Migrant Workers. *See* International
  Convention for the Protection of the
  Rights of All Migrant Workers
United States, 70, 85, 114, 156, 157, 186
  drug war, 171
  Iraq occupation, 12
  refugee acceptance, 160
  Ukrainian relations, 40
United States Visitor and Immigrant Status
  Indicator Technology (US-VISIT),
  241
Universal Declaration of Human Rights,
  20–21, 192
uprisings, 76, 253

Ural Mountains, 209
U.S. Border Patrol, 35, 242
U.S. Bureau of Customs and Border
  Protection, 233, 242
U.S. Department of Defense, 243
U.S. Department of Homeland Security,
  235, 241
U.S. Immigration and Customs
  Enforcement (ICE), 234, 235
U.S.-Mexico border, 18, 23, 40, 205, 210,
  231–37, 241, 242
Uzhgorod, Ukraine, 41–43, 191

Valetta, Malta, 67, 68, 70
vandalism, 200, 228
Vella, Matthew, 68–69
Verhaegen, Jacky, 154–55, 187–88
Vic, Spain, 186
Vietnamese migrants, 31, 114
vigilantism, 104–5, 180, 232
Vinc, Jan, 38
violence. *See* brutality; murder; racial
  violence; rape
Virtual Border Watch, 236
visas, 17–19, 66, 112, 115, 250
  Schengen Area, 27, 34, 35
Vouros, Dimitrios, 95–96
Vyšné Nemecké, Slovakia, 38, 39

Wackenhut, 239
Wakefield, England, 136–37
Walking Borders. *See* Caminando Fronteras
Wallenberg, Raoul, 161
walls, fences, etc. *See* fences, walls, etc.

Warhol, Andy, 222–23, 224
Warsaw, 166, 169, 226
weapons smuggling, 33, 35, 168, 236
weather-related disasters, 243
Weber, Roger, 26–27
Weise, Frank-Jürgen, 248
Welcome (film), 202
Welcome to Europe, 196, 197
West African migrants, 49, 52, 62, 72,
  134–35, 153. *See also* Cameroonian
  migrants; Congolese migrants; Malian
  migrants; Nigerian migrants;
  Senegalese migrants; Sierra Leonean
  migrants
Western Sahara, 3, 196
West Indian migrants, 21
White, Arnold, 18
Who Are We? (Huntington), 232
Widdecombe, Ann, 110
workers, migrant. *See* migrant workers
World War I, 18, 132
World War II, 37, 90, 161, 162, 209, 218–20

X-ray machines, 30, 35, 38, 114

Yugoslavia, 46

Zapatero, José Luis, 228
Zeebrugge, Belgium, 4
Zimbabwean migrants, 230–31
Zimbabwe–South Africa border. *See* South
  Africa–Zimbabwe border
La Zona (film), 243–44
Zweig, Stefan, 17, 18

Celebrating 20 Years of Independent Publishing

Thank you for reading this book published by The New Press. The New Press is a nonprofit, public interest publisher celebrating its twentieth anniversary in 2012. New Press books and authors play a crucial role in sparking conversations about the key political and social issues of our day.

We hope you enjoyed this book and that you will stay in touch with The New Press. Here are a few ways to stay up to date with our books, events, and the issues we cover:

- Sign up at www.thenewpress.com/subscribe to receive updates on New Press authors and issues and to be notified about local events
- Like us on Facebook: www.facebook.com/newpressbooks
- Follow us on Twitter: www.twitter.com/thenewpress

Please consider buying New Press books for yourself; for friends and family; or to donate to schools, libraries, community centers, prison libraries, and other organizations involved with the issues our authors write about.

The New Press is a 501(c)(3) nonprofit organization. You can also support our work with a tax-deductible gift by visiting www.thenewpress.com/donate.